Putting Folklore
to Use

Putting Folklore to Use

MICHAEL OWEN JONES

Editor

THE UNIVERSITY PRESS OF KENTUCKY

Putting Folklore to Use has been selected as a
Publication of the American Folklore Society,
New Series, Patrick B. Mullen, General Editor.

Copyright © 1994 by The University Press of Kentucky

Scholarly publisher for the Commonwealth,
serving Bellarmine College, Berea College, Centre
College of Kentucky, Eastern Kentucky University,
The Filson Club, Georgetown College, Kentucky
Historical Society, Kentucky State University,
Morehead State University, Murray State University,
Northern Kentucky University, Transylvania University,
University of Kentucky, University of Louisville,
and Western Kentucky University.

Editorial and Sales Offices: Lexington, Kentucky 40508-4008

Library of Congress Cataloging-in-Publication Data

Putting folklore to use / Michael Owen Jones, editor.
    p.   cm. — (Publication of the American Folklore Society. New
series)
  Includes bibliographical references and index.
  ISBN 0-8131-1825-5 (cloth : alk. paper) : —
  ISBN 0-1831-0818-7 (paper : alk. paper) :
  1. Applied folklore—United States. 2. Folklore—United States—
Research. 3. United States—Social life and customs. I. Jones,
Michael Owen. II. Series: Publications of the American Folklore
Society. New series (Unnumbered)
GR105.P88 1993
398′.0973—dc20
                                       93-2101

This volume is dedicated to the memory of
Dr. Sue Samuelson (1956-1991).

An academician at heart, she paved the way in applied folkloristics
from expert witness in legal proceedings to human resources
development, marketing, and public relations.

Contents

PART III.
Enhancing Identity and Community

Preface

This is the first book to describe ways of applying concepts and insights from folklore studies to a broad range of situations and social concerns. It has its antecedents in works on folklore in museums, education, and the public sector but differs from them in several ways. First, though it is intended primarily for folklorists, the essays should be of interest and use to practitioners in other fields. Second, the authors of these dozen essays go beyond speculation or theory to describe actual applications of which they have direct knowledge, in most instances having been involved occupationally. Third, the book is more skills-oriented than its predecessors. It identifies particular knowledge, abilities, and techniques of folklorists valuable to many professions and useful in trying to solve a variety of problems.

Authors of essays in Part I demonstrate how utilizing folklore can promote learning, problem solving, and the conservation and presentation of folklore. Judith Haut shows how a teacher can achieve the goals of pluralistic education by acting like a folklore fieldworker, thereby reducing intergroup stereotyping and increasing students' self-esteem while simultaneously developing independent learning skills. Jo Farb Hernandez examines recent trends in different types of museums; she concludes with specific recommendations for including folklore programming, explaining its value to learning. Marjorie Bard discusses the uses of narratives in diagnosis and intervention with homeless persons, illustrating applications for policy and programs. Finally, Benita Howell advocates folklore or folklife research as a crucial part of environmental planning.

Writers in Part II focus on how values, concepts, and approaches from folklore studies can improve the quality of life. David Hufford considers how health care can be rendered more effective if practitioners become aware of a variety of ways of thinking about the causes and cures of illness—achieved in part by adopting a fieldworker's point of view when interviewing patients. Kristin Congdon proposes ways to democratize art therapy, sensitizing the art facilitator to the value and implications of everyday creativity and traditional aesthetics and thereby helping to improve communication in therapeutic settings. Sara Selene Faulds analyzes how to improve the design of public spaces through an emphasis on symbolic behavior in face-to-face interaction. Michael Owen Jones proposes taking a folkloristic approach to the study of organizational behavior as well as incorporating concepts and methods from folklore research into efforts at organization development. In the final essay in this section, Elke Dettmer explores a possible role for folklore studies in developing a more responsible tourism.

Authors in Part III discuss ways of utilizing folklore research that, for whatever else may be accomplished, can enhance identity and a sense of community. Betty Belanus reviews some of her experiences during the past decade as a public sector folklorist who has put folklore to use in schools, museums, and parks and recreation programs not only to educate but also to stimulate appreciation of and pride in local traditions. David Shuldiner describes folklore programming for and with the elderly in ways that promote a sense of self-worth. Sue Samuelson examines her experience in public relations work for a professional association, helping reflect and create a self-image. In the last essay, Patricia Atkinson Wells sets forth an agenda for helping rural communities survive and even thrive.

Of course, there are other applications of folklore and its study. Several journalists, including Mark Twain, George Korson, and Charles Kuralt, have reported folk traditions, and several folklorists with M.A. or Ph.D. degrees have found employment in journalism. Many librarians learn and tell myths, legends, and folk tales (sometimes as part of their job description); and individuals with advanced degrees in folklore studies have become librarians. Photographers, filmmakers, and videographers often document examples of folklore and aspects of folklife, and increasingly folklorists serve as consultants to media projects. State humanities councils have hired folklorists as program officers and selected academic folklorists to sit on their boards of directors.

Space does not permit including essays on all applications. The topics selected include areas in which folklore has long been considered relevant (such as education), institutions or agencies in which many folklorists have been employed in recent years (e.g., the public sector, such as museums and arts councils), and fields that are likely to draw increasingly heavily on folklore studies as well as employ more folklorists in the future (e.g., health, aging, organization development, and environmental planning). The criteria used to select authors were a combination of who is noted for a particular application, who could provide the necessary overview and case studies (as evident from earlier conference papers or publications), and who was ready and willing to prepare an essay.

The volume is loosely structured. A chapter in the section on promoting learning, for example, is just as likely to have implications for improving the quality of life and enhancing identity and community. It seemed, however, that one or another of the three themes into which the book is divided dominated each article. Moreover, it made sense to move from promoting learning and conserving examples of folklore to questions of how this can improve the quality of life, essential aspects of which are self-esteem and closeness to others. Common principles throughout the chapters are methods of folkloristics as well as skills and abilities of folklorists that may be applied to another field, how one applies them, and some issues in application. Overall, there is a deep-seated concern for appreciating and understanding folklore and, through it, people, and for utilizing this respect for tradition and understanding of symbolic behavior to help solve social issues and improve the world in which we live.

One purpose of this book is to provide guidance and direction to folklorists who are considering applying their training, skills, and knowledge to the problems of human welfare, such as aiding the homeless, caring for the elderly, or improving workplace conditions. Another is to inform practitioners in professional fields about using folklore studies to augment their own specializations, thereby enhancing the quality of education, health care, urban planning, and other services extended to the public.

Regardless of the type of social application, an underlying assumption is that knowledge of folklore is vital. People tell stories. They celebrate, ritualize, play, and use figurative language. These traditional, symbolic forms and processes are universal in the species. Particular examples may express values, transmit precepts, teach and reinforce norms, or occupy leisure. Or they may project anxieties, express joy and satisfaction, provide meaning, and in other ways help people make sense of their world, cope, and act. Whatever their functions and consequences, the very existence of these forms and processes defines homo sapiens. To be effective, therefore, efforts to alter conditions, attitudes, or behavior must take into account the presence and impact of traditions and symbolic interaction.

As the field of folklore studies continues to gain ground in academe, and the number of practitioners outside the academy increases, the applications are likely to multiply and diversify. We hope this book contributes to these developments by showing how folklore research is being applied in a dozen ways in our society today.

Applying Folklore Studies: An Introduction

Michael Owen Jones

*It implies lack of faith in your field or profession
not to see its relation to the life around you.*
—Benjamin A. Botkin (1952)

Folklore has been the object of curiosity, documentation, and speculation for centuries. Plutarch (40-120 A.D.), author of *Roman Questions*, wrote the first formal treatise on folklore, grappling with the origins and meanings of a people's beliefs and customs just as contemporary folklorists do. The eighteenth-century Scottish poet Robert Burns collected ballads and composed poetry in the "folk" idiom, much as did American folksong revivalists in the 1960s, some of whom became well-known folklorists. The brothers Grimm recorded tales from the lips of their housekeeper, Frau Katherina Viehmann, publishing them and others in the two-volume *Kinder- und Hausmärchen* (1812-1815), in which they hypothesize the history and dissemination of these stories, particularly in relation to German identity. Despite the long interest in people's songs, stories, sayings, and rituals, folklore research did not exist as an academic discipline in most countries until recent years. Folklore was studied, however, and put to use in search of a usable past or for other personal, political, administrative, or humanitarian purposes.

In this introduction I survey the foundations of folklore studies, set forth several concepts, and describe skills and knowledge of the folklorist that have practical application. Throughout the essay I consider issues that arise when folklorists engage in applied activities. My purpose is to lay the groundwork for the rest of the book, which presents a dozen different applications of folklore studies in the United States today.

First, some basic terms. In 1846 the Englishman William Thoms coined the Anglo-Saxon compound "Folk-Lore." He intended it to replace "popular antiquities," in vogue since the eighteenth century. Among other designations are "oral traditions" (used at least as early as 1777), the French *traditions populaires*, and the German *Volkskunde* (an eighteenth-century term, literally "knowledge of the common folk"). In 1909, Sven Lampa at the University of Lund lectured on *folkliv* (a term that appears as early as 1847), the Swedish equivalent of the German *Volksleben* and the forerunner of "folklife" (used at least as early as 1897 when William Parker Greenough published *Canadian Folk-life and Folk-lore* [New York: G.H. Richmond][1]), a term that Don Yoder championed in the United States in the 1950s.

To differentiate the subject matter of folklore or folklife from its methods of documentation and analysis, "folkloristics" began to be used in the mid-1960s. Influenced by German scholarship, the term implies a systematic and disciplinary approach. Some folklorists prefer "folklore studies," suggesting a field of study but perhaps not a strict discipline (others prefer "folklife," which they feel encompasses more than "folklore"). "Applied folklore," employed occasionally in the 1940s and 1950s—particularly by Benjamin A. Botkin—found currency by the late 1960s and early 1970s. With the growing popularity in the 1980s of "folklore studies" to designate the field, "applied" began to be used in conjunction with this term instead of with "folklore" alone. "Applied folklore studies" or "applied folkloristics" suggests a discipline in its own right with theory and methods.

Whether they use the term "folklore," "folklife," or "oral traditions," most folklorists probably would agree that the forms and processes studied have in common at least three characteristics. They are symbolic, they are learned or generated in people's firsthand interactions, and they are traditional, exhibiting continuities and consistencies in thought and behavior through time and space, respectively.

"Attack the problem, not the person," "If you want people to tell you the truth, then 'don't shoot the messenger,' " "If you want to get to know someone, walk a mile in his shoes," and other proverbs and traditional sayings are colorful, encapsulate the wisdom of many, and evoke a multiplicity of images and ideas. The stories that people tell are not simply a dispassionate reporting of facts but dramatic performances vividly portraying some aspect of an event, in the process engaging teller and listener alike in a host of associations and possible inferences. Rituals convey meanings that transcend the mundane, invoking associations and feelings that otherwise are often ignored, discounted, or suppressed in our workaday lives. In other words, something visible is taken to stand for the invisible, whether ideas, qualities, or feelings. Even customs are symbolic. As "our" way of doing things, these traditions define behavior and express identity.

In addition, the sayings, stories, and customs called folklore arise in the interactions of people and therefore are shaped by participants' personalities, social identities and relations, and shared experiences. A "story," for example, is not a "text," as in literature. Rather, it is the entire performance, including linguistic as well as paralinguistic and nonverbal behavior, with "digressions," "asides," and feedback; and it is a product of an interaction between the narrator and the auditors who assume particular social roles and identities during the storytelling event.

Finally, because they are repeated, emulated, or reproduced, those symbolic behaviors labeled folklore are "traditional." That is, they have both a social and a historical character, exhibiting similiarities in assumptions, attitudes, and ways of doing things through space and time. To be traditional also means that customs, stories, rituals, beliefs, and other symbolic forms become imbued with value—either positively or negatively—and are perpetuated, altered, extinguished, or revived.

Among the forms and processes of folklore are jargon, argot, proverbs, traditional sayings, and nicknaming; myths, legends, and anecdotes; jokes and kidding; rumors and gossip; costume, the making of personal items at work, and the personal decoration of space; recreation, games, and play; celebrations, festive events, parties, and cooperative work efforts; traditional expressions of belief; ceremonies, rituals, and rites of passage; and customs and social routines. Much could be added to this list. There are dozens of kinds of stories, for instance, from exempla to sagas, floating legends, memorates, and personal experience narratives; and there are many types of rites and rituals. In addition, folklorists have identified such phenomena as ethnic display events, small group festive gatherings, and the proto festival (a celebration that may become institutionalized as an annual community event).

In their work, folklorists consciously seek evidence of continuities in what people do and think. They document the stories that people tell, the figurative language they use, the rituals they engage in, the songs they sing. Folklorists interpret these traditional, expressive forms and examples according to one or more of several perspectives. Viewing folklore as an index of historical processes, some researchers use examples of folklore to reconstruct the past or to examine historical events and movements. Others treat folklore as an aspect or manifestation of culture, and as an index to cultural processes. They examine how aspects of workers' culture, say, reflect workview, socialize newcomers to an occupational setting, enculturate values, or mirror social and cultural change; or they investigate cultural identity expressed through folklore, or ways that examples of folklore help immigrants adjust to a new culture or sometimes hinder intercultural communication and understanding. Increasingly more researchers conceptualize folklore as a behavioral phenomenon. They explore traditional, symbolic forms as expressions of psychological states and processes (e.g., projection or transference, wish fulfillment, an aspect of the grieving process, a means of coping or adjustment), or examine such cognitive and interactional processes as learning, communication, and social dynamics.

In addition to documenting and interpreting examples of traditional, symbolic behavior in people's everyday lives, many folklorists also present these examples and their intepretation in museum exhibits, films, festivals, phonograph recordings, and radio programs. Some folklorists attempt to help a people perpetuate some of their traditions, acting as "stewards" and "cultural conservationists" on their behalf by documenting the traditions, making them public, trying to get others to appreciate them, assisting in the development of apprenticeship programs, and so on. Other folklorists apply their training in yet other ways to help solve problems related to education, aging, urban design, and cultural pluralism.

Delineating "genres" of folklore and developing constructs and perspectives are a necessary part of folklore studies. But before discussing folklore knowledge further, we need to consider such questions as the following: To what uses have folklore and its study been put historically and why? Should contemporary folklorists step down from the ivory tower of academe and engage in applications? What does "applied folkloristics" mean?

Folklore Studies in Theory and Practice

Although the terms "applied folklore" and "applied folkloristics" are relatively new, the notion of systematically documenting and utilizing traditions is not. According to William A. Wilson in *Folklore and Nationalism in Modern Finland* (Bloomington: Indiana University Press, 1976), in 1630 Gustav II Adolf, King of Sweden, decreed that traditions from which could be inferred the way of life of ancient times be taken down. A collection of "antiquities" could demonstrate to older European countries that Sweden, which then ruled Finland and other areas, had a long history as a nation. In 1666 an antiquities council was founded in Stockholm. Eight years later the council implored the Finnish clergy to gather data on the old narrative songs because they contained "much truth about the heroic deeds of the forefathers" (pp. 20-21).

In the eighteenth century, writes Wilson (p. 17), Finland mounted a reconstruction program to recover from the ravages of the Great Northern War. Aimed at finding better means of governing and of improving productivity, the program first required thorough documentation and analysis of prevailing conditions. From the 1730s to about 1800, scores of young men set out to describe their home regions. They published more than one hundred scholarly treatises that recorded agricultural techniques, architectural traditions, health practices, foodways, wedding and funeral customs, calendar observances, recreational activities, legends, proverbs, and superstitions, as well as flora and fauna.

One use of folklore in Germany in the late eighteenth and early nineteenth centuries was nationalistic. Johann Gottfried Herder and other members of the Romantic movement were distressed over the abandonment of German language and literature in favor of French. The Romantics' conviction that folk poetry contained the essence of a nation's creative heritage led to attempts to retrieve the ancient traditions in order to uncover traces of heroic, noble past. Folklore was documented but also often rewritten and transformed into a kind of literary discourse about a nation's values, virtues, and manners. This occurred in Finland, Scotland, Ireland, and many other countries during the nineteenth and early twentieth centuries.

In the United States at the end of the nineteenth century, many of the members of the American Folklore Society (founded in 1888) were governmental workers and museum professionals (particularly from the Bureau of American Ethnology), along with some writers, academics, and librarians. According to Simon J. Bronner (editor), in *Folklife Studies from the Gilded Age* (Ann Arbor: UMI Research Press, 1987), "Between 1890 and 1903, ten presidents of the American Folklore Society, when they took office, held professional affiliations with ethnological museums" (p. 20). Besides putting folklore on display in natural history museums, folklorists made their subject a key educational and tourist attraction at the World's Columbian Exposition in Chicago in 1893. In addition, Stewart Culin published extensively on traditions of American Chinese whose presence had caused labor and racial strife and whose immigration had been restricted by Congress in 1882 (Bronner, pp. 87-89). Billed by the *Philadelphia Inquirer* in 1887 as "the friend of all the persecuted Chinamen," Culin was motivated to consider, in his words, folklore's "application to the problems arising in the question of restricting immigration." For a dozen years the aide-de-camp to General George Crook in the Southwest (and elected president of the American Folklore Society in 1896), John G. Bourke took extensive notes on local Indian and Mexican-American folklore, including foodways, to better prepare his soldiers to survive in hostile surroundings (Bronner, p. 183).[2]

Another use was that of helping immigrants adjust. For example, Jane Addams established Hull House in the industrial district of Chicago on September 18, 1889. She made this settlement a place where groups of people could gather together to celebrate familiar holidays, dress in traditional costume, sing the old songs, and reminisce about days gone by. In 1900 she created a Labor Museum at Hull House with products, photographs, and demonstrations. By showing similarities in the historical development of textile processes, pottery, metalworking, and other handcrafts, the museum linked Greeks, Syrians, Italians, the Irish, and Russians to one another, revealed a continuity between experiences in the old country and the new, and built a bridge between immigrants and their children. Within a decade, some of Addams's ideas had gained general acceptance. In 1910 popular magazines printed articles rejecting the melting pot simile and proposed instead the metaphor of a mixing bowl in which the characteristics of each nation are preserved.[3]

William I. Thomas and Florian Znaniecki's *The Polish Peasant in Europe and America* (Boston: Richard C. Badger, 5 volumes, 1918-1920) continued the social justice wing of Progressive reform, paying attention to folk customs as a guide to social assistance. In 1908, Thomas was appointed director of the Helen Culver Fund for Race Psychology and given $50,000 "to study [in his words] an immigrant group in Europe and America to determine as far as possible what relation their home mores and norms had to their adjustment and maladjustment in America."[4]

Phyllis H. Williams prepared and published a volume on folklife specifically for purposes of application. Called *South Italian Folkways in Europe and America: A Handbook for School Workers, Visiting Nurses, School Teachers, and Physicians* (New Haven: Yale University Press for the Institute of Human Relations, 1938), each of the book's chapters begins with a section on culture and traditions in Italy, taken from data compiled by Giuseppe Pitré, a physician by profession and folklorist by avocation, and published in *Biblioteca delle Tradizioni Popolari Siciliane* (Polermo: L. Pedone-Lauri, 25 volumes, 1871-1913). Then follows a section on current traditions based on Williams's own observations of more than five hundred Italians in the United States over an eleven-year period. Finally, each chapter ends with specific advice regarding adjustment. "When social workers have acquired a fair knowledge of the differences that regional backgrounds make in Italian immigrants, their ability to approach individuals and family groups acceptably is greatly enhanced," writes Williams. "Types of food, attitudes toward the government, and mortuary rites vary from section to section. The rest of this book is an attempt to provide in detail both the subtle and the recognizable distinctions and something of the body of belief and practice that lies behind them" (p. 16).

In the 1940s Rachel Davis DuBois, a social worker, utilized two techniques to increase understanding among people of different ethnic backgrounds. One was the group conversation in which neighborhood participants, under the guidance of a facilitator, recalled childhood experiences, trying to get back to a time when they accepted their traditions and their neighbors. The technique became festive and ritualistic as well as therapeutic through the interpolation of songs, dances, and games suggested by the conversation and by concluding the session with a symbolic song, dance, or ceremony.

DuBois also used the *parranda*, a Puerto Rican term for "progressive party," in which several families hold open house with guests traveling from one home to the next. She had children leave the classroom to visit the homes of families of various cultural backgrounds. They ate different types of food and took part in songs, games, and dances as well as learned about customs through coversation and interview. These in turn were reported back in the students' compositions and integrated into the school experience through "intercultural assemblies."[5]

Writing extensively on the subject and practicing what she preached, Dorothy Mills Howard championed folklore's application to education. Her essay "Folklore in the Schools" (1950) makes her philosophy abundantly clear. "The purpose of this article is to demonstrate by concrete example that folklore has a justifiable place in the schools, not as a separate subject, or for the purpose of making folklorists of children, or as an academic, book exercise but as an integral part of a co-ordinated program for child growth and development where children become aware of the folklore process, what it is, and how it operates in their own lives and in their community."[6]

Public agencies in the United States have long played a role in applied folklore, from the Bureau of American Ethnology, founded in 1879, to the Works Progress Administration's Federal Project Number One, which operated between August 2, 1935, and August 31, 1939. The latter included folklore documentation, festivals, or publications by the Federal Art Project, Federal Music Project, Federal Theatre Project, Federal Writers' Project, and Historical Records Survey. There was also the National Research Council's Committee on Food Habits, dedicated to the belief that studies of cultural patterns and customs revolving around food are crucial to solving nutritional problems.

Several individuals legendary in folklore circles today participated in some of these programs. Herbert Halpert, director of the music division of the National Service Bureau, was associated with the Federal Theatre Project (later he established the folklore library, archive, and teaching program at Memorial University of Newfoundland). Ethnomusicologist Charles Seeger was with the Federal Music Project and was vice chairman of the Joint WPA Folklore Committee.

In addition, from 1928 to 1932 Robert W. Gordon served as the head of the Archive of American Folk-Song (originally established at the Library of Congress on July 1, 1928, it finally received congressional funding in 1937). He was succeeded by John A. Lomax (1932-1942), whose son Alan served as assistant in charge from 1937 to 1942. The elder Lomax had been employed by the Historical Records Survey, and he was the national advisor on folklore and folkways to the Writers' Project from June 25, 1936, to October 23, 1937. John Lomax is noted for his collections of cowboy songs and tunes in the 1910s; he and Alan discovered and made famous many traditional musicians, including Huddie ("Leadbelly") Ledbetter.

Benjamin A. Botkin was appointed national folklore editor of the Federal Writers' Project in 1938. He had studied at Harvard and Columbia, earning his doctorate in 1931 at the University of Nebraska in English and anthropology under ballad scholar Louise Pound, and then taught at the University of Oklahoma where he collected regional lore and started *Folk-Say*, a newsletter filled with local miscellany. He was appointed director of the folksong archive in 1942 but resigned three years later to devote himself to writing and editing, having recently enjoyed success as the compiler of a best-selling book on American folklore.

Botkin was succeeded as head of the Archive of American Folk-Song by Duncan Emrich (1945-1956), Rae Korson (1956-1969), Alan Jabbour (1969-1974), and Joseph C. Hickerson (1974-). Having also been known as the Folklore Section (1946-1954) and the Archive of Folk Song (1954-1981), the institution was renamed the Archive of Folk Culture on October 1, 1981.

More recently, three national organizations have been responsible for much of the government-sponsored applications of folklore. In 1967 Ralph Rinzler, a performer and member of the Greenbriar Boys and popularizer of North Carolina folk musician Doc Watson, founded the Smithsonian's Folklife Festival. Retired in 1984 and recently named assistant secretary emeritus, Rinzler intended the festival both to celebrate traditional art forms in America and to educate the public about them. The Office of Folklife Programs at the Smithsonian Institution continues the festival (along with research, exhibits, films, and publications), with Richard Kurin, the director, defending the annual event as an advocate for cultural equity.[7]

The Folk Arts Program of the National Endowment for the Arts was established in 1974. First directed by Alan Jabbour and then by Bess Lomax Hawes, the program funds local traditional festivals, workshops, demonstrations in schools, and other activities that present folk art and artists, in part to help perpetuate traditional art forms, skills, and knowledge. This program has also provided the first years of funding for folk arts coordinator positions in arts councils. By the late 1980s, fifty of the fifty-six states and territories as well as several cities had hired people with training in folklore or ethnomusicology to coordinate the documentation and presentation of traditional arts, performers, and craftsmen.

On January 2, 1976, President Ford signed a congressional bill, the American Folklife Preservation Act (P.L. 94-201), which established the American Folklife Center as the nation's first national agency devoted to folk culture and its study, preservation, and presentation. Located in the Library of Congress, the Center, which is headed by Alan Jabbour (a medievalist and classical violinist cum fiddler), provides technical assistance, carries out model documentary projects, and organizes public forums in the name of "cultural conservation."[8]

Individuals trained in folklore have also pursued careers in museum work and administration, performing groups and arts management, journalism, parks and recreation departments, social work, the medical and legal professions, and business. Among UCLA's earliest M.A. recipients, for example, are Barret Hansen, better known as "Dr. Demento" of radio fame; Ed Kahn, a film writer and producer; Anthony Shay, founder and director of a folk dance troupe; and Ed Cray, the author of numerous popular books and now an instructor of journalism at the University of Southern California. Karana Hattersley-Drayton, trained in folklore at the University of California, Berkeley, did cultural programming for the National Park Service at Fort Mason in San Francisco for several years. With degrees in folklore from Indiana University, Rayna Green was employed by the American Association for the Advancement of Science to stimulate interest in culturally-based science, William Ivey directs the Country Music Foundation in Nashville, and Steve Ohrn conducts research and curates exhibits for the State Historical Society of Iowa. Karen Creuziger and Malachi O'Connor—graduates of the folklore and folklife program at the University of Pennsylvania—work for management consulting firms, the first in San Diego and the second in Philadelphia.

Others have founded their own organizations, such as Margy McClain who directs Urban Traditions, a not-for-profit organization in Chicago serving schools and government agencies; Rebecca Conard, a principal in a private firm in Santa Barbara specializing in environmental issues and land use policies; and Sondra Thiederman in San Diego who consults with businesses, universities, and other organizations regarding the multicultural workplace. (All have degrees in folklore from UCLA.)

The folk studies program at Western Kentucky University was specifically "designed to provide a usable master's degree that made its graduates marketable in the burgeoning field of folklore."[9] Many have found employment as arts coordinators, oral historians, museum curators, and parks and recreation department personnel. Other folklorists teach, although not necessarily in the university or in folklore programs.

Folklore in and out of Academe

"I contend that it is no business of the folklorist to engage in social reform, that he is unequipped to reshape institutions, and that he will become the poorer scholar and folklorist if he turns activist," insisted Richard M. Dorson in 1971. He published his remarks at the end of a special issue of a journal on applied folklore. Among the articles about folklorists helping to improve educational systems, urban planning, and health care, only Dorson's essay challenged the application of folklore studies. "We cannot afford much diversion from our primary responsibilities as scholars to seek and record the truth about man and his ways," he wrote. Beyond being an educator, "I hesitate to give advice on how to make the world better, or happier, or freer, through folklore."[10]

One reason for Dorson's objecting to folklorists putting their research to use is the long history of abuse or misuse of folklore. All too often the documentation of traditions during the preceding two hundred years had been inspired by nationalism or employed as a tool of colonialism and totalitarianism. A spate of books and articles appeared in the 1960s and 1970s warning against the perversion of folklore research for political ends, holding up as examples Nazi Germany's exploitation of the Aryan myth, Soviet Russia's glorification of its power elite as heroes, and Red China's indoctrination of children in its government's philosophy through folk songs, dance, and puppetry. Some of the articles were published in the *Journal of the Folklore Institute* (now called *Journal of Folklore Research*), which was founded and edited by Dorson, who directed the Folklore Institute at Indiana University from 1957 until his death in 1980.

Commercial exploitation also posed a threat. For decades Dorson railed against popularizers like Benjamin A. Botkin, author of numerous "treasuries" including *The Treasury of American Folklore*, a Book-of-the-Month Club selection when it was published in 1944 and rarely if ever out of print since then. Dorson's famous concept of "fakelore," which he coined in 1950, was stimulated by such works. He intended the term to designate the fabrication of stories, songs, and other "traditions" for financial gain, whether in the form of advertising, popular treasuries, television hootenannies, or community boosterism. Through fakelore, explains Barbara Kirshenblatt-Gimblett about Dorson's use of the term, "the hapless consumer was duped into thinking he was getting the genuine folklore article, and folklore as an academic discipline was discredited with each new treasury and literary tall tale."[11]

"Dorson's mission was to make the discipline of folklore legitimate and honorable in the university," writes Bruce Jackson. "He attacked anything and anyone he thought stood in the way of that goal."[12] This is a second reason for Dorson's rejection of applied folklore, and perhaps also why his critiques of popular works by Botkin, Emrich, and others were sometimes harsh.

In the nineteenth and early twentieth centuries, folklore was largely an adjunct to philological studies and literature. For many historians and anthropologists, customs, legends, and other forms of folklore were useful but secondary in their pursuit of the past or as a way to understand a culture. Dorson admits having "stumbled into folklore from a training in American cultural and intellectual history," earning a Ph.D. at Harvard in 1943 where he wrote a dissertation on "New England Popular Tales and Legends," with the help of a Celticist.[13]

The first academic folklore program in the United States was not approved until 1939. Established by Ralph Steele Boggs, the curriculum of folklore in the English department at the University of North Carolina, Chapel Hill, continues to grant the master of arts degree.

A short-lived department of American folklore was established at Frank-lin and Marshall College, Lancaster, Pennsylvania, in 1948. Headed by Alfred L. Shoemaker, its other faculty included Don Yoder and J. William Frey. Lasting through the 1951-52 academic year, it offered six courses.[14]

By 1950 Indiana University offered both the Ph.D. and the M.A. degree from the folklore department, chaired by Stith Thompson. The University of Pennsylvania followed suit in 1964 with a graduate program in folklore and folklife under the direction of MacEdward Leach. In the same year the Cooperstown Graduate Programs initiated a two-track M.A. in American folk culture or museum studies, directed by Louis C. Jones (a college teach-er turned historical association administrator). Now discontinued, it was application-oriented, preparing students for employment in museums, ar-chives, and historical societies. In 1965 UCLA's folklore and mythology pro-gram (known from the late 1940s as the Folklore Group, headed by Wayland D. Hand, who was hired in 1937 specifically to teach folklore courses) was empowered to confer the master of arts degree and in 1978 the doctorate. The University of Texas has an interdepartmental program in folklore and ethnomusicology that grants advanced degrees, guided for many years by Américo Paredes. In 1970, Western Kentucky University established an M.A. degree program in folk studies chaired by Lynwood Montell.

The University of Oregon has a combined folklore and ethnic studies program within the English department. Utah State University offers a mas-ter's degree through a joint program of folklore, Western history, and litera-ture. Folklore at the State University of New York, Buffalo, is combined with mythology and film studies in a Ph.D. program. Several institutions offer a concentration in folklore within anthropology (e.g., the University of California at Berkeley), Slavics (Harvard University), English (e.g., Ohio State University), American studies (George Washington University, the University of California at Davis, and so forth), and other fields. Today, more than five hundred colleges and universities list courses on folklore.

Conceptions of "Applied Folklore"

In addition to the specter of political and commercial abuse of folklore and subversion of the academic mission, there was the question of what ap-plied folklore is. The letter of invitation to participants at a conference on applied folklore in 1971 contained the following definition, agreed upon by a committee of Richard Bauman, Robert H. Byington, Henry Glassie, Rayna Green, and Harry Oster:

We define applied folklore as the utilization of the theoretical concepts, factual knowledge, and research methodologies of folklorists in activities or programs meant to ameliorate contemporary social, economic, and technological prob-lems.[15]

It was this notion of applied folklore as an instrument of social reform and the folklorist as a change agent to which Dorson, a participant in the conference, objected when he wrote that the folklorist is not equipped to reshape institutions, has no business trying to do so, and will become the poorer scholar if he turns activist.

The American Folklore Society's Committee on Applied Folklore later dropped the advocacy rhetoric in order to gain general support from their colleagues for establishing a Center for Applied Folklore. According to Robert Byington, who chaired the committee during the twelve months between the society's annual meetings in 1971 and 1972, applied folklore became simply "an expansion of the folklorists' customary activities (research, fieldwork, publication and teaching), particularly teaching, into areas beyond the walls of the academy." Some committee members even denied having a social or political platform, he contends.[16]

A decade before, in an article in *New York Folklore Quarterly* (1961), Botkin had proposed an applied folklore center. It was to be largely a repository for materials and a clearinghouse for disseminating folklore (e.g., through publication) but also a service center promoting festivals, training community leaders for folklore programs, guiding social workers in the use of folklore, and providing courses in folklore for teachers. The American Folklife Center's establishment in 1976 and the development of the Smithsonian's Office of Folklife Programs have fulfilled some of the functions envisioned for both Botkin's Applied Folklore Center and the American Folklore Society's Center for Applied Folklore.

There have been other conceptions of applied folklore. To Dorson the term had three meanings, all of which are operative today. One was social reform, "the obligation of the folklorist to ameliorate the lot of the folk." Another was putting folk wisdom and know-how to use—for example, the utilization of home remedies by modern medical science. A third, which he advocated, was the "application of folklore concepts and content to teaching and research in other fields," such as history and literature.[17]

To Botkin, "It is only when he [the folklorist] gets *outside* of folklore into social or literary history, education, recreation, or the arts, that he becomes an 'applied' folklorist." For Botkin, the "pure folklorist" was too much a purist, thinking "of folklore as an independent discipline," as Dorson did. By contrast, "the applied folklorist prefers to think of it as ancillary to the study of culture, of history or literature—of people."[18] Botkin thought of his books as examples of applied folklore because they use "folk-say" as "folk literature" and "folk history," help "keep alive folk expressions that might otherwise be lost," and exemplify "giving back to the people what we have taken from them and what rightfully belongs to them."[19] By associating himself with Rachel Davis DuBois, Ruth Rubin, and others experienced in social work and education, Botkin gained ideas about broader applications for folklore, which he wrote about in one essay, whether or not he actually practiced them in his own endeavors.

Those favoring the term and work of applied folklore studies often make an assumption articulated by W.F.H. Nicolaisen at the applied folklore conference in 1971. He contended that "the basic notion of applied . . . appears to be the utilization of the results of pure research, theoretical study, academic inquiry—call it what you like—for the purpose of enriching human life in a very practical way." While cognizant of past abuses in the use of folklore, Nicolaisen writes, "I'm optimistic enough to think that the application of theoretical results is normally intended for the betterment of the human condition and not the reverse." [20] Application, then, is a value-laden concept.

For others like David Hufford, "applied folklore" is best defined in neutral terms. But historical misapplications have given it "a number of rather more limited definitions" or generated opposition to it. These misapplications, writes Hufford, include folklore used to justify and enhance political ideologies, well-meaning but naive attempts at revivalism, and the "frequently silly and misguided attempts to apply so-called folklore to education through song books, over-organized teaching of folk dance, and so forth." [21] Elsewhere Hufford writes, "My definition of applied folklore is simply the application of concepts, methods and materials from academic folklore studies to the solution of practical problems," rather like engineering and other fields that have their theoretical as well as applied side. "Such an application of academic folklore knowledge to practical problems provides an excellent setting for the empirical testing of folklore hypotheses and generates by necessity a richly interdisciplinary approach," [22] he contends.

In sum, applied folklore may mean or connote ameliorating social ills, utilizing traditional knowledge and techniques in modern science and technology, drawing on insights from folklore studies to illuminate issues in other (usually academic) fields, enriching human life, or applying concepts and hypotheses from folklore theory to solve practical problems of whatever nature. All these ideas assume research, intervention, and a body of theory and knowledge. A broader conception of applied folklore studies might be stated as follows:

The field of applied folkloristics ethically utilizes concepts, methods, and theories from the discipline of folklore studies as well as its own specialization to provide information, the formulation of policy, or the initiation of direct action in order to produce change or stability in behavior, culture, or the circumstances of people's lives including environment and technology. [23]

Major elements in this conception warrant brief discussion. First, explicit reference to ethics at the very beginning of the statement warns against misapplication and emphasizes the need for moral considerations at every step. It also conveys the spirit of ameliorative definitions intent on reforming institutions and improving life without having to explain or defend what "socially desired" or "betterment" is.

Second, the notion that instrumental activities are informed by research, concepts, and theories means that the field of applied folklore *studies* encompasses far more than "applied folklore." In its narrowest sense, applied folklore involves using only forms and examples of folklore, such as simply publishing a compilation of folktales or teaching a folk dance (without knowing the history, performance context, meanings, and significance of the forms or examples of folklore).

Applied folklore studies in the broader sense is illustrated by a two-day conference called "Presenting Folk Arts," held in June 1990 at Cornell University. Produced by the New York State Council on the Arts and directed by Robert Baron, who heads the council's Folk Arts Program, the event was designed to introduce presenting organizations (arts organizations that present performances produced by others rather than themselves) to the performing *folk* arts. Because many presenters want to offer folk arts but lack the necessary knowledge of how to locate and choose them or how to present folk artists appropriately on stage, the conference focused on these matters. The first panel discussed selecting artists as well as presenting them in ways that are appropriate to the organization and compatible with the cultural and aesthetic values of the performers. Other panels dealt with performing venues (from proscenium stage to the community dance party), how to bring existing audiences in to see unfamiliar traditions as well as how to reach new communities, and ways of educating audiences for both understanding and enjoyment. For all these issues there is a growing body of research, methods, and theory developed by folklorists involved in public sector programming. This research and technology constitutes part of the unique field of applied folklore studies.

Third, in applied folkloristics, the utilization of research may involve not only providing information or advice but also helping formulate policy or initiating direct action, or a combination of these. At the American Folklore Society meeting in 1989, for example, Shalom Staub of the Pennsylvania Heritage Affairs Commission reported on the Pennsylvania Department of Transportation's announced alternative routes to relieve traffic congestion along Route 30 in Lancaster County. Not considered in the cost of such construction was the adverse impact on the Amish and other plain sect communities densely concentrated in the area. In bisecting farms and church districts and thus cutting off internal transportation routes, "the

proposed road threatened the social fabric of the Amish community."
PennDOT eventually accepted the notion of an "Ethnic Culture Survey,"
inviting Staub to design it. "My study plan called for an ethnography of
Amish land use, perceptions and use of space, and transporation patterns";
in other words, the research would provide basic information on traditional
behavior, values, and customs. "PennDOT later required that these perspectives be factored into new proposed alternative routes." [24] Thus the
study became a key element in policy planning and program development.

Fourth, including in the conception of applied folklore studies both
"change" and "stability" as possible purposes or outcomes of the intervention recognizes the complexity of situations involving people's traditions. All too often consultants to organizations dwell on change, having
been called in to intervene in a dispute or to enhance communications or
improve cooperation; they don't understand the impact or potential value
of history, custom, and tradition. On the other hand, folklorists involved in
cultural conservation may be too readily inclined to preserve, present, or
perpetuate folklore just because it constitutes a group's arts and traditions;
they are unwilling to admit possible dysfunctions socially or psychologically and the need for change.

Fifth, practical folkloristics includes applications not only to institutions and social relations but also to the realms of individual behavior, culture, technology, and the environment. Child psychologists, family therapists, and marriage counselors can learn from folklorists about the kinds
of ritualistic behavior and narrative performance that people generate,
their role in communication, and their consequences as interactional strategies. Anthropologists, social workers, and educators concerned about intergroup tensions can utilize concepts and skills from folklore studies in
documenting, interpreting, and presenting folklore that teach one to appreciate the diversity of culture and to value multiculturalism.

As far as technology is concerned, for more than two decades specialists in artificial intelligence have experimented with programs that mimic
human storytellers. Sheldon Klein, one of the first to explore folklore from
this perspective, has worked on computer models of dialects and myth
structure, and he has applied principles from Vladimir Propp's *Morphology
of the Folktale* to create a Folk Telling System. James Meehan, inventor of a
narrative-producing program called Talespin, and Scott Turner who created Minstrel, understand that a study of storytelling can reveal how people communicate, which in turn may be used to help computers better
communicate with people. [25]

In regard to environment, Kurt Dewhurst and Marsha MacDowell of
the Michigan Traditional Arts Program, Michigan State University Museum, were engaged in 1990 to conduct a "Low-Level Radioactive Waste

Authority (LLRW) Project Folklife Cultural Survey." Its purpose was to provide information about the impact of a project on people's traditions and customs as well as help shape policy and action regarding the project. A major theme at "Cultural Conservation: Reconfiguring the Cultural Mission: The First National Conference," Library of Congress, Washington, D.C., May 16-19, 1990, was that environmental impact reports should incorporate research on potential cultural impact. State and local governments should "require . . . a review of cultural resources alongside the architectural and archaeological review" accompanying development projects.[26]

The last matter to consider is whether teaching is an example of applied folklore studies. Many instances of applied folklore ultimately involve "education" (through training, instruction, or enlightenment), or invoke education as a justification (such as public folklife programming of festivals and arts demonstrations). On the other hand, teaching in academe often entails trying to influence attitude and behavior, not just conveying information. In the final analysis, whether or not classroom instruction exemplifies the pragmatic side of folklore studies depends on circumstances, content, and especially purpose. When the intent is "not necessarily or even primarily to train new generations of professional folklorists, but to develop in students a sensitivity to traditional culture and the esthetic dimension of life, and to foster an appreciation for cultural diversity," writes Richard Bauman, teachers "are engaging in applied folklore up to their very ears."[27]

Putting Folklore to Use

By the late 1960s or early 1970s the burgeoning folklore programs and courses had turned out more people with degrees in folklore studies than could be absorbed back into these programs and even in other departments. In addition to universities producing a surfeit of graduates in theoretical fields like folklore studies, demands continued for greater relevancy, accountability, and advocacy—to do something to try to solve problems in race relations, health, housing, and the workplace. Increasingly more English majors, historians, and philosophers sought and found employment outside academe. So did folklorists.

Applied Folklore Studies in the Public Sector

Henry Glassie (now on the folklore faculty at Indiana University) was the first "state folklorist" in the modern sense of "folk arts coordinator" (much earlier, Henry V. Shoemaker held the title of state folklorist of Pennsylvania, 1948-1952, apparently the first in the country[28]). While a graduate student at the University of Pennsylvania, Glassie was employed (beginning in 1966) as director of the Ethnic Arts Survey for the Pennsylvania Historical and Museum Commission to begin surveying traditions in the state and develop an archive of resources. By 1974 Maryland and Tennessee employed folklorists in state arts agencies to build resource files of artists, establish liaisons with traditional craftsmen and performers, study marketing of the folk arts, and engage in similar activities. According to Charles Camp, who has directed folk arts programming for the Maryland Arts Council since 1976, fifteen state folklore programs "sprang up between 1976 and 1979."[29] By the mid-1980s the number had more than doubled and included territories and cities as well as states.

Most of these folk arts programs are lodged in state councils on the arts. Examples are Alaska, Alabama, California, Hawaii, Iowa, Illinois, Louisiana, Massachusetts, Maine, Minnesota, Mississippi, Montana, New Jersey, Nevada, New York, Oklahoma, Rhode Island, Tennessee, Utah, Washington, and Wisconsin, among others. The Southwest Folklife Center is based at the University of Arizona. Other programs are under the auspices of state historical societies or preservation centers, as in Iowa, Kansas, New Jersey, and South Dakota. Some folklore programs are found in combined arts and humanities organizations, such as the American Samoa Council on Culture, Arts and the Humanities, and the Ohio Joint Program in the Arts and Humanities. Since the mid-1980s the City of Los Angeles Cultural Affairs Department has boasted a Folk and Traditional Arts Program; the Cultural Arts Division of the City of Oakland, California, also has a Folk Arts Program. In New York, the Brooklyn Arts Council and the Queens Council on the Arts employ folklorists. Some county arts councils also have folklorists on their staffs. Finally, the state of Florida has its own folklore-related organization—the Bureau of Florida Folklife Programs—which is independent of other government agencies. Employing up to a dozen folklorists, the bureau has produced many records, videotapes, slide/tape programs, and other programming about ethnic, regional, and occupational traditions in the state.

In addition to individuals employed in state or city arts councils, historical societies, and other government agencies as "folk arts coordinators," "cultural conservationists," or "folklife specialists," there are those who have founded or who work for not-for-profit corporations. As private organizations rather than government agencies, the not-for-profits theoretically have greater lattitude in programming and in advocacy or activist efforts,[30] although such potential has not always been realized. The oldest of these not-for-profits is the National Council for the Traditional Arts. Based in Washington, D.C., it is directed by Joe Wilson. A second organization is the World Music Institute in New York City, and a third is the Ethnic Arts Center in New York City.

In the 1970s, folklorist William Ferris (who is now director of the University of Mississippi's Center for the Study of Southern Culture) and Judy Peiser founded the Center for Southern Folklore in Memphis, Tennessee, which Peiser directs. Pat Jasper and Kay Turner guide the activities of Texas Folklife Resources, based in Austin. After working with Urban Gateways in Chicago, Margy McClain established Urban Traditions. Hal Cannon and Elaine Thatcher run the Western Folklife Center in Salt Lake City, which is a spin-off from their earlier work with the Utah Arts Council. Jane Beck, formerly the folk arts coordinator for the Vermont Arts Council, established her own Vermont Folklife Center. Steve Zeitlin, whose wife Armanda Dargan is at the Queens arts council, directs City Lore, Inc., in New York City.

Many folklorists employed in both government agencies and private, not-for-profit organizations refer to their field as "public sector folklore" rather than applied folklore studies. In recent years confusion has arisen regarding the relationship between the two. The term "applied folklore" originated at least twenty years before "public sector folklore" or "public folklife programming." For a decade the American Folklore Society had an Applied Folklore Section. In 1983, however, it merged with the Public Sector Section, losing its name and identity. This has led some to suppose that public sector folklore has superseded applied folklore.

Because so many folklorists are now employed by government agencies and not-for-profits geared toward providing arts, educational, and cultural services to the general public, the notion of "public sector" rather than applied folklore is appealing and seems appropriate. The sobriquet "public sector" helps unify diverse programs, even if not all projects are funded with public monies, carried out by public agencies, or of benefit to the general public; folklorists are united by a common name, and presumably in common cause. The term "public sector" sounds innocuous enough, even humanitarian. It thus escapes some of the connotations of "applied folklore" (whether the political misuses and abuses or the reformist rhetoric).

Changing the name does not alter two facts, however. One is that public sector folklore is one kind of applied folklore or applied folkloristics. To document forms of traditional, symbolic behavior and then present the performers or craftspeople and information about traditional activities in public events, as public sector folklorists do,[31] does not differ conceptually from researching traditional, symbolic behavior in regard to health or aging and then providing information, planning programs, or developing policy in order to help bring about change benefiting the ill and the aged.

Conceptually, then, public sector folklore programming is one example among many of applied folkloristics. Only one essay in this book concerns the activities of a folklorist in "public service" (i.e., employed in government agencies providing educational, arts, or cultural programming). The remainder examine applications of folklore studies in the realms of education, museum exhibitions, medicine, art therapy, urban planning, aiding the homeless, organization development, tourism, aging, public relations, and economic or community development. Folklorists also use their skills as archivists, librarians, journalists, photographers, marketers, and program officers of humanities councils, to name a few other fields.

The second fact is that public folklife programming, like other examples of applied folkloristics, is a form of intervention. As David Whisnant writes, "To engage with public issues and act in the public arena is to intervene—inescapably—in the lives of individuals and in the institutions that embody their collective will and vision. The question is not whether we shall intervene, but how and with what effects, amid what particular set of historical, cultural, and political circumstances, and in the service of what values and social vision."[32] It is for this reason that the conception of applied folklore studies stated earlier begins with explicit reference to ethics. Even when "intervention" is used in a positive sense of interceding with the express purpose of resolving conflict, reducing tensions, or removing the causes of stress, there are likely to be far-reaching, unanticipated consequences.

Whisnant's warning clearly applies to situations of hard advocacy and activism in which goals are to redress social ills by affecting policy in government, education, health, and business or industry. But it also applies to the more subtly expressed mission in public sector folklore, for example, the statement of purpose of the NEA Folk Arts Program "to honor and make visible the stylistic and cultural variety that has made life in the United States an exciting challenge and an adventure in human understanding. . . . To encourage those community or family based arts that have endured through several generations, that carry with them a sense of community."[33] Hard decisions have to be made as to which examples of stylistic and cultural variety should be honored and made visible through government funding, and which community or family traditions are to be valorized and perpetuated while others languish.

The same points apply in regard to a more recent term, "cultural conservation," coined by Alan Jabbour and his staff at the American Folklife Center[34] and promulgated in *Cultural Conservation: The Protection of Cultural Heritage in the United States*, coordinated by Ormond H. Loomis (Publications of the American Folklife Center, no. 10 [Washington, D.C.: Library of Congress, 1983]). To some, the term conjures up images of putting native Americans on "reservations" or of "endangered species" in "preserves," "sanctuaries," and zoos. In the first published statement of concern, Lisa Null warned of the possibility that artificially sealing off elements of culture would result in their being "embalmed or arrested in suspended animation." Moreover, "selecting, conserving and manipulating cultural exchanges can play havoc with scholarly values of detachment and objectivity. They are certainly not responsibilities for the faint of heart." In response, Marjorie Hunt and Peter Seitel insist that "it is possible to foster the continued vitality of 'endangered species'—natural or cultural—without dismantling or derailing national and international economic, political and social institutions." They refer to an exhibit at the Festival of American Folklife about cultural conservation, which, among other things, "documents efforts on the part of the keepers of tradition themselves to conserve their own culture in the face of a changing social and physical environment." [35]

Robert Cantwell has raised questions about the concept of "culture" in cultural conservation, about "natural" and "unnatural" cultural growth, and about how to determine, "in a non-legislative context, 'the will of the people.' " Essentially, " 'Cultural conservation' denotes a competition within official culture for control of the cultural environment." [36] According to Frank de Caro, who reviewed the first national conference (1990) on "Cultural Conservation: Reconfiguring the Cultural Mission," "conference participants repeatedly expressed their dissatisfaction with" the term. "What does it mean to *conserve* culture? Does it differ from *preservation* as in historical preservation? Can we really presume to conserve anything so dynamic as culture? Does it really describe what 'cultural workers' do?" he asks. "Yet it is a brilliant term from a public relations standpoint" (not unlike Jabbour's references to "stewardship" [37]), one that evokes "ideals that resonate with the positive and the widely accepted." It serves to bring together not only folklorists but also anthropologists, planners, museum curators, civil servants, historians, and others; [38] a virtue, as long as the term is recognized as largely symbolic and serious questions continue to be raised.

Some of the other issues and concerns that have arisen in the past two decades are a function of the period, with conceptual and logistical problems looming large when folk arts or public folklife programming was just getting started. While there are basic similarities, issues also differ somewhat, depending on whether the application is folk arts programming, museum exhibitions, folklore in education, craft assistance programs, urban planning, organization development, and so on. In what follows I mention only a few of the topics receiving particular attention in the literature.

One area of concern, especially early in the history of public sector work, has been conceptual and logistical. Charles Camp has written most about the subject. This is not surprising, given the fact that he has been directly involved in public programming since 1974, when he began working at the Smithsonian's Festival of American Folklife and then two years later was hired by the Maryland Arts Council. In "Developing a State Folklife Program," in *Handbook of American Folklore* edited by Richard M. Dorson (Bloomington: Indiana University Press, 1983), Camp writes that a fundamental problem is that "arts administrators often consider the plural 'folk arts' as the common man's versions of the fine arts. Thus a skilled wood-carver becomes a 'folk da Vinci' and a badly rendered portrait is termed 'folklike' in its crudeness or naivete" (p. 518). In their programming, therefore, some folklorists are restricted to those traditional forms having a fine arts counterpart, which greatly distorts the picture of aesthetic expression in everyday life.

Another difficulty, notes Camp, is that those trying to develop state folklife programs "must view a politically defined area (the state) as a distinct culture area, and then create research and presentation strategies appropriate to both the folkloric materials to be found within the state and the constituencies served." Compounding the problem is that folklorists, who like to see themselves primarily as educators rather than civil servants, begin to be treated as a kind of scholar-in-residence, a conception that greatly limits what they can accomplish and creates misunderstanding "by fellow *workers* (not *colleagues*) as well as the public," Camp contends (p. 520).

In addition, "in a field with so few practical precedents, reasonable goals and a means for measuring the state folklorist's efforts are difficult to define," writes Camp (p. 520). "The objectives of most state folklore programs have something to do with furthering public awareness, appreciation, and support of traditional culture," but such aims are vague. Typical measurements include attendance figures at festivals, concerts, and exhibitions as well as the number and variety of groups involved in state folklife programming "as participants in workshops, as correspondents, or as field information sources" (p. 522).[39]

Yet another set of problems for folk arts coordinators revolves around the appropriateness and defensibility of standard presentational models and techniques, such as festivals, concerts, exhibits, and lectures—but particularly festivals. In an article in 1980 titled "Six Reasons Not to Produce Folklife Festivals," Charles Camp and Tim Lloyd argue that the justification for folk festivals has not been confirmed by actual experience. The contention that festivals bring information and understanding of folk culture to a wide and varied audience is dubious in that many festival goers are regulars from middle-class backgrounds who attend for the enjoyment and who are given a highly conventionalized, formulaic program of musical performances, dancing, craft demonstrations, and food for sale. The authors write, "If festivals are to begin to live up to their educational claims, those responsible for their direction and planning are going to have to realize that folklife festivals, as currently produced, do not present folk culture, even when they present tradition-bearers; and that the information presented in them, which is intended to lead to public knowledge and understanding of folk culture, is not presented in a form which that public associates with education." [40]

Part of the difficulty might be with the authors' notions of "folk culture" and "tradition-bearers," older terms implying that only certain individuals communicate or behave through traditional, symbolic forms and processes. Also important is the idea of "education." Those involved in developing folklore programs for the public must justify their activities to adminstrators, politicians, and funding sources. Because they have advanced degrees and are inclined to think of themselves more in terms of educators than bureaucrats, folklorists in government agencies or not-for-profit organizations tend to plan, implement, and defend programs by claiming educational purposes. But perhaps education is too rigidly defined in terms of the formal educational model in which the folklorists have been trained rather than in regard to a model and theory of informal, experiential learning. Finally, as Leslie Prosterman suggests in "Folk Festivals Revisited," in *Practicing Anthropology* (1985), American folk festival construction has been based largely on foreign or exotic models and recent mass-culture commercial forms. What is needed is for festival theory and technology to pay more attention to traditional American templates—the customary, indigenous, less institutionalized festivals found locally and regionally in the United States (p. 16).

There is also growing concern about ethical issues in the deliberate staging of cultural pluralism by festival organizers serving as cultural brokers. In "Why We Do the Festival," Richard Kurin, director of the Office of Folklife Programs at the Smithsonian Institution, offers numerous justifications for the Smithsonian's annual Festival of American Folklife on the National Mall. Basically, the festival encourages "the preservation and transmission of traditional cultural repertoires"; in doing so, the festival is explicitly political, serving as "an advocate for human cultural rights, for cultural equity, for cultural diversity in the context of the Smithsonian—a national institution founded with democratic, enlightened ideals." [41] "The Festival, then, is among other things a kind of morale-builder," writes Robert Cantwell in "Conjuring Culture: Ideology and Magic in the Festival of American Folklife"; "it strengthens the self-esteem of folk artists . . . and may enrich their understanding and appreciation of the culture of which they are the bearers. The Festival, moreover, provides a kind of training ground for the representation of culture." [42] Richard Bauman and a group of folklore graduate students at Indiana University interviewed performers, demonstrators, and presenters at the festival. Their report suggests a certain degree of success overall but a variety of problems as well, ranging from a lack of organization and specific direction (according to some participants) to professional rivalry among several staff and unfulfilled expectations for a number of demonstrators.[43]

In "The Brokering of Ethnic Folklore: Issues of Selection and Presentation at a Multicultural Festival," Susan Auerbach (former director of the Folk Arts Program, Cultural Affairs Department, Los Angeles) confronts head-on the matter of how festival organizers "select, define, manipulate, and sometimes alter the cultural symbols and strategies of ethnic groups." She contends that organizers of the Smithsonian's annual festival and other festivals modeled on it "create new forms of ethnic interaction and promote a fledgling national folk festival culture, with its own standards of in-group competence and performance." Using her experiences with Los Angeles's "Cityroots Festival: A Celebration of New Immigrant Traditions" (1987) as a basis, she explores how festival organizers "must confront issues of stereotyping, traditionality, acculturation, and, ultimately, the implications of cultural pluralism as a belief system."[44] Among the decisions to be made (some of which are influenced politically and ideologically as well as philosophically) are what groups to highlight in the festival, which segments of the ethnic community to invite as participants, whether to include the young or the old performers (the ethnic groups often prefer the former as evidence of the traditions' continuity, while folklorists often prefer the latter as evidence of survival), which particular individuals to invite, and what traditions from each group to include or exclude.

Such a seemingly simple matter as making food available for sale involves issues of stereotyping as well as traditionality and authenticity, observes Auerbach. For example, festival planners deliberately chose food vendors who would make those traditional dishes well known to themselves but not familiar to the general public. Yet, "the very stereotypes which festival culture opposes may be those symbols which constitute the most common meeting ground between strangers," writes Auerbach. She cites the case of the Korean cooks at Cityroots who wanted to offer an old standby, barbecue ribs, arguing that Americans already were familiar with the dish; "We want them to like our food. If we make something else, they might decide that they don't like Korean food," and, by extension, not respect the Korean people. Organizers and cooks eventually compromised on another meat dish, *bulgogi*, which has a similar taste to barbeque ribs but is generally unknown to non-Koreans.[45]

Issues of authenticity and context have also confronted curators who present folk artists in museums, according to Charlie Seemann. Regarding the first matter, "Too often museums take the path of least resistance and use performers who interpret or recreate folk arts because these people are easiest to get and are practiced performers." The other problem concerns changes in behavior and performance that occur when "an art or craft is removed from its natural context in family or community and moved into the museum."[46]

Other matters of concern in regard to museums, as M. Jane Young points out, include how "concepts from folklore theory can be used . . . to present a more dynamic and accurate picture of the relationship between people and things." In particular, she refers to the "performance-centered approach" that emphasizes the "process and total performance with audience and performer, user-maker, participant and onlooker." A logical extension is exhibitions that include, say, Zuni interpetations of Zuni history as well as interpetations by anthropologists, archeologists, and historians. Exhibits would also show multifaceted aspects of an event, for example, both the positive and negative impact of acculturation.[47]

The fact that so much programming in the folk arts has depended on a few governmental agencies for funding has not escaped attention. Bruce Jackson notes that in its second year (1975), the Folk Arts Program of the National Endowment for the Arts then headed by Alan Jabbour, awarded half a million dollars in grants. In 1976 the amount more than doubled. In 1980, Bess Hawes, who had headed the program since its third year, oversaw the distribution of $2.27 million, and in 1981 $3.1 million. "All Folk Arts grants are voted on by a panel, but Hawes selects all panel members herself," writes Jackson. "Federal folklore power, then, has been wielded by a small group of people for more than a decade."[48]

Some questions and issues focus on marketing of folk art, which was the subject of a special issue of *New York Folklore* (1986) edited by Rosemary O. Joyce. Others concern political and ethical issues precipitated by folklore programming threatening the existing power structure in a community, as discussed by Jean Haskell Speer and others in Burt Feintuch's volume, *The Conservation of Culture: Folklore and the Public Sector* (Lexington: University Press of Kentucky, 1988). Doris Dyen has confronted this and related problems, developing a "partnership approach" between the folklorist and the community that makes "the 'public' an active rather than a passive partner in any programming effort."[49] What she proposes in the realm of public sector programming resembles "participatory action research" advocated by William Foote Whyte and others for use in, especially, organization development.

Another issue, recently debated in the pages of the *American Folklore Society Newsletter* by Elliott Oring and the society's president, Barbara Kirshenblatt-Gimblett, is whether the AFS—which has been a scholarly society since its founding a century ago—can also function as a professional organization, serving the needs of not only those in academe but also folklorists occupationally involved in the application of folklore studies, particularly the freelance and consulting folklorist.

Yet other concerns are how to train this new breed of professional folklorist and how developing careers in applied work will fit into existing status systems based on the academic model.[50] Answering these questions requires identifying some of the skills and knowledge of folklorists that can be and often are applied in different realms.

Folklorists' Skills and Knowledge

Folklorists possess a number of skills and abilities that serve them well regardless of the area of application. One, of course, is knowledge of the many different forms and processes of traditional, symbolic behavior. All people tell stories, celebrate, ritualize, play, and use metaphorical expressions; they participate in traditions that convey meanings, recall past experiences, and act as symbols. Folklorists study these phenomena to discover how people interact, communicate, instruct, persuade, conceptualize, create, mark transitions, project anxieties, cope with the environment, and solve dilemmas in human relations. In the process, they also learn what defines homo sapiens as a species, namely, the fact that people behave in remarkably similar ways (i.e., folkloristically), despite differences in language, religion, or color of skin.

Another skill is knowing how to isolate examples of folklore conceptually from the continuum of human experience, record them, and analyze them. Folklorists take this ability for granted, but it seems quite mysterious to many social workers, urban planners, organization behavioralists, and others.

A third skill is being able to make sense of the data. To some, folklore is an aesthetic phenomenon primarily; performers, craftspeople, and art forms are to be appreciated for their own sake, honored, and celebrated through specially devised presentational modes (e.g., festivals, demonstrations, or folk-artists-in-the-classroom programs). Viewing folklore as an index of historical processes, some researchers have used it to reconstruct the past or to examine historical events and movements. Yet others treat folklore as an element of culture and index of sociocultural processes; they examine how traditions reflect worldview, socialize individuals and enculturate values, or mirror social and cultural change. Increasingly more researchers are conceptualizing folklore as a behavioral phenomenon and are exploring symbolic forms as an index of psychological states and processes or studying cognitive and interactional processes, such as learning, communication, and social dynamics.

In the first few pages of *Folklore and Folklife: An Introduction* (Chicago: University of Chicago, 1972), which he edited, Richard M. Dorson lists a baker's dozen "skills, perspectives, and methods that set the folklorist apart from the anthropologist, the historian, the literary critic, the sociologist, the psychologist, and the political scientist" (p. 6). The entire list (pp. 6-7) consists of the following: *fieldwork*, the *use of archives*, the *use of the folk museum*, *mastery of bibliographic tools*, the *use of indexes* that classify folklore forms (e.g., the types and motifs of folk tales), skill at *annotating* oral traditions to establish their pedigree and create a comparative base, the use of special *terminology* (i.e., constructs like "esoteric-exoteric factor," "oral formulaic composition," and "proto-memorate"), *using printed sources* to detect examples of folklore and to analyze them in relationship to oral forms, the knowledge of several languages in order to engage in *international communications* so as to have comparative data, knowledge of the *history of folkloristics*, and enough familiarity with literature to investigate *literary uses of folklore*, with anthropology to explore the *relationships of folklore to culture*, and with history to comprehend the *historical validity of oral traditions*. One could also add familiarity with musicology, linguistics, geography, sociology, and psychology, writes Dorson.

Although most are academically oriented, some of these skills have practical applications and consequences. Willard B. Moore, Elizabeth Harzoff, Jay Anderson, and other folklorists not only know how to utilize folk or open air museums, they are or have been employed in them to help develop or implement programs in cultural history interpretation or cultural resource management. Others like Joe Hickerson, Margaret Read MacDonald, and Marsha Maguire are archivists or librarians whose training in folklore was essential to landing a job in which they work with special collections. Doing fieldwork has been a vital part of public sector work that requires locating traditional performers and craftspeople to participate in arts and cultural programming.

Overall, we can infer from Dorson's list five fundamental skills and abilities resulting from training in folklore studies. One is that, in their research and analysis, folklorists are multidisciplinary and interdisciplinary. Many are as conversant with "acculturation," "anxiety reduction," and "group dynamics" used by anthropologists, psychologists, and sociologists as they are with basic concepts in literature and history. Borrowing from dramaturgy and other fields, they have evolved keywords like "art," "performance," and "praxis" to guide the study of behavior, culture, and society.[51]

Second is that folklorists have well-developed interviewing and participant observation skills. Documenting behavior, feelings, and attitudes in situations in which they naturally exist or occur provides qualitative information which the survey techniques relied on in many professions do not achieve. Folklorists are able to grasp complex social situations as well as present information in less ethnocentric ways than the layperson. Questioning rarely threatens interviewees. Folklorists have the ability to communicate sensitively and obtain information relatively painlessly from individuals across cultural, educational, and economic backgrounds. Also, they usually direct their queries toward the expressive, aesthetic, and social aspects of human experience. In the process of interviewing, folklorists are able to ask global questions, put interviewees at ease by treating them as experts on the subject, and suspend personal judgments about who or what the interviewees are and really need, which is common in ethnography but new in the service professions.[52]

Third, folklorists, like many anthropologists, are able to bridge communication gaps created by cultural differences.[53] Folklorists can also perceive the larger whole, which many cannot do because of disciplinary blinders; this skill encourages alternative views and responses to problems.

Fourth, folklorists are comparatists. As Robert A. Georges demonstrates in an article on the subject in *Western Folklore* (1986), isolating the telling of a story is a comparative act in that one identifies it as a story, or a particular kind of story, on the basis of other phenomena with which one compares it. Whatever is done with the data involves comparison, contends Georges. Amassing an archive, for example, or publishing a collection of materials, requires comparing data within an ordering system and makes information available for others to use in studies of structure, content, or style, all of which entail comparison. The oldest perspective in folklore studies, once considered *the* folklore method—namely, the historic-geographic approach —insists on comparing elements in texts or artifacts in order to ascertain ultimate origins and establish laws of continuity and change. Inferring psychological, cultural, or social meanings and functions from folklore also requires comparisons to isolate the phenomena and to test hypotheses.

It was his use of comparatism more than anything else that sets Plutarch aside as the first folklorist. In his enormously influential *Parallel Lives* he relies on detailed comparisons to bring out detailed parallels: "What Plutarch discovered was the extraordinarily repetitive automatism of human behaviour in politics, especially under stress. Political activities are so stereotyped and repetitious that individuals in different periods and societies can have almost identical careers." In *Roman Questions* Plutarch provides several alternative answers to each question he raises about a belief or custom. He also compares different regions, which makes him "unusually sensitive among ancient writers to change in folk beliefs over time."[54]

In both theoretical and practical folkloristics, this comparatist orientation helps assure an interdisciplinary or multidisciplinary approach. It leads to a search for alternative solutions to problems. And it reinforces a propensity toward cultural relativism.

Finally, folklorists have a particular set of values and outlook. What they value is human creativity, expressiveness, commensuality, and respect for history and tradition. They consider valuable and important what others often overlook: the patterns of behavior, expressive movements, figures of speech, festive events, storytelling, the communication of traditional knowledge, and other symbolic activities in which people engage in their daily interactions. When she was director of the Project on Native Americans in Science at the American Association for the Advancement of Science, Rayna Green wrote about the qualifications of folklorists:

They are trained to take texts, pots, pictures and designs apart, to develop taxonomies and make lists, without getting lost in cultural descriptions of the whole. They are trained to follow up information gained in one interview with information gained elsewhere. And they are trained to look at and where scientists never look—at those artistic, expressive materials that are the antithesis of science and the essence of culturally-based science.[55]

Folklorists consider those whose traditions they record to be experts; they treat those whose expressive behavior they document with great respect, as star performers. Most folklorists are populists. This attitude is reinforced by a field of study preoccupied not so much with the common person as with what makes us all members of a common species.

According to Alf H. Walle, who is trained in both marketing and folklore studies, there are several skills that most folklorists do *not* possess, to their disadvantage. Foremost of these is the lack of "broad, state of the art expertise in management and marketing." The "cultural resource specialist," therefore, must compete with arts management professionals who do "possess a cluster of organizational, managerial, and marketing skills." In addition, "applied anthropologists have a long history of working with bureaucrats and in predicting, monitoring, and mitigating social change," which, again, most folklorists lack. He cites Bonita Howell, an anthropologist who "has been particularly active in cultural conservation and has encouraged anthropologists to vie for dominant roles in folklife and cultural conservation activities."[56] (Unlike most anthropologists, however, Howell, who authored an essay in this volume on environmental planning, has considerable knowledge of folklore studies and empathy with folklorists.)

Folklorists themselves must be held accountable for this situation. To many, the very concept of "organization" (not to mention management) has been anathema. Witness the flap a few years ago when Robert S. McCarl and Robert Byington, and later Archie Green, Mia Boynton, and David E. Whisnant, attacked the idea of studying "organizational folklore."[57] That the motives and research agendas of proponents of organizational research could be grossly misrepresented by antagonists, in some instances for purposes of self-aggrandizement, with little comment by other members of the American Folklore Society, suggests how well-entrenched the antiorganizational sentiment was. Perhaps the remarks by Bess Lomax Hawes, who headed the Folk Arts Program of the National Endowment for the Arts, express the feelings of many public sector folklorists in the past, if not the present. "I used to think that issues involving structure and organization were not worth spending a lot of time on and that only substance and content were really important," she writes. "Perhaps the past seven years in federal service have bureaucratized me, though I hope not to the point of paralysis. Be that as it may, I certainly have more respect than I had when I came in for the limiting and shaping powers of definition, structure, and form."[58]

The worry over competition from other fields, voiced by Walle, also pervaded the 1990 American Folklife Center's meeting on "Public Sector Training and Minority Participation." According to a memorandum called Summary Report on the Meetings prepared by Timothy Lloyd, assistant to the director, "other fields, including anthropology, cultural studies, and ethnic studies, have appropriated materials and approaches folklorists once considered their own, and have established themselves in the academy and in public opinion in places where folklorists should be. Thus . . . our discipline needs to become more active in professional and public education about folklore and the work of folklorists."[59] A collection of essays such as this one, it is hoped, will help in this public education endeavor. Considering the many skills that folklorists possess, along with their knowledge of people's traditional symbolic behavior, much good can be accomplished by folklorists if given the opportunity.

Conclusion

In this chapter I have given attention to folklorists in the public sector. Nowadays, there are more of them; or else they are more outspoken, and better organized. Only a handful of trained folklorists have been involved in medicine to the extent that David Hufford has. Not many folklorists have published on the traditional and symbolic uses of space by residents of our cities, as Sara Selene Faulds has done. Few folklorists who have become travel agents or guides have related their training in folkloristics to tourism, like Elke Dettmer.

A second reason for this emphasis is that those involved in public sector folklife have written more about conceptual, administrative, ethical, and political problems than have those involved with other applications.

Such issues pervade applied folklore studies, however, and are not particular to one area.

Finally, folklore has been a university subject for only forty years but an object of scrutiny for millennia. Although public sector programming is now in the limelight, much of the attention to folklore in the past was for other practical reasons and professional use—by physicians, politicians, administrators, educators, and so forth.

Not all folklorists want to work for arts councils. In future, more will likely seek employment in journalism, education, human resources development, public relations, cultural resources management, and other areas like those dealt with in this book. Perhaps the largest potential realm of application of folklore studies is the school system. Many who have taken folklore classes have been teachers. But it was only a dozen or so years ago that Richard M. Dorson and Inta Gale Carpenter asked, "Can Folklorists and Educators Work Together?"[60] Beginning in the late 1960s, Roger Abrahams, Richard Bauman, Sylvia Grider, Margaret (Meg) Brady and other folklorists consulted with the Southwestern Educational Laboratory in Austin, Texas. Richard Blaustein, at the Center for Excellence at East Tennessee State University, works closely with educators and curriculum planners. The annual summer Fife Conference at Utah State University, directed first by William A. (Bert) Wilson and now by Barre Toelken, has long been oriented to teachers and librarians. Urban Traditions in Chicago works closely with the school system. The Los Angeles Unified School District wants an annual institute on folklore for public school teachers. And folklorists in Michigan, New York, Indiana, and elsewhere in the country have developed curriculum materials for public education.

Some public sector folklorists insist that they are looked down upon by their colleagues in academic programs. Because they do not have time for in-depth research and their publication records are modest, they feel that their work somehow doesn't measure up. These perceptions may be changing. The semiannual *Public Programs Newsletter* has become a weighty tome in which members report on activities and debate issues. The *Journal of American Folklore* now solicits reviews of exhibits, catalogues, conferences, and other creative work by public sector folklorists. The number of conferences and published collections of essays on applied folklore, cultural conservation, and public sector folklore has increased significantly. The status of applied folklorists will continue to rise as they develop and articulate a discipline with its own concepts, methods, and theories.

Increasingly folklore programs are offering courses in applied folklore studies not only because more graduates will seek careers outside academe but also because there is a growing literature, body of issues, and set of skills to teach. A meeting at the American Folklife Center in June 1991 on public sector training and minority participation emphasized that public sector folklore is not separate from academic theory. The chairs of folklore programs estimated that 60 percent of their graduates find employment outside academe; hence the need for training of students in applied folkloristics, and even the hiring of faculty with both academic and applied experience.

Some folklore courses currently taught are obviously more relevant than others to practitioners, e.g., courses on fieldwork, folk medicine, belief and ritual, and organizational culture and symbolism. No matter how esoteric or arcane the subject, however, much other folklore instruction is also valuable. This is because of the questions raised. Typically folklorists attempt to establish what the traditions are and analyze the themes, structures, and rules that underlie them. They inquire about how and why examples of folklore are generated, perpetuated, modified, extinguished, or revived. They also seek to uncover meanings, uses, and functions.

Such questions help differentiate the field of folklore studies. Their repetition drives home the fact that folklorists deal with certain data in particular ways for specific reasons. Students are taught to identify, value, and understand the traditional, symbolic forms and processes called folklore that are common to human beings everywhere and that define the species. Although certain courses may make applications more apparent, almost any curriculum in folklore studies is, ultimately, useful.

Notes

1. I am indebted to Simon J. Bronner for calling this reference to my attention and for many other historical facts, such as information on the American folklore program at Franklin and Marshall College, the Cooperstown Program, the Pennsylvania Dutch Folklore Center, and the work and writings of Victorian American folklorists. See the enlightening volume edited by Simon J. Bronner, *Folklife Studies from the Gilded Age: Object, Rite, and Custom in Victorian America* (Ann Arbor: UMI Research Press, 1987), especially his "Introduction," pp. 1-49; and also issues of the *Folklore Historian* (1984-present), published by the History and Folklore Section of the American Folklore Society. For more information about "ethnic display events," "small group festive gatherings," and "protofestival," which are mentioned in this section, see respectively Larry W. Danielson, "The Ethnic Festival and Cultural Revivalism in a Small Midwestern Town" (Ph.D. diss., Indiana University, 1972); Linda T. Humphrey, "Small Group Festive Gatherings," *Journal of the Folklore Institute* 16 (1979): 190-201; and John A. Gutowski, "The Protofestival: Local Guide to American Folk Behavior," *Journal of the Folklore Institute* 15 (1978):113-32.

2. More recently General Edward Geary Lansdale compiled an extensive collection of folksongs of American troops in the Vietnam War, making use of them as a technique of psychological warfare and a means of conveying intelligence, according to Lydia M. Fish in "General Edward G. Lansdale and the

Folksongs of Americans in the Vietnam War," *Journal of American Folklore* 102 (1989): 390-411.

3. Daniel Levine, *Jane Addams and the Liberal Tradition* (Madison: State Historical Society of Wisconsin, 1971), 157; see also pp. 145-47. See also Jane Addams, *Twenty Years at Hull-House, with Autobiographical Notes* (New York: Macmillan, 1938), 235-46, 256.

4. See William I. Thomas and Florian Znaniecki, *The Polish Peasant in Europe and America*, edited and abridged by Eli Zaretsky (Urbana: Univ. of Illinois Press, 1984), 1, 2, 9.

5. Benjamin A. Botkin, "Applied Folklore: Creating Understanding Through Folklore," *Southern Folklore Quarterly* 17 (1953): 203-4; see also Rachel Davis DuBois, *Neighbors in Action: A Manual for Local Leaders in Intergroup Relations* (New York: Harper and Brothers, 1950), especially pp. 87-89.

6. Dorothy Mills Howard, "Folklore in the Schools," *New York Folklore Quarterly* 6 (1950): 99-107; the quote is from p. 99.

7. Richard Kurin, "Why We Do the Festival," in Thomas Vennum, Jr., ed., *1989 Festival of American Folklife* (Washington, D.C.: Smithsonian Institution Press, 1989).

8. For origins of the term "cultural conservation," see Alan Jabbour, "Director's Column, *Folklife Center News* 8 (Oct.-Dec.): 2-3. See the challenge by Lisa Null, "Letters to the Editor," *American Folklore Society Newsletter* 14 (October): 2, 3; and the reply by Marjorie Hunt and Peter Seitel, "Response to Null," *AFSN* 14 (October): 3, 6. For other works promoting or exploring the subject, see Ormond Loomis, coordinator, *Cultural Conservation: The Protection of Cultural Heritage in the United States* (Washington, D.C.: Library of Congress Publications of the American Folklife Center, no. 10), and Burt Feintuch, ed., *The Conservation of Culture: Folklorists and the Public Sector* (Lexington: Univ. Press of Kentucky, 1988).

9. Chad Berry, "The Graduate Program in Folk Studies at Western Kentucky University," *Folklore Forum* 19 (1986): 175.

10. Richard M. Dorson, "Applied Folklore," in Dick Sweterlitsch, ed., *Papers on Applied Folklore* (Bloomington: Folklore Forum Bibliographic and Special Series, no. 8, 1971), 40.

11. Barbara Kirshenblatt-Gimblett, "Mistaken Dichotomies," *Journal of American Folklore* 101 (1988): 140. On his concept of "fakelore," see Richard Dorson, *American Folklore and the Historian* (Chicago: Univ. of Chicago Press, 1971), 2-14.

12. Bruce Jackson, "Ben Botkin," *New York Folklore Quarterly* 12 (1986): 24.

13. Dorson, *American Folklore*, 4.

14. See Simon J. Bronner, "A Prophetic Vision of Public and Academic Folklife: Alfred Shoemaker and America's First Department of Folklore," *Folklore Historian* 8 (1991): 39-50. Also at Franklin and Marshall was the Pennsylvania Dutch Folklore Center, which sponsored an archive, outdoor museum, public seminar, and a tabloid-format periodical called *The Pennsylvania Dutchman*. In 1958 the center was incorporated, changing its name to the Pennsylvania Folklife Society and its publication to *Pennyslvania Folklife*. See Don Yoder, *Discovering American Folklife: Studies in Ethnic, Religious, and Regional Culture* (Ann Arbor: UMI Research Press, 1990), 4, 5; and Don Yoder, "Folklife in Pennsylvania: An Historical Survey," *Keystone Folklore*, n.s. 1 (1982): 8-20.

15. Robert H. Byington, "What Happened to Applied Folklore?" in Charles Camp, ed., *Time and Temperature: A Centennial Publication of the American Folklore Society* (Washington, D.C.: American Folklore Society, 1989), 78. For some reason, the Committee on Applied Folklore's definition was not published in the special issue on the subject in 1971, although Henry and Betty-Jo Glassie did quote most of it, leaving out "social, economic, and technological" between the words "contemporary" and "problems." See page 31 of their article, "The Implications of Folkloristic Thought for Historic Zoning Ordinances," in Sweterlitsch, *Papers on Applied Folklore*, 31-37.

16. Byington, "What Happened to Applied Folklore?" 78.

17. Dorson, "Applied Folklore," 40.

18. Benjamin A. Botkin, "Applied Folklore: Creating Understanding Through Folklore," *Southern Folklore Quarterly* 17 (1953): 199.

19. Botkin, "Applied Folklore," 199, 204; and Benjamin A. Botkin, "WPA and Folklore Research: Bread and Song," *Southern Folklore Quarterly* 3 (1939): 10.

20. William Nicolaisen, "The Mapping of Folk Culture as Applied Folklore," in *Papers on Applied Folklore*, ed. Dick Sweterlitsch (Bloomington: Folklore Forum Bibliographic and Special Series, no. 8, 1971), 23.

21. David Hufford, "Some Approaches to the Application of Folklore Studies," in Sweterlitsch, *Papers on Applied Folklore*, 6.

22. David Hufford, "Folklore Studies and Health," *Practicing Anthropology*, 1-2 (1985): 23.

23. To an extent, this conception is influenced by the definition of applied anthropology set forth in John van Willigen, *Anthropology In Use: A Bibliographic Chronology of the Development of Applied Anthropology* (Pleasantville, N.Y.: Redgrave, 1980), 3.

24. Shalom Staub, "Charting a Course Back (and Forward) to Applied Folklore," unpublished paper given at the American Folklore Society meeting, Philadelphia, 1989.

25. Suzanne Waldenberger, "Today's MINSTREL: Computer Generated Narrative," unpublished report, UCLA Folklore and Mythology Archive, 1987.

26. Dewhurst and MacDowell's fact-finding and assessments are included in various sections of Richard W. Stoffle, ed., *Cultural and Paleontalogical Effects of Siting a Low-Level Radioactive Waste Storage Facility in Michigan: Candidate Area Analysis Phase* (Ann Arbor: Institute for Social Research, University of Michigan, 1990). In regard to the conference on cultural conservation, see the review by Frank de Caro, published in *Journal of American Folklore* 104 (1991): 85-91.

27. Richard Bauman, "Proposal for a Center of Applied Folklore," in Sweterlitsch, *Papers on Applied Folklore*, 1.

28. See Yoder, "Folklife in Pennsylvania," 14-16.

29. Charles Camp, "Developing a State Folklife Program," in Richard M. Dorson, ed., *Handbook of American Folklore* (Bloomington: Indiana Univ. Press, 1983), 518.

30. Margy McClain, "The Role of Folklore in Not-for-Profit Organizations." Unpublished paper given at UCLA, Jan. 9, 1991.

31. This characterization comes close to the definitions of "public folklore" and "folklife programming" as defined, respectively, by Bruce R. Buckely, "Forty Years Before the Mast: Sailing the Stormy and Serene Seas of Public

Folklore," *New York Folklore* 15 (1990): 1, and Doris Dyen, "Individual and Community: Defining the Goals of Public Folklife Programming," *Kentucky Folklore Record* 32 (1986): 91.

32. David E. Whisnant, "Public Sector Folklore as Intervention: Lessons of Past, Prospects for the Future," in Feintuch, *Conservation of Culture*, 233.

33. Betty Belanus, "Evaluating Public Sector Folklore: The Tennessee State Parks Folklife Project," Ph.D. dissertation, Folklore, Indiana University, 1990, 54.

34. Jabbour, "Director's Column," 2-3.

35. Null, "Letters to the Editor," 2-3; and Hunt and Seitel, "Response to Null," in the same issue, pp. 3 and 6.

36. Robert Cantwell, "Conjuring Culture: Ideology and Magic in the Festival of American Folklife," *Journal of American Folklore* 104 (1991): 148-63. See also the criticism of Cantwell's essay and his response in *Journal of American Folklore* 104 (1991): Peter Seitel, "Magic, Knowledge, and Irony in Scholarly Exchange: A Comment on Robert Cantwell's Observations on the Festival of American Folklife" (pp. 495-96); and Robert Cantwell, "Response to Peter Seitel" (pp. 496-99).

37. Alan Jabbour, "On the Values of American Folklorists," *Journal of American Folklore* 102 (1989): 292-98.

38. Quotes are from Frank de Caro's review, cited in note 26, pp. 86-87.

39. Similar measures were employed decades earlier when Allen Eaton designed the specular America's Making Exhibit during the 1920s to impress upon the nation the rich diversity and worthiness of immigrant groups. In his book *Immigrant Gifts to American Life: Some Experiments in Appreciation of the Contributions of Our Foreign-Born Citizens to American Culture* (New York: Russell Sage Foundation, 1932), 63-66, Eaton presents statistics and anecdotal evidence of interest measured by several factors. One was attendance ("the largest number on record for any two consecutive weeks since the gallery had been dedicated nine years before"). Others focused on the foreign-born themselves (the subjects of the exhibit), including their increased interest in organizations in the U.S. sponsoring them, in classes conducted in public schools for their benefit, in applications for citizenship, and in changed attitudes toward this country and its government.

40. Charles Camp and Timothy Lloyd, "Six Reasons Not to Produce Folklife Festivals," *Kentucky Folklore Record* 26 (1980): 72. See also Henry Willett, "Re-Thinking the State Folk Arts Program (Or, Alternatives to the Festival)," *Kentucky Folklore Record* 26 (1980): 12-15. For a critique of Camp and Lloyd's essay, as well as an excellent consideration of a range of festive events and what they have in common, see Magda Zelinska-Ferl, "Festive Events: In Pursuit of Meaningful Experiences," Ph.D. dissertation, University of California, Los Angeles, 1991 (particularly Chapter I, "On Studying Festive Events: An Introduction," pp. 4-24, and Chapter V, "Festivals: How Educational Are They? A Case of the Smithsonian Folklife Festival," pp. 103-30).

41. Page 10 of Richard Kurin, "Why We Do the Festival," in Frank Proschan, ed., *Program Book* (Washington, D.C.: Smithsonian Festival of American Folklife, Smithsonian Institution, 1989), 8-21.

42. See Cantwell, "Conjuring Culture," 150.

43. Richard Bauman, Patricia Sawin, and Inta Carpenter, *Reflections on the Folklife Festival: An Ethnography of Participant Experience* (Bloomington: Folklore Institute, Indiana University, Special Publications, No. 2, 1992).

44. Pages 225 and 226 in Susan Auerbach, "The Brokering of Ethnic Folklore: Issues of Selection and Presentation Issues at a Multicultural Festival," in Stephen Stern and John Allan Cicala, eds., *Creative Ethnicity: Symbols and Strategies of Contemporary Ethnic Life* (Logan: Utah State Univ. Press, 1991), 225-38.

45. Auerbach, "Brokering of Ethnic Folklore," 230.

46. Charlie Seemann, "Presenting the Live Folk Artist in the Museum," in Charlie Seemann and Patricia Hall, eds., *Folklife and Museums: Selected Readings* (Nashville: American Association of State and Local History, 1987), 61.

47. M. Jane Young, "The Value of Things: Folklore and the Anthropological Museum Exhibit," *Practicing Anthropology* 1-2 (1985): 19.

48. Bruce Jackson, "The Folksong Revival," *New York Folklore* 11 (1985): 201.

49. Doris J. Dyen, "Two Concepts of Public Programming: The Partnership Approach and the Folk Cultural Exposition," *Kentucky Folklore Record* 30 (1984): 17. See also her article, "Individual and Community," 91-109. Also see William Foote Whyte and Kathleen King Whyte, *Learning from the Field: A Guide from Experience* (Beverly Hills: Sage, 1984), 163-91, and William Foote Whyte, ed., *Participatory Action Research* (Newbury Park, Calif.: Sage, 1991).

50. This set of questions is similar to the concerns raised by John Bushnell in "The Art of Practicing Anthropology," in Michael V. Angrosino, ed., *Do Applied Anthropologists Apply Anthropology?* (Athens: Southern Anthropological Society Proceedings, no. 10, distributed by the Univ. of Georgia Press, 1976), 10.

51. Simon J. Bronner, "Art, Performance, and Praxis: The Rhetoric of Contemporary Folklore Studies," *Western Folklore* 47 (1987): 75-101.

52. James W. Green and James W. Leigh, "Teaching Ethnographic Methods to Social Service Workers," *Practicing Anthropology* 11:3 (1989): 8-10.

53. Walter Goldschmidt and Peggy Reeves Sanday, "Postschrift: The Present Uses of Anthropology: An Overview," in Walter Goldschmidt, ed., *The Uses of Anthropology* (Washington, D.C.: American Anthropological Association Publication, no. 11, 1979), 258.

54. W.M.S. Russell, "Plutarch as a Folklorist," in Venetia J. Newall, ed., *Folklore Studies in the Twentieth Century: Proceedings of the Centenary Conference of the Folklore Society* (Totowa, N.J.: Rowman and Littlefield, 1980), 374, 375. Writes Russell, p. 375: "the methods used by Plutarch . . . entitle him to be considered a pioneer of folklore study." See also F.B. Jevons, ed., *Plutarch's Romane Questions, Translated A.D. 1603 by Philemon Holland* (London: David Nutt, 1892), v: "Plutarch's *Romane Questions* may fairly be said to be the earliest formal treatise written on the subject of folk-lore. The problems which Plutarch proposes for solution are mainly such as the modern science of folk-lore undertakes to solve; and though Plutarch was not the first to propound them, he was the first to make a collection and selection of them and give them a place of their own in literature."

55. Rayna Green, "Culturally-Based Science: The Potential for Traditional People, Science, and Folklore," in Newall, *Folklore Studies in the Twentieth Century*, 212. See also Lynwood Montell, "Academic and Applied Folklore: Partners

for the Future," *Folklore Forum* 16 (1983): 159-74, who quotes Green, 168-69.

56. Page 269 in Alf H. Walle's article "Cultural Conservation: Public Sector Folklore and Its Rivals," *Western Folklore* 49 (1990): 261-75.

57. See Robert Byington, "Letter to the Editor," *The American Folklore Society Newsletter* 14 (Feb. 1985): 4; Mia Boynton, "Folklore in the Industrial Workplace," *New York Folklore* 14:1-7 (p. 1); Archie Green, "At the Hall, in the Stope: Who Treasures Tales of Work?" *Western Folklore* 46 (1987): 153-70 (p. 168); Robert S. McCarl, "Letter to Editor," *The American Folklore Society Newsletter* 13 (Dec. 1984): 2, 5, and "Letter to the Editor: Reply to Michael Owen Jones," *The American Folklore Society Newsletter* 14 (June 1985): 2, 5; and Whisnant, "Public Sector Folklore as Intervention," 243. McCarl tacked on to several articles statements attacking and misrepresenting organizational folklore; see for example, "Accident Narratives: Self Protection in the Workplace," *New York Folklore* 14 (1988): 35-44; and "Occupational Folklife in the Public Sector: A Case Study," in Feintuch, *The Conservation of Culture*, 132-53.

For counters to some of the misplaced criticism of organizational folklore studies, see Alf H. Walle, "Letter to the Editor," *The American Folklore Society Newsletter* 14 (June 1985): 2, 3; Simon J. Bronner, *American Folklore Studies: An Intellectual History* (Lawrence: Univ. Press of Kansas, 1986), 125-28; Michael Owen Jones, "On Folklorists Studying Organizations: A Reply to Robert S. McCarl," *American Folklore Society Newsletter* 14 (Apr. 1985): 5, 6, 8; Michael Owen Jones, "Is Ethics the Issue?" in Peter J. Frost, Larry F. Moore, Meryl Reis Louis, Craig C. Lundberg, and Joanne Martin, eds., *Organizational Culture* (Beverly Hills: Sage, 1985), 235-52; and Michael Owen Jones, "Why Folklore and Organization(s)?" *Western Folklore* 50 (1991): 29-40.

58. Bess Lomax Hawes, "Aspects of Federal Folklife," *Practicing Anthropology* 1-2 (1985): 4-5 (the quote is on p. 5).

59. Timothy Lloyd, "Report from American Folklife Center Meeting on Public Sector Training and Minority Participation," *American Folklore Society Newsletter* 20:5 (Oct. 1991): 3-5.

60. Richard M. Dorson and Inta Gale Carpenter, "Can Folklorists and Educators Work Together?" *North Carolina Folklore Journal* 26 (1978): 3-13.

For Further Information

For information about Plutarch, see references to Russell and Jevons in footnote 54. Many people have written about the uses of folklore in literature; see, for example, Mary Ellen Brown, *Burns and Tradition* (London: Macmillan, 1984); Carl Lindahl, *Earnest Games: Folkloric Patterns in the Canterbury Tales* (Bloomington: Indiana University Press, 1987); and Steven Swan Jones, *Folklore and Literature in the United States: An Annotated Bibliography of Studies of Folklore in American Literature* (New York: Garland, 1984). The term "usable past" is from Simon J. Bronner, *American Folklore Studies: An Intellectual History* (Lawrence: Univ. Press of Kansas, 1986), Chapter 1, "The Usable Hidden Past of Folklore," pp. 1-38.

For further information about basic concepts and terms, see Dan Ben-Amos, "The Concept of Motif in Folklore," in Venetia J. Newall, ed., *Folklore*

Studies in the Twentieth Century: Proceedings of the Centenary Conference of the Folklore Society (Totowa, N.J.: Rowman and Littlefield, 1980), 17-36; Bronner, *American Folklore Studies*; Jan Harold Brunvand, *The Study of American Folklore: An Introduction* 3rd ed. (New York: Norton, 1986); Alan Dundes, *The Study of Folklore* (Englewood Cliffs, N.J.: Prentice-Hall, 1965); George H. Schoemaker, ed., *The Emergence of Folklore in Everyday Life: A Fieldguide and Sourcebook* (Bloomington, Ind.: Trickster Press, 1990); Barre Toelken, *The Dynamics of Folklore* (Boston: Houghton Mifflin, 1979); Don Yoder, "The Folklife Studies Movement," *Pennsylvania Folklife* 13 (1963): 43-56. My emphasis on repetition and reproduction is from Robert A. Georges, "Folklore," in David Lance, ed., *Sound Archives: A Guide to Their Establishment and Development* (Milton Keynes, England: International Association of Sound Archives, 1983), 134-44.

In the *Dynamics of Folklore*, Toelken includes a section titled "Applied Folklore as a Basis for Action," pp. 353-67. See also Benjamin A. Botkin, "Delegate's Report on the 34th Annual Meeting of the American Council of Learned Societies," *Journal of American Folklore* 65 (1952): 182-83, from which is taken the statement that serves as the epigram to my chapter in this book; "Applied Folklore: Creating Understanding Through Folklore," *Southern Folklore Quarterly* 17 (1953): 199-206; and "Proposal for an Applied Folklore Center," *New York Folklore Quarterly* 17 (1961): 151-54.

Also see Dick Sweterlitsch, ed., *Papers on Applied Folklore* (Bloomington, Ind.: Folklore Forum Bibliographic and Special Series, no. 8, 1971), and also his article, "Applied Folklore: Debate Goes On," *Folklore Forum* 4: 15-18. Strangely the definition of applied folklore proposed at this time was not printed in its entirety until recently in Robert H. Byington's "What Happened to Applied Folklore?" in Charles Camp, ed., *Time and Temperature: A Centennial Publication of the American Folklore Society* (Washington, D.C.: American Folklore Society), 77-79. Although he did not use the term "applied folklore studies," David J. Hufford came close to it in the title of his article "Some Approaches to the Application of Folklore Studies," in Sweterlitsch, *Papers on Applied Folklore*, 166-75. I used the term "applied folklore studies" in 1981 in the title of a session of papers, and in my own essay, at the California Folklore Society Meeting, April, UCLA, and finally began to employ it in print beginning with "Is Ethics the Issue?" in Peter J. Frost, Larry F. Moore, Meryl Reis Louis, Craig Lundberg, and Joanne Martin, eds., *Organizational Culture* (Beverly Hills: Sage, 1985), 235-52.

Few seem to have tried to define either applied folklore or applied folklore studies. Although Lynwood Montell writes about "Academic and Applied Folklore: Partners for the Future," *Folklore Forum* 16 (1983): 159-74, giving examples of applied folklore, he does not really explain either academic or applied folklore as constructs. Surprisingly, neither does Barbara Kirshenblatt-Gimblett in her well-received essay, "Mistaken Dichotomies," *Journal of American Folklore* 101 (1988): 140-55. In his "Reflections on 'Keywords' in Public-Sector Folklore," *Practicing Anthropology* 1-2 (1985): 4-5, Archie Green mentions such terms as fieldwork, invention, intervention, and advocacy. He characterizes the latter: "folklore advocates are simply those employed in non-teaching roles" (p. 4), a definition of advocacy that some might find disappointing and one with which some in teaching roles might take issue.

On the Romantics and the nationalistic use of folklore, see Ellen J. Stekert, "Tylor's Theory of Survivals and National Romanticism: Their Influence on Early American Folksong Collectors," *Southern Folklore Quarterly* 32 (1968): 209-36. In "Who Benefits from Folklore?" (*German Volkskunde: A Decade of Theoretical Confrontation, Debate, and Reorientation [1967-1977]*, edited and translated by James R. Dow and Hannjost Lixfeld [Bloomington: Indiana Univ. Press, 1986], 41), Dieter Kramer writes, "During the periods of absolutism and the Enlightenment, early 'folklore' was to a great extent an 'administrative auxiliary science.' It was very much in the interest of politics directed toward social change, i.e., toward 'improving conditions.' "

Increasingly more people are writing about folklore and the U.S. federal government. See Susan Dwyer-Shick, "The Development of Folklore and Folklife Research in the Federal Writer's Project, 1935-1943," *Keystone Folklore Quarterly* 20 (1975): 5-31; "Review Essay: Folklore and Government Support," *Journal of American Folklore* 89 (1976): 476-86; and "The American Folklore Society and Folklore Research in America, 1888-1944" (Ph.D. dissertation, Folklore and Folklife, University of Pennsylvania, 1979). In addition, see the first chapter of Betty Belanus's Ph.D. dissertation in Folklore at Indiana University, "The Structure of Public Sector Folklore: The Tennessee State Parks Folklife Project" (1990); Jerold Hirsch, "Cultural Pluralism and Applied Folklore: The New Deal Precedent," in Burt Feintuch, ed., *The Conservation of Culture: Folklorists and the Public Sector* (Lexington: Univ. Press of Kentucky, 1988), 46-67; and several articles in Feintuch's book, such as his "Introduction: Folklorists and the Public Sector," 1-16, Erika Brady's "The Bureau of American Ethnology: Folklore, Fieldwork, and the Federal Government in the Late Nineteenth and Early Twentieth Centuries," 35-45, and various appended documents. See also Peter Thomas Bartis, "A History of the Archive of Folk Song at the Library of Congress: The First Fifty Years" (Ph.D. dissertation, Folklore and Folklife, University of Pennsylvania, 1982); Bruce Jackson, Judith McCulloh, and Marta Weigle, eds., *Folklore/Folklife* (Washington, D.C.: American Folklore Society, 1984).

In regard to Botkin, see especially Jerold Hirsch, "Folklore in the Making: B.A. Botkin," *Journal of American Folklore* 100 (1987): 3-38; Bruce Jackson, "Benjamin A. Botkin (1901-1975)," *Journal of American Folklore* 89 (1976): 1-5, and "Ben Botkin," *New York Folklore* 12 (1986): 23-32; and Ronna Lee Widner, "Lore for the Folk: Benjamin A. Botkin and the Development of Folklore Scholarship in America," *New York Folklore* 12 (1986): 1-22. The latter writes in note 3, page 21: "One-half million copies of *A Treasury of American Folklore* were sold during the first three years of publication. Some twenty editions had appeared by 1971, and forty years after its initial appearance the book remains in print."

In recent years Botkin has had his apologists, some of whom attempt to portray him as the hero of applied folklore. In preparing this chapter I read both what Botkin wrote on the subject and considered at length his statements quoted by others. Try as I might, I have been unable to interpret his conception of applied folklore (which is vaguely stated at best)—when applied to himself and his activities—as anything more than justifying his compilations as "lore for the folk," to use Widner's phrase. As Botkin wrote and others often quote, he aspired to give "back to the people what we have taken from them and what rightfully belongs to them, in a form . . . which they can understand and use" (see "WPA and Folklore Research: 'Bread and Song,'" *Southern Folklore Quarterly* 3 [1939] :10). While this might be applying folklore for one's own benefit first (by publishing popular treasuries) and for the general American populace secondarily, it scarcely seems to be applied folkloristics in the modern sense.

To mention just a few of the publications on political uses of folklore that appeared in *Journal of the Folklore Institute*, which was founded and edited by Richard M. Dorson, see I. Bazgoz, "Folklore Studies and Nationalism in Turkey," 9 (1972): 162-76; S. Eminov, "Folklore and Nationalism in Modern China," 12 (1975): 257-77; A. Haque, "The Uses of Folklore in Nationalistic Movements and Liberation Struggles: A Case Study of Bangladesh," 12 (1975): 211-40; R. Klymasz, "Folklore Politics in the Soviet Ukraine: Perspectives on Some Recent Trends and Developments," 12 (1975): 177-88; and F. Oinas, "The Political Uses and Themes of Folklore in the Soviet Union," 12 (1975): 157-76. For some examples from the *Journal of American Folklore*, see J. Dow, "German *Volkskunde* and National Socialism," 100 (1987): 300-304; C. Kamenetsky, "Folklore as a Political Tool in Nazi Germany," 85 (1972): 221-35; and W. Mieder, "Proverbs in Nazi Germany: The Promulgation of Anti-Semitism and Stereotypes Through Folklore," 95 (1982): 435-64. Also see G. Ortutay, "The Science of Folklore in Hungary Between the Two World Wars and During the Period Subsequent to the Liberation," *Acta Ethnographica* 4 (1955): 6-89; L. Snyder, "Nationalistic Aspects of the Grimm Brothers' Fairy Tales," *Journal of Social Psychology* 33 (1951): 209-23; Betty Wang, "Folksongs as Regulators of Politics," *Sociology and Social Research* 20 (1935): 161-66: and A.C. Yen, "Red China's Use of Folklore," *Literature East and West* 8 (1964): 72-87. See also Simon J. Bronner, "The Use of Folklore in the Shaping of American Ideology, 1880-1990," *International Folklore Review* 6 (1988): 21-25, whose thesis is that "in this formative period for professional cultural studies [1880-1900], scholars self-consciously prepared a menu of culture which fed the appetite of policymakers and opinion moulders" (p. 21).

For information about folklore programs and teaching folklore, see Ronald L. Baker, "Folklore and Folklife Studies in American and Canadian Colleges and Universities," *Journal of American Folklore* 99 (1986): 50-74; Elliott Oring, "Preface," in *Folk Groups and Folklore Genres: An Introduction* (Logan: Utah State Univ. Press, 1986), ix-xiv; Bruce Jackson, ed., *Teaching Folklore* (Buffalo: Documentary Research, Inc., rev. ed., 1989); and Ralph Steele Boggs, "Folklore in University Curricula in the United States," *Southern Folklore Quarterly* 4 (1940): 93-109.

Robert Baron and John Suter describe the "Presenting Folk Arts" Conference and Showcase held at Cornell University in June 1990 in *Public Programs Newsletter*, vol. 8, no. 2 (Oct. 1990), 9-15. The newsletter is an excellent source for anyone interested in public folklore and folklife programming, particularly the arts. It is published by the Public Sector Section of the American Folklore Society. For subscription information, write to the AFS at 4350 North Fairfax Drive, Suite 640, Arlington, VA 22203.

Several special issues of journals and book-length collections of essays have been devoted to different aspects of applied folklore. See, for example, "Folklore in the Schools," *Keystone Folklore Quarterly* (1978); "Folk Festival Issues," edited by David E. Whisnant, *John Edwards Memorial Foundation*, special series, no. 12 (1978); "Folklore in the Schools," *North Carolina Folklore Journal* (1978); "Folklore and the Public Sector," *Kentucky Folklore Record* (1980); "The State of Folkloristics," *New York Folklore* (1983); "Applied Folklore," edited by Leslie Prosterman, *Practicing Anthropology* (1985); "Marketing Folk Art," edited by Rosemary Joyce, *New York Folklore* (1986); Patricia Hall and Charlie Seemann, eds., *Folklife and Museums: Selected Readings* (Nashville: American Association for State and Local History, 1988); "Folk Arts in New York State: A Public Forum," edited by Deborah Blincoe and John Forrest, *New York Folklore* (1989); and "Folklore in Education," edited by Nancy J. Nusz, *Southern Folklore* 8 (1991).

For an extensive bibliography on folklife and education as well as numerous examples of applications, see Marsha MacDowell, ed., *Folk Arts in Education: A Resource Handbook* (East Lansing: Michigan State University Museum, 1987). See also the collection of essays, bibliographies, filmography, and sample lesson plans compiled by Judith E. Haut and Michael Owen Jones, *Folklore Conference: Hearing Their Stories: Narrating, Self, and Cultural Diversity in the Classroom* (Los Angeles: Academic Publishing Service, University of California, 1991).

Benita J. Howell has been most active in regard to applying folklore research to environmental planning. See such works as *A Survey of Folklife Along the Big South Fork of the Cumberland River* (Knoxville: University of Tennessee, Department of Anthropology, Report of Investigations No. 30, 1981); "Folklife Research in Environmental Planning," in William Millsap, ed., *Applied Social Science for Environmental Planning* (Boulder: Westview Press, Social Impact Assessment Series, no. 10, 1984), 127-39; and "Folklife in Planning," *CRM [Cultural Resources Management] Bulletin*, 10:1 (Feb. 1987): 14, 15, 29. See also Ed Evans, "Folklorist [Gregg Richie] Searches Out Poets, Quilters, Musicians Among Clover Fork Residents," *US Army Corps of Engineers District Digest* 91 (July 1991): 10-11.

For applications of folklore studies to organizations, see Polly Stewart, "The Folklorist as Academic Administrator," in *Time and Temperature: A Centennial Publication of the American Folklore Society*, ed. Charles Camp (Washington, D.C.: The American Folklore Society), 18; Michael Owen Jones, "Why Folklore and Organization(s)?" *Western Folklore* 50 (1991): 29-40; Michael Owen Jones, ed., "Emotions in Work: A Folklore Approach," *American Behavioral Scientist* 33:3 (Jan./ Feb. 1990); and Michael Owen Jones, Michael Dane Moore, and Richard Christopher Snyder, eds., *Inside Organizations: Understanding the Human Dimension* (Newbury Park, Calif.: Sage).

In regard to marketing, see John F. Sherry, Jr., "Some Implications of Consumer Oral Tradition for Reactive Marketing," in Thomas Kinnear, ed., *Advances in Consumer Research*, vol. 2 (Ann Arbor: Association for Consumer Research, 1984).

For a recent work on folklore and health, see Diane E. Goldstein, ed., *Talking AIDS: Interdisciplinary Perspectives on Acquired Immune Deficiency Syndrome* (St. John's: ISER Research and Policy Papers, No. 12, Memorial University of Newfoundland, 1991).

Some of the applications in anthropology are similar to those in folklore studies, and issues may overlap. See, for example, Michael V. Angrosino, ed., *Do Applied Anthropologists Apply Anthropology?* (Athens: Southern Anthropological Society, distributed by the Univ. of Georgia Press, 1976); Constance P. deRoche, "Empathy and the Anthropological Imagination," *Practicing Anthropology* 11:3 (1989): 7; Elizabeth M. Eddy and William L. Partridge, eds., *Applied Anthropology in America* (New York: Columbia Univ. Press, 1978); Walter Goldschmidt, *The Uses of Anthropology* (Washington, D.C.: A Special Publication of the American Anthropological Association, No. 11, 1979); Robert T. Trotter, II, ed., *Anthropology for Tomorrow: Creating Pratitioner-Oriented Applied Anthropology Programs* (Washington, D.C.: A Special Publication of the American Anthropological Association in Collaboration with the National Association for the Practice of Anthropology, No. 24, 1988); John van Willigen, *Anthropology in Use: A Bibliographic Chronology of the Development of Applied Anthropology* (Pleasantville, N. Y.: Redgrave); and John van Willigen, Barbara Rylko-Bauer, and Ann McElroy, ed., *Making Our Research Useful: Case Studies in the Utilization of Anthropological Knowledge* (Boulder: Westview Press, 1989). These works also consider some of the skills of ethnographers.

In regard to folklorists' values and orientation, see also Alan Jabbour's American Folklore Society's centennial presidential address, "On the Values of American Folklorists," *Journal of American Folklore* 102 (1989): 292-98. Related to this subject is the matter of career choice. See Bruce R. Buckley, "Forty Years Before the Mast: Sailing the Stormy and Serene Seas of Public Folklore," *New York Folklore* 15 (1990): 1-15; Bruce Jackson, "The Folksong Revival," *New York Folklore* 11 (1985): 195-203; and Richard A. Reuss and Jens Lund, eds., *Roads into Folklore: Festschrift in Honor of Richard M. Dorson* (Bloomington, Ind.: Folklore Forum Bibliographic and Special Series, No. 14, 1975). In his introduction to the latter work, Reuss writes (p. 1), "Some were influenced to a large degree by their avid contacts with popular folklore materials, either through the folksong revival or printed collections. Some took up folkloristics as a career as an outgrowth of a search for ethnic identity. . . . Some gravitated toward our discipline as a substitute for other subject areas that for one reason or another were unsatisfying. . . . A number of writers state or imply that they became folklorists ultimately because in our field of endeavor it seemed possible to be both scholarly and genuinely involved with people."

PART I

*Promoting Learning,
Problem Solving,
and
Cultural Conservation*

1

How Can Acting Like
A Fieldworker
Enrich Pluralistic Education?

JUDITH E. HAUT

While living on the island of Saipan in 1975 I began to investigate how children perceived their own ethnic identities,[1] interviewing the members of a sixth grade class at a local elementary school. Most of the children in the class were Chamorro, Saipan's indigenous inhabitants. A few were Carolinian, their families originally from the Caroline Islands in Micronesia.

I found that the children evaluated themselves negatively in contrast with Americans but positively in relation to all other groups we discussed— Koreans, Japanese, and other Micronesians. The most upsetting comparison to American children was from one eleven-year-old boy who said, as he pinched the brown skin on his forearm, "I'm not smart, look at my skin." Feeling some consternation, I asked, "Who ever told you that your skin had anything to do with how smart you are?" He said, "Nobody. I looked at my reader and it is for second-graders in America."

I knew that English was the boy's third language: he had already learned Chamorro and Carolinian. I also knew many Saipanese children assumed that all Americans are white. Though I reassured him that his book was for children who, unlike him, were reading in their first language, I felt his distress and realized that no educational experience should be this painful. By looking in his reader, this child had reached conclusions about others and about himself that no teacher should want or probably would expect. This child's misperceptions dramatically illustrate the need for cross-cultural, multicultural, and home-cultural studies—i.e., for pluralistic education.

Goals in Pluralistic Education

Folklorists have a number of avenues through which their training might be applied to education. They can provide assistance in the development of curriculum for geography, culture studies, social studies, and/or comparative literature. They might also aid teachers in understanding the main forms of folklore the children themselves engage in outside the classroom.

Although it is normally the data from folklore fieldwork—e.g., legends, myths, or descriptions of folklife—that are applied in educational settings, I believe that folklorists also have much to offer as a result of their own experiences in doing face-to-face research with people. In this chapter I will explore why I believe the methods of folklore fieldwork are useful for expanding and meeting the goals of pluralistic education. Before describing folklore fieldwork, however, I want first to define what I mean by "pluralistic education," at least for present purposes.

In my experience, pluralistic education is based on the notion that the United States has many ethnic groups. Pluralistic education not only accepts that observation but, tempered with a folkloristic orientation, also embraces the idea that each person belongs to multiple groups that may be identified on the basis of one or more of the following: religion, age, race, ancestors' or the individual's country of origin, economics, gender, special interests, and so forth. Pluralistic education uses these two basic ideas—the multiethnic make-up of our society and the multiple identities of each individual—as the basic premise for stimulating student excitement and interest about what human beings do.

Pluralistic education seeks to lessen dissonance in the classroom by incorporating a variety of learning and interactional styles. Two additional goals of pluralistic education are to increase self-esteem and to reduce intergroup stereotypes. It seeks to increase students' self-esteem by promoting the students themselves as resources (i.e., using what the students themselves know as the subject matter), and by encouraging the students to analyze the information they bring to the classroom. In *Teaching and Learning in a Diverse World* (1987), Patricia G. Ramsey links these goals by hypothesizing that "higher self-esteem mitigates the need to prove one's ascendancy over others" (p. 113). She speaks to the need for children to "express and explore their own ideas and perceptions of the world" (p. 118).

I believe folklore fieldwork methods and resultant data have an important role to play in education, especially as it moves away from an educational model predicated upon the deficiencies of children to one which acknowledges what the child brings to the classroom. Through the appropriate exposure to and utilization of folklore methods and materials, children can increase feelings of self-worth by exploring their perceptions of the world, delight in the diversity of their peers and the world at large, and develop critical thinking and independent learning skills. Following a brief characterization of folklore fieldwork, I will present and discuss some of my specific fieldwork and classroom experiences with students. Through an acquaintance with the processes of fieldwork, educators will be better able to assess the usefulness and the limitations of the outputs of fieldwork—such as published collections of folktales or children's games—for their own classrooms.

What Is Folklore Fieldwork?

For the purposes of this chapter, fieldwork means a systematic approach to answering our questions about our own and others' behavior, culminating in some sort of reported description and analysis. For the folklorist, the specific behaviors or activities under scrutiny are those that we consider to be "traditional"—i.e., those that we assume to exhibit historical and geographical continuities and consistencies. Research is carried out in the situations in which these behaviors naturally occur (in contrast to, say, library, archive, or laboratory research).

The most rudimentary requirements for folklore fieldwork are curiosity and the skills for appropriately and adequately serving that interest. By "appropriate" I mean utilizing acceptable and ethical means of obtaining information: this may include protecting interviewees' identities, learning about informal hierarchical authorities (social channels), observing what may be very subtle rules of discourse (who can ask what of whom and in what specific circumstances), and finding common ground before exploring differences. By "adequate" I refer to the production of a full description and analysis, which are inseparable. The goal is to move beyond the assumptions and perspectives we carry into the fieldwork experience; to engage in fieldwork, we hypothesize, observe, question, and participate while trying to defer judgment. We make inferences and eventually reach generalizations. Finally, good fieldworkers also let themselves be the subject of inquiry.[2]

What benefit can the methods and materials of folklore fieldwork provide for pluralistic education? When students practice the basics of folklore fieldwork—observing, asking questions, analyzing, and reporting—they utilize concepts that enhance their ability to notice diversity with interest; they also learn appropriate ways in which to answer questions about that diversity. Learning to identify what the question is, as well as how to ask it, is essential quality of good fieldwork as well as of the independant learner. Furthermore, the methods and materials of folklore fieldwork can help teachers discover and practice new communication strategies as well as internationalize the curriculum by using easily available folklore publications.

How Can Fieldwork Methods Help the Student?

Bringing data from fieldwork into the classroom can mean using published collections of, say, narratives or children's games from around the world in order to internationalize the curriculum. Or it can entail utilizing the activities of the children so students see themselves reflected in the classroom, e.g., employing traditional games in the teaching of math, vocabulary, or spelling. A third, more subtle and perhaps far more powerful means is to encourage children to be the resources and the analysts through teaching them the techniques of a fieldworker and thus stimulating their interest, engagement, and analysis. Because narratives have such broad application in the classroom—for language arts, bilingual programs, geography, history, and even public speaking—I will use this genre as an example of application.

Storytelling is a ubiquitous activity. Everybody tells stories—from the child who describes how he managed to get to the top of the tree to pull down the kite or how he and his friends managed to toilet paper the scout leader's house without getting caught, to the child who delights her friends at a slumber party with scary stories. Because of its broad and familiar use, children can relate to the data and study of storytelling while seeing both similarities and differences between themselves and others.

Narrative or folktale collections provide a readily available resource for internationalizing studies at the elementary or secondary school level. Because folkloristics has a long history of comparative studies, rich resources and indexing aids are available. For example, Alan Dundes's anthology, *Cinderella: A Casebook* (New York: Wildman, 1983) covers the many forms of Cinderella or Cinderella-like stories as well as the different scholarly approaches used to study these tales. From Germany's Aschenputtel to Java's Kleting Kuning and on to America's Disney-created Cinderella, the geographic breadth of these stories combined with the students' probable familiarity makes this a good start for either a comparative study of oral narratives or a discussion of some of the traditional sources for written literature or film. Several sources for locating similar comparative materials are listed in the further readings section.

For many folklorists, finding versions and variants of what is conceived to be the same story (or ballad or game) is proof of tradition and oral transmission. In the classroom, using different versions of the same tale illustrates that storytellers narrate in specific situations and often for special purposes, oftentimes altering the account to emphasize a point. Having students tell stories and describe the different ways they have heard or told what seems to be the "same" story leads to a discussion of rhetoric. We tell stories to an audience—of one or many. Our purpose in relating a story, whether of a personal experience or a story we heard at home or on the street corner, may differ from one situational context to another. Ask the students: "Do you tell stories the same way to your friends as you do to a parent?" One may narrate the "same" personal experience story to illustrate one's wit or the gullibility of another simply by shifting emphasis in the telling.

Furthermore, by being asked if certain stories are told in particular settings or circumstances (such as parties, on the way to school, or during part-time jobs) or only with specific groups of people, the individual student may begin to see that she or he belongs to several groups. With the realization that having multiple identities is a common human characteristic, students can also acknowledge their different ways of interacting based on the role or group of the moment. This may contribute to modifying the common concept that any one group of students can be labeled as belonging to a culturally homogenous body. Remember, any individual has multiple identities.[3]

Students as Fieldworkers

Students gain confidence in exploring diversity as they are encouraged to see that they can act as fieldworkers; it is appropriate to notice differences among people and it is possible to learn techniques for investigating and understanding those differences. Many of the basic skills folklorists use— participant observation, inference, and reporting—are already part of elementary-age students' repertoire.

For example, in a discussion with fifth- and sixth-graders about storytelling, the children began to describe the kinds of scary stories they tell each other and why they do so. In recapitulating their own responses about storytelling, I told them, "When you hear stories like these, you're participating in folklore. When you think about why you tell these stories— 'it's fun, it's scary, it's like a roller coaster'—you're analyzing the functions. And when you talk about it here with your friends, you are reporting. In short, you are doing what any good folklorist does." Significantly, using and analyzing folklore data builds upon skills the children already possess.

Encouraging students to further develop their fieldwork skills does not mean that they need to go out into the community to interview people. Bringing in data or visitors from the outside and then asking the children for their own observations and questions will contribute to their refining the fieldworker's attitude: stimulating their curiousity as well as helping them learn the appropriate means for generating questions, puzzling over possible answers, analyzing, and inferring.

Like stories, published information about the wide geographic variation of games as well as their immediacy for children make them a highly useful topic for multicultural purposes and for eliciting from children their conceptions about fieldwork. During a recent folklore presentation for upper elementary school children in the Los Angeles area, I suggested that the children imagine not having available mass-produced toys. "What would you do? What would you play with?" The children talked excitedly about making their own playthings. Then I demonstrated a game played much like jacks, involving the use of a lime and eight small stones. I told them I had learned it on Pohnpei in the Central Caroline Islands. Having first established that we sometimes play with items readily found in the environment, the use of a lime as a ball did not seem to be a quaint or exotic culture trait. In fact, the students were intrigued with the game. They also wanted to know more about what these children do—their playthings and games, their way of life, and the physical description of their island.

While locating the respective geographic areas on a map, I described similar games with their differing names, rules, and playing pieces. The students described their own games of jacks in greater detail, debating over how many pieces were really needed for play. When they noted that both boys and girls play, the teacher and I reflected aloud that rarely in our childhood did boys play jacks—a matter that then led to remarks by all of us on possible changes in girl/boy domains in our society. Brian Sutton-Smith and B.G. Rosenberg describe some of these changes in "Sixty Years of Historical Change in the Game Preferences of American Children," in *Child's Play*, edited by R.E. Herron and Brian Sutton-Smith (1971: 18-50).

At one point I asked the children, "How would you study this game if you saw a child playing it?" They responded by posing a number of questions, such as "What is it called?" "How do you play it?" "What is its purpose?" "Why are you playing it?" These are some of the basic questions that a folklorist doing fieldwork would consider in an attempt to understand the activity from an insider's perspective.

I also asked the children to tell me what they learned from playing jacks themselves, or from hearing about jacks-like games. They mentioned eye-hand coordination, excitement, playing with friends, and timing. Then one child said, "Other kids do the same things we do."

The initial recognition that other people share remarkable similarities is an important step in developing an ability to delight in diversity. Over the course of the school year the sensitive teacher might try to expand the simple discovery that all people have ways of playing, demonstrating happiness or sorrow, providing for the survival of their children, and so forth but that all people do so in profoundly diverse ways. Through enacting the role of folkloristic fieldworker in and out of the classroom, teachers and students will acquire the skills and attitudes that are an essential part of pluralistic education.

It is apparent from this example of jacks that folklore in the curriculum can also pique interest in and provide novel ways of approaching such subjects as geography and history. Jacks even has relevancy to math instruction, as it involves principles of subtraction and division. Because of familiarity in form or content, folklore has an immediacy with which students can readily identify, tending to stimulate further inquiry. In classroom discussions involving children's folklore, the children do not have to be told that their ideas count; it becomes self-evident.

The example of jacks suggests yet other ways to develop teaching strategies and to affect the educational process, namely generating skills in independent learning and critical thinking through a fieldwork model. The students became self-motivated, spontaneously asking essential questions about who played the jacks-like game I had described and demonstrated. Furthermore, they demonstrated how they would go about trying to study an unfamiliar game on their own. Through this activity and discussion, these children were learning to identify, document, and interpret certain forms of expressive behavior by asking questions, posing and testing hypotheses, and reassessing their assumptions about taken-for-granted aspects of everyday life. The skills required for this process are vital to critical thinking—a process whose essence is delayed judgment, i.e., weighing and assessing data rather than jumping to conclusions or functioning in terms of stereotypes and oversimplification. In short, the students had the opportunity to reaffirm that they have the ability to be both the resource and analyst of their own traditions as well as the interested observer and interpreter of other people's expressive behavior.

How Can Fieldwork Methods Help the Teacher?

Thus far I have spoken of the advantages for students in learning about the methods and materials of folkore research. There are benefits for teachers as well. Though it may seem contradictory in terms of age and professional status, the teacher can comfortably and profitably assume the role of learner in and out of the classroom. As Ramsey writes in *Teaching and Learning in a Diverse World*, "It is the teacher who makes the goals of accepting, respecting, and appreciating oneself and others an honest and authentic dynamic in the classroom. . . . As a person, the teacher provides a model and the inspiration for children to adopt a pluralistic point of view" (1987: 40).

Like their students, teachers need the opportunity to become flexible decision-makers. Professionally trained folklorists might explore the options of entering into limited partnerships with classroom teachers. A folklorist might engage in research that could result in descriptions of the various communication strategies students use among their peers or within their families. For example, what kinds of narrating behaviors are encouraged in the home? How might verbal and written classroom excercises be modified so that the student finds something familiar at school?

Such a partnership has the potential for longterm benefits beyond affecting a few specific lessons. Often, folklorists are called upon to provide some ideas for enrichment during a brief workshop for teachers. By working with teachers over an extended period of time, the folklorist provides suitable data from fieldwork. In addition, the folklorist also models for the teacher the methods of folkloristic research.

The process of fieldwork meets some of the changing goals of education theory in that it epitomizes experiential learning useful to teacher and student alike. Finally, pluralistic education ultimately is not limited to ethnicity and intercultural understanding so much as it concerns the recognition, understanding, and appreciation of multiple identities related to a variety of experiences. Conducting folkloristic fieldwork can put pluralistic education into actual practice.

In some respects, my teaching experiences at the University of Guam during the late 1970s illustrate the benefits of overlapping roles as teacher and fieldworker. In addition to teaching folklore and education courses in the Bilingual/Bicultural Training Program in the College of Education, I taught writing courses through the English department.

Because I conceived of myself as both fieldworker and teacher, I looked for opportunities to fill these complementary roles. My fieldwork experiences contributed information that helped my teaching; my teaching, especially as I reflected on classroom discussions and presentations that didn't work, raised issues for my fieldwork inquiries. Nor were these roles played out in separate arenas. I continued to be a fieldworker in the classroom and during office hours, observing and interviewing people. One result was that instead of being data-oriented I became communication-oriented. What could enhance our interactions? And how might these interactional skills, as well as the data resulting from their use, be shared with the students so that their curiosity about one another could be stimulated and they could be directed to raise and answer their own questions? Matters such as these are applicable to all teaching situations.

I noticed that lively classroom discussions were precipitated equally by using traditional narratives familiar to some of the students and by describing my life experiences that illustrated points of similarities and differences in our lives. Just as occurs in the course of doing good, qualitative fieldwork, the curiosity and the assumptions that aid or hinder communication are interpersonal, not one-sided. For example, I infer that students responded to me as they perceived me in a variety of roles: teacher, young person, married, white (haole), mainland American, Jewish, a folklorist, and so forth. During office hours I found myself answering questions about my parents' occupations, the home and area where I was raised, my religious practices, my siblings, and why I had no children yet.

In time, my office resembled a sitting room, with a pandanus mat on the floor, a pot of tea on the bookcase, and pictures of my family and in-laws on the wall above my desk. In this setting, through conversing with students about our activities, families, and expectations, I was able to make inferences regarding communication styles. Students talked about what they felt was the contradiction between how they were expected to act at home and what they were expected to do at the university.

Several colleagues also talked to me about what they felt was a contradiction between their expectations of proper student responses in class and actual student behavior. One common complaint was that students did not look the professors in the eye. Only one professor boasted that she knew her students respected her because they looked right at her. One day a young Chamorro woman from Saipan provided a valuable insight into my colleague's interpretation. The young woman described how that same teacher had publicly harassed and embarrassed a student for being tardy to class. "When we respect someone we don't look right at them," she said. "But we hate Professor ———, so we stare at her."

We cannot, of course, assume that eye contact (or lack thereof) means the same thing to every Chamorro student at the University of Guam. What is inferrable is that there are advantages to acting like a fieldworker, i.e., suspending judgment while observing, asking questions, and in other ways obtaining information to help answer or resolve puzzling issues.

In all settings, effective teaching involves being available to the students on a one-to-one basis, a human-to-human basis, in order to learn what is being communicated in the classroom besides the three R's. Communication problems between teachers and students often derive from perceived differences in values. Fieldworkers face similar confrontations and likewise struggle over whether or not to change their own behavior or to expect others to change theirs.[4] Similarly, many pedagogical decisions rest on values or notions about appropriate behavior from the teacher's own life experiences and are not limited to "cross-cultural" situations.

For example, while teaching a summer session course at the University of Guam attended by several older elementary school teacher-assistants with little or no previous college experience, I noticed that several papers to a terminology quiz contained identical answers. Announcing to the class that I felt some of the answers were identical, I asked that the people involved please make an appointment to come to my office to talk to me. I never approached or identified them. Shortly thereafter, three women came in together. When asked why the papers had some identical answers, they said, "You know that in our culture it is important to cooperate; so we were helping each other." They continued, "We are used to doing things together." I replied that I used the quiz to determine if the basic terms were being understood so that I could both evaluate their progress and moniter my own teaching.

I remember feeling very ambivalent about the situation. I wondered if the sole issue was the women's need to help each other or if they were also exploiting my naiveté. (I was in my late twenties, they were in their forties; I was a statesider newly arrived in Guam, they were Chamorro and of Guam.) I feared they were "cheating" and using "their culture" as a false front. In other words, I suspected that they knew they were supposed to do the test separately but did not. At the same time I felt guilty because I was supposed to be the culturally sensitive folklorist. As a solution, I asked them to do the other exams separately but amended the requirements for the collecting project so that it could be completed cooperatively. In subsequent years I began to feel comfortable relying on cooperative tasks. My interaction with the students, as well as my unresolved conflict, precipitated revisions in my own teaching style.

As I have thought about this and other experiences, I have come to see that cultural identity is only a part of the multiple roles we enact. In the above example, cultural and personal values as well as assumptions about roles demarcated by age, residency, and acquired status affected classroom communication. The choices we make about curriculum materials can also have a positive or unexpected influence on the student.

Curriculum Prospects and Potential Problems

One way in which teachers sometimes seek to improve communication in the classroom is to provide students with familiar materials. Some, for example, may teach reading with typescripts of traditional narratives. But teachers should think carefully, both about the materials and their own attitudes, before using folklore materials in this format.

Folklore data is the output of human interaction, but the synopsized or isolated texts that we often use as part of our attempts to bring traditional materials into the classroom fail to reflect this. Misuse of folklore materials can inadvertently lead to diminished self-esteem, negative stereotypes, or increased feelings that people are so different as to be considered incomprehensible or irrational. This happens, for example, when people characterize "folklore" as being limited to old stories and things that aren't quite true. Such a connotation might well color and compromise the effective use of folkloristic material in the classroom. Students who characterize the information they provide as "just folklore," with the term carrying the underlying meaning of "untrue," might well interpret the information as invalid or not as useful as the information in a textbook. In making such an interpretation, students devalue themselves as well. It is therefore important for teachers and students to characterize folklore more neutrally—perhaps simply as expressive behaviors that we infer to exhibit continuities through time and space—and to address the symbolic nature of much of what we identify as folklore.

A second caution is also in order for the use of folklore data: there is no one right version. Oral narratives differ because people construct stories anew each time they engage in narrating. Oral narrative is different from written literature. People narrate in response to specific storytelling contexts; the audience, season, or perception that the storytelling is a primary or secondary activity to other work may profoundly influence how a storyteller tells a story at that moment. Sometimes people characterize these factors as having an undue influence on an imagined "pristine, original tale" and a loss of "pure" tradition. But it is a part of the human ability to actively construct and make use of a variety of sources for narrating. The notions of a "pure" tradition, and the fall from that standard, might lead to a loss of self-esteem as students then often end up apologizing for having less than "pure" folklore. Furthermore, the use of a cleaned up, literary version of a folktale—itself a composite of multiple versions—sets up an impossible contrast for the student who hears oral stories at home or from friends. People tend to apologize for the stories they tell: "This is not as good as the one in such and such a book."

When using folk tales in the classroom, speaking of what *storytellers* do—not what the story does—shifts the focus to the narrating process. Calling attention to how storytellers make use of what they see and know, for example, and exploring how they draw upon this experience and knowledge, portrays human beings as creating and communicating through the process of storytelling rather than being passive and uncritical.

Some teachers might be tempted to bring quilters, healers, or musicians into class for the students to watch in hopes that they will learn to appreciate special skills and the people who practice them. These experiences do present excellent fieldwork opportunities for the students. Bringing in outside presenters can expand the students' experiences, illustrate theoretical discussions and, most importantly, humanize the curriculum. On the other hand, bringing in outside presenters such as basket weavers, water dowsers, or ballad singers may unwittingly reinforce the very stereotypes that students might hold about old people or people from particular communities.

It is appropriate and important to introduce students to the wide variety of human behaviors surrounding work and art. On the other hand, if doing so merely reinforces ideas about "what old people do," "what black folks do," or "what Appalachian folk do" then we haven't helped the student. One solution might be to balance the presenters in the class. For example, if an elderly person comes in as a storyteller, also find a teenager or a child from a different grade who tells urban legends so that the children realize experientially that folklore is not limited to the past or to the elderly.

Another solution is to plan the visitation to maximize interaction between the guest and the students. Help the students frame questions so that the visitor is encouraged to talk about the processes of producing or demonstrating a particular skill. In the course of the preparation, the students may have the opportunity to discuss what makes questions appropriate or inappropriate: can we ask the same things of young people and old people, of men and women? The student may also discover that the presenter has other roles or identities than simply that of a maker of baskets or singer of ballads.

Folklore Concepts Enhance Curriculum and Style

Through modeling and encouraging the development of fieldworker skills and attitudes, teachers foster an environment in which children are enabled to be both the resource and the analyst for the study of expressive human behavior. The student and teacher are placed in a cooperative relationship. Jerome Bruner, in his essay "The Act of Discovery," in *Beyond the Information Given* (1973), calls this the "hypothetical mode of teaching," wherein the students have the opportunity to ask questions and to make meaningful discoveries for themselves (p. 403).

In his essay, "Multiethnic Education in the U.S.A.: Practices and Promises," James Banks writes, "Ethnic diversity is a positive element in a society because it enriches a nation and increases the ways in which its citizens can perceive and solve personal and public problems" (Trevor Corner, ed., *Education in Multicultural Societies* [New York: St. Martin's, 1984], 68). The goal of using folkloristic methods and materials in the classroom is to provide teachers and students with the conceptual tools they need to assimilate information about diverse peoples, develop communication strategies, and become independent curious learners.

As I have discussed in this chapter, acting like a folklore fieldworker can help attain these goals of pluralistic education. Folklorists can move beyond providing materials for enrichment by teaching or modeling fieldwork techniques as they provide site-specific research. Such practices and applications as the following may have far-reaching results:

> • First, using data from folklore studies, particularly drawing from comparative materials, internationalizes the curriculum without the student having to leave the classroom.
> • Second, learning and practicing the skills of folkloristic fieldwork may contribute to increased self-esteem and to positive classroom in-

teraction, hopefully lessening some of the negative intergroup stereo-typing. As students come to realize that they belong to multiple groups and that even the members of any one group express themselves dif-ferently, they may cease to see themselves, or be seen by others, as comprising a homogeneous group. In turn, this allows students and teachers to challenge stereotypic notions predicated on such group membership.

• Third, the information from and the methods of folklore field-work are particularly useful for teachers attempting to devise classroom strategies that minimize the dissonance between themselves and the students.

• Fourth, the enactment of fieldwork in even so limited a setting as allowing students to interview an outside guest speaker nurtures the students' ability to actively enjoy learning about other people in appro-priate and systematic ways.

• Finally, as the teacher and the students gain proficiency in utiliz-ing folkloristic research methods and data, pluralistic education—which celebrates the varied make-up of our society and the multiple identities of each individual—becomes an integral aspect of all that occurs in the classroom.

Notes

I want to thank Dr. Teri Keeler and Professor Michael Owen Jones for their com-ments on earlier drafts of this essay.

1. Saipan is in the Northern Marianas Islands, directly north of Guam. Fol-lowing World War II, it was administered by the United States as part of the Trust Territory of the Pacific; it is now a commonwealth of the United States. I am grateful to Linsa Falig, teacher at San Roque Elementary School, for her help in interviewing the students.

2. For a discussion of the personal nature of fieldwork, see Robert A. Georges and Michael O. Jones, *People Studying People: The Human Element in Fieldwork* (Berkeley: Univ. of California Press, 1980).

3. See Beth Blumenreich and Bari Polanski, "Re-evaluating the Concept of Group: ICEN as an Alternative" in Gerald Cashion, ed., *Conceptual Problems in Contemporary Folklore Study* (Bloomington, Ind.: Folklore Forum Bibliographic and Special Series, 1974), 12-18.

4. Cf. Georges and Jones, *People Studying People*, especially pp. 113-17.

For Further Information

Stereotyping begins at an early age; it may well be that early and positive experi-ences in the schools are one of the few strategies to promote positive intergroup attitudes. For an indication of how early stereotyping begins, see Mary Ellen Goodman, *Race Awareness in Young Children*, rev. ed. (New York: Collier, 1964), and Gordon Allport, *The Nature of Prejudice*, abridged ed. (Garden City: Doubleday Anchor, 1958). For a survey of the subject, as well as specific classroom strategies, see Patricia G. Ramsey, *Teaching and Learning in a Diverse World: Multicultural Education for Young Children* (New York: Teachers College Press, 1987). Her distinction regarding the use of traditional and contemporary images in children's literature (p. 207) easily translates to the use of fieldwork data; it is essential to find contemporary information. For an example of an ongoing anti-bias curriculum in education as well as insight into the actual development of the program, see the video, "Anti-Bias Curriculum," Louise Derman-Sparks, executive producer. To order, write to Pacific Oaks Extension Services, 714 W. California Blvd., Pasadena, CA 91105. In California, the current purchase price for the video is $40.28; outside California it is $38.00.

James Banks also discusses the need for educational intervention against stereotyping in "Multiethnic Education in the U.S.A.: Practices and Promises," in Trevor Corner, ed., *Education in Multicultural Societies* (New York: St. Martin's, 1984), 68-95. See also Alan Dundes, "A Study of Ethnic Slurs: The Jew and the Polack in the United States," *Journal of American Folklore* 84 (1971): 186-203; Dundes contends that if children know about these slurs then they can fight against them. William Hugh Jansen, "The Esoteric-Exoteric Factor in Folklore," in Alan Dundes, ed., *The Study of Folklore* (Englewood Cliffs: Prentice-Hall, 1965) (originally published in *Fabula: Journal of Folktale Studies* 2 [1959]: 205-11), describes a model of stereotyping: what one group of people thinks another group thinks of them.

For discussions of folklore and identity, see Alan Dundes, "Defining Identity through Folklore" in Anita Jacogbom-Widding, ed., *Identity: Personal and Socio-Cultural: A Symposium*, Uppsala Studies in Cultural Anthropology 5 (Uppsala: Acta Universitatis Upsaliensis, 1983), 235-61 as well as Elliott Oring's essay, "Ethnic Groups and Ethnic Folklore," in Elliott Oring, ed., *Folk Groups and Folklore Genres: An Introduction* (Logan: Utah State Univ. Press, 1986), 23-44. For folklore associated primarily with children, see Jay Mechling's article, "Children's Folklore," in the same volume, pp. 91-120; Mechling provides an excellent annotated bibliography for the study of children's lore.

There are several anthologies or handbooks that describe educational strategies with multiethnic students or that provide suggested experiences for creating multiethnic studies. Roger Abrahams and Rudolph C. Troike's *Language and Cultural Diversity in American Education* (Englewood Cliffs: Prentice-Hall, 1972) contains articles covering different aspects of expressive behavior and conflicts with the system of American education. The volume moves away from viewing pluralistic education on a deficit model. This anthology includes Susan Phillips's essay "Acquisition of Roles for Appropriate Speech Usage," 167-83, in which she describes attitudes about speaking and silence among the children of the Warm Springs Reservation and the need for non-Indian teachers to understand these. Claire Farrer describes the play activities of Mescalero Apache children and potential conflicts in the classroom in "Play and Inter-Ethnic Communication" in David F. Lancy and B. Allen Tindall, eds., *The Anthropological Study of Play: Problems and Prospects. Proceedings of the First Annual Meeting of the*

Association for the Anthropological Study of Play (Cornwall: Leisure Press, 1976), 86-92.

James A. Banks, *Teaching Strategies for Ethnic Studies*, 2nd ed. (Boston: Allyn and Bacon, 1979), argues for an ethnic orientation throughout the general curriculum, rather than presenting isolated teaching units on holidays or special heroes. He includes an overview of basic instructional problems in teaching ethnic studies, chronologies of major immigration groups to the United States, and sample multiethnic units. For an overview of the changing demographics of California schools and a piercing look at the experiences of young immigrants, see Laurie Olsen, project director, *Crossing the Schoolhouse Border: Immigrant Students and the California public Schools*, California Tomorrow Policy Research Report (1988). To order, contact California Tomorrow at 849 South Broadway, Suite 831, Los Angeles, CA 90014.

For essays written by post-secondary teachers who infuse multicultural content or style into their teaching, see Liucija Baskauskas, ed., *Unmasking Culture: Cross-Cultural Perspective in the Social and Behavioral Sciences* (Novato, Calif: Chandler and Sharp, 1986). This book includes bibliographies and film aids. For curriculum suggestions using folklore in the public schools, see Richard M. Dorson and Inta Gale Carpenter, "Can Folklorists and Educators Work Together?" *North Carolina Folklore Journal* (Special Issue: Folklore in the Schools) 26(1978): 3-13.

The applications of folklore in education are the focus of the 1978 special double issue of *Keystone Folklore Quarterly* 22 (1-2). For discussions of the possibilities and problems inherent in applying ethnography to education, see Perry Gilmore and Allan A Glatthorn, eds., *Children in and Out of School: Ethnography and Education* (Washington D.C.: Center for Applied Linguistics, 1982). Handbooks that provide specific strategies and lesson plans for using folklore in the classroom are also available. For example, teachers will find lesson ideas, bibliographies, and introductory essays in Marsha MacDowell, ed., *Folk Arts in Education: A Resource Handbook* (East Lansing: Michigan State University); for ordering information regarding this publication as well as *Hmong Folk Arts: A Guide for Teachers* and other booklets, write to The Museum, Michigan State University, East Lansing, MI 48824-1045. Betty Belanus coordinated an educational project sponsored by the Indiana Historical Bureau. The resulting handbook, *Folklore in the Classroom* (Indianopolis: Indiana Historical Bureau), is available for a small fee from the Indiana Historical Bureau, 140 North Senate Dr., Indianapolis, IN 46204. Also of interest are Vada E. Butcher, Toby H. Levine, and James A. Standifer, *Jumpstreet: A Story of Black Music—Secondary School Teaching Guide* (a publication of WETA TV, Washington, D.C. and Program for Educational Opportunity, University of Michigan, available from Dr. Charles D. Moody, University of Michigan, Ann Arbor, MI 48109); Deidre R. Foreman, *Louisiana Culture: Curriculum Guide* (1982; available from Deidre R. Foreman, Social Studies Supervisor, Calcasieu Parish Schools, 1724 Kirkman, P.O. Box 800, Lake Charles, LA 70602); and Sylvia Grider, *Children's Folklore: A Manual for Teachers* (White Springs: Bureau of Florida Folklife Programs, 1988; write to the Bureau, P.O. Box 265, White Springs, FL 32096).

The following articles describe learning style and contexts. See Jerome Bruner, "The Act of Discovery," in Jeremy Anglin, ed., *Beyond the Information Given* (New York: Norton, 1973), 401-12 (originally published as "Human Problem Solving," *Harvard Educational Review* 31 [1961]), and Harry Wolcott, "The Anthropology of Learning," *Anthropology and Education Quarterly* 13 (1982): 83-108.

For an overview of folklore archives see Jay Mechling, "Oral Evidence and the History of American Children's Lives," *Journal of American History* 74 (1987): 579-86. Although oriented to the history teacher, he provides a general characterization of available resources.

Teenagers will quickly grasp the idea that folklore deals with current issues if they read portions of Jan Harold Brunvand, *The Vanishing Hitchhiker* (New York: Norton, 1981). For accurately recorded narratives from oral tradition, see *The Folktales of The World* series edited by Richard Dorson. Some of the nations represented are Chile, China, England, France, Germany, Greece, Hungary, Ireland, Israel, Japan, Mexico, and Norway. The series is published by the University of Chicago Press. For a single volume reference, see Richard Dorson's *Folktales Told Around the World* (Chicago: Univ. of Chicago Press, 1978), which presents narratives from oral tradition with international multiple versions and scholarly commentary. To find numerous literary versions of narratives, see Margaret Read McDonald, *The Storytellers Sourcebook: A Subject, Title and Motif-Index to Folklore Collections for Children* (Detroit: Neal-Schuman, 1982). The essays in Alan Dundes, ed., *Cinderella: A Casebook* (New York: Wildman, 1983), provide a broad range of theoretical perspectives as well as comparative data about Cinderella-like tales.

The Library of Congress offers a discography of oral narrative. Jack Tales and tales in Gullah dialect are included in the series from field collectors. There is no charge for the catalog; request the Folk Recordings catalog from The Archive of Folk Culture, Library of Congress, Washington, D.C. 20540. For an excellent example of background material before bringing storytellers into the classroom, see the materials developed by Patricia Atkinson Wells and Patricia Hall, "I Hear/I Tell." The materials may be ordered from Patricia Wells at 426 Eventide Dr., Murfreesboro, TN 37130. There is a small fee.

Another excellent resource for teachers, Margaret Gibson and George Rich's "Demystifying The Concept of Culture: A Teacher's Guide to the Cross-Cultural Study of Games and Play," Monograph IV in the Bilingual Education Training Series (1978), includes background information, observation projects, and bibliography. This publication—#ED 174-739—may be ordered from the ERIC Document Reproduction Service, 3900 Wheeler Ave., Alexandria, VA 22304-6409. Creditcard orders may be placed at 800-227-3742.

The articles and bibliography in the special issue of *Western Folklore* 39 (1980) on children's folklore, edited by Sylvia Grider, cover such topics as children's narratives, cooties, counting-out rhymes, and hospital lore. Other basic resources for the study of children's play and games include Iona Opie and Peter Opie, *The Lore and Language of Schoolchildren* (Oxford: Clarendon, 1959), and Iona Opie and Peter Opie, *Children's Games in Street and Playground* (Oxford: Clarendon, 1969). For American data, see Mary Knapp and Herbert Knapp, *One Potato, Two Potato: The Secret Education of American Children* (New York: Norton, 1976); as well as Simon J. Bronner's book, *American Children's Folklore* (Little Rock: August House, 1988). For a historical contrast to the American descriptions, see the unabridged replication of the 1903 edition of William Wells Newell, *Games and Songs of American Children* (Toronto: Dover, 1963). The sections, "Folklore Sources" and "Games in Education," in Elliott M. Avedon and Brian Sutton-Smith, eds., *The Study of Games* (New York: Wiley and Sons, 1971), provide extensive bibliography and suggestions for the incorporation of games into the classroom.

For an understanding of the conflicts and intricate processes of fieldwork, see Robert A. Georges and Michael O. Jones, *People Studying People: The Human Element in Fieldwork* (Berkeley: Univ. of California Press, 1980). For a description of the personal nature as well as some of the practical matters of fieldwork, see Barre Toelken, *The Dynamics of Folklore* (Boston: Houghton Mifflin, 1979), especially pp. 291-304. See also James P. Spradley, *The Ethnographic Interview* (New York: Holt, Rinehart and Winston: 1979). For reports of projects carried out by college undergraduates, see James P. Spradley and David McCurdy, *The Cultural Experience: Ethnography in Complex Society* (Chicago: Science Research Associates, Inc., 1972).

For an anthology of brief essays covering the wide breadth of genres and methods in folkloristics, see Richard Dorson, editor, and Inta Gale Carpenter, associate editor, *Handbook of American Folklore* (Bloomington: Indiana Univ. Press, 1983), and the lengthier articles in Richard Dorson, ed., *Folklore in the Modern World* (The Hague: Mouton, 1978). In the latter volume, see especially Roger Abrahams and Susan Kalčik, "Folklore and Cultural Pluralism," 223-36.

2

Folklore in Museums: Issues and Applications

Jo Farb Hernandez

Recent years have witnessed a surge in the numbers of museum exhibitions focusing on or including folkloristic artifacts and themes. The numbers of folklorists on museum staffs or serving as advisory consultants for exhibitions, interpretative programs, and collection acquisitions have also grown dramatically. These trends have not been limited to living history or folklife museums but have become manifest across the range of museum types, sizes, and area of concern. The issues raised by these folklorists or in these exhibitions parallel folkloristic research in academia and in other public sector fields. (I have in mind such matters as those concerning the process and extent of creativity within traditional or culturally determined aesthetic parameters, or the relative strengths of the influences promoting continuity versus those promoting change, both inter- and intragenerationally.) Moreover, the specialized nature of the public presentation of museum scholarship provides an excellent forum for the resolution of these issues and concerns and may therefore serve as a model for the field as a whole.

Utilizing objects and collections as a basis, museums have the opportunity to present information and educate their visitors in an enjoyable, non-threatening way. In past years, unfortunately, this education was too often Eurocentrically biased. When alternative or ethnic images were examined, they were most often subjugated to the metaphor of the melting pot: quaint reminders of colorful customs that some day would be little more than intriguing relics of a folksy past.

But American museums are changing as the reality of the increasingly pluralistic society of the United States overtakes the notion of a singular culture whose ultimate objective is a homogenized, westernized whole. We are learning that aesthetic norms are not handed down from on high (i.e., Western Europe) but are culturally (as well as often age, gender, and geographically) specific. Within this new conceptualization, we cannot but accept that a society of such diversity would enjoy multiple aesthetics and cultural values.

Folklorists are helping museum personnel to realize that the presentation of alternative objects and images revealing these multiple aesthetics can only serve to expand visitors' understanding of the themes, and, more important, can help change those perceptions that are based on an outdated reality that may negatively impact daily life—globally as well as locally. Further, in this new win-win situation, presentation of alternative images can open up a dialogue helping to empower diverse constituencies with the validation that the museum can bestow, while it increases museum attendance and broadens the outreach of public programming.

It is apparent, however, that the treatment of these issues, as evidenced by the manner of presentation of material culture displays, is handled quite differently in different types of museums. In this chapter I chart the ways in which several kinds of museums present (or could present) such material, and explore the various issues that are raised (and, hopefully, resolved) through such exhibitions. I also suggest how incorporating folklore and traditional artifacts can enhance the educational function of museums while simultaneously providing positive experiences for visitors and broadening the museum's participation in community life.

Art Museums

As I suggest in an article called "Folk Art in the Fine Art Museum," the very concept of "folk art" is often best insinuated rather than explicitly pointed out in an art museum exhibition. By being circumspect, curators can thereby encourage audiences to approach the material on display without the preconceived notions of naiveté, lack of sophistication, simplicity, and quaintness that seem to have worked themselves into our national consciousness when we hear the term "folk art."

Just as important, however, is the reality that both "folk art" and "fine art" can be responded to either exclusively or concurrently in the same two ways: (1) formally, with reference to color, shape, composition, and so forth, or (2) contextually, with reference to the art historical, social, economic, geographic, and personal influences on the artist at the time of the work's creation. Although the latter may be a more educated way to evaluate the object, the two responses are equally valid and simply provide different kinds of aesthetic experiences for the viewer.

Issues regarding the amount of supplementary contextual information to include in an art exhibition are continuously being debated by museum directors, curators, and exhibit designers. The current prevailing wisdom seems to be to include basic information but not to overwhelm the viewer with such copious material that the object is subjugated or that its aesthetic power is diminished. For, unlike a living history museum in which the commonplace object perhaps tells the story better than the singular masterpiece, the art museum *does* choose its material on the basis of superior aesthetic qualities.

Additional contextual information, along with critical analyses of the artist's oeuvre, are often found in accompanying publications ranging from simple photocopied sheets to elaborate four-color catalogs. Lectures, panels, workshops, and performances may highlight other aspects of the artist's life and times, which will provide a greater depth of understanding about the work.

Art museums tend to hold true to this manner of presentation whether the material is a retrospective of a contemporary painter or the masterpieces of unknown tribal artists from a traditional nineteenth-century village. The objects are isolated on the wall or on pedestals, individually and often dramatically lit, and individually labeled. However, this focus on aesthetics (and "preciousness") need not detract from an understanding of the culture within which these expressive behaviors were manifested.

To illustrate this thesis, I would like to use a Mexican Indian Dance Mask exhibition as an example. The masks in this exhibition were installed according to the dances or dance complexes in which they appeared, not on the basis of pure design, geography, or age. The curator wanted to remind the audience that these were not simply beautiful or intriguing visual objects but that they were produced to function as necessary accoutrements to a folkloric performance or event. The human factor was further stressed by including several complete costumes (with masks) in the display, by continuously showing slides portraying the masks being "danced," and by presenting an exhibit of still photography, also focusing on the masks being worn in context. Performances by a folklorico group on the opening day—not of choreographed crowd-pleasing exotic, but of traditional masked dances—further emphasize that the masks were meant to be viewed in motion rather than statically hanging on a wall.

Through these means as well as the bilingual wall labels, educational panels, and catalog, the museum was able to address folkloristic issues about continuity and change, the process of creativity, and the importance of context (stressing the constant dynamism that accompanies each masking performance); it could also consider the social, cultural, and religious functioning of the artifacts within the broader context. Other issues examined pertained to the various beliefs associated with these dance-dramas, and the influences upon the evolution of artifact design, construction, use, and so forth. Those members of the audience who chose to utilize the supplementary educational material that we had available were able to enhance their enjoyment of the dramatically presented display of powerful visual objects. Information concerning traditional construction processes and technology, the social and cultural framework that surrounded the production and use of the artifacts, beliefs, and change along the cultural continuum rounded out the concepts illustrated by the exhibition's visual elements. Several different examples of masks from the same dance emphasized the individual variation that can occur within a given form. Yet on the surface, the exhibition was purely an art display, presenting superior quality objects, with apparently little in common with the contextually created scenes of a natural history museum.

History and Natural History Museums

Unlike the art museum whose primary function is to present the finest aesthetic masterpiece, perhaps only secondarily relating it to the contextual and personal environment that influenced its production, the history or natural history museum is more concerned with using artifacts to reveal the distinctive factors that as a whole constitute local, regional, or national sagas of development.

Although the early development of these institutions saw a greater emphasis on the mighty and memorable (e.g., the bed that Washington slept on), growing numbers of curators realize that they can present a more thorough and democratic history if they also include traditional artifacts to tell their story. This new trend bucks the earlier wisdom (that folkloric truths did not necessarily echo historical fact) with the understanding that how people see themselves and their history is equally as valid an interpretation as that propounded by a trained historian from academia.

In order for this manner of presentation to interpret the past successfully and faithfully, however, the curatorial decisions must be made by or with the advice of a folklorist, in conjunction with members of the group itself; the knowledge of the traditional values a group considers important is critical and can only be elucidated by a professional in the field. This basic esoteric/exoteric counterpoint (first propounded by William Hugh Jansen in his 1959 article) provides a significant opportunity to offer a comprehensive education about the subject, for differing interpretations of the same artifact or manifestation of expressive behavior can mirror the multifaceted aspects of the objects or event, as well as the differing perspectives responding to the experience. In this way, the museum may leave the question of final historical interpretation up to the viewer and can educate through open-ended questions inspiring dialogue rather than indoctrinating through a dogmatic presentation of seemingly unassailable facts.

An example of an innovative presentation of artifacts produced in a traditional way by authentic practitioners of the tradition could be illustrated through a display of Native American baskets. Alongside scholarly interpretations by anthropologists and historians that attempts to place the material in an economic, social, cultural, geographic, and ritual context, labels might also include excerpts from oral history tapes made by past or present-day creators, videos of baskets being created, photo enlargements of creators with their comments and in context, and so forth. The focus of the presentation thus moves away from the "typical" basket used to epitomize the historical context to a focus on the individual, and on the variation and specificity that are always evident within a group. Emphasizing individual behavior within the group's parameters concomitantly requires an examination of the larger issues of evolving customs, diverse attitudes, and continuity versus change that might be lost by emphasizing the similarities between objects rather than their differences.

The physical aspect of display presentations in a history or natural history museum often includes the attempted recreation of contextual scenes in which the objects are arranged as they would have been in their original environment. In these cases, individual labeling of each artifact is often not provided, except perhaps for outstanding specific items. But this is not of as great a concern as it is in the art museum, for the use of more common or ordinary objects actually serves to present local history in a more realistic light.

Recent technological advances in interactive computer programming can be innovatively adapted in museums of this nature. In a pioneering example, the Oakland Museum's History Information Stations use a touch-screen videodisc computer to provide information about each of more than six thousand objects in their California history hall. The system also makes possible viewing videotaped interviews with scholars who discuss concepts illustrated by the artifacts, and clips of oral histories of Californians who had participated in or been influenced by the historical movements or events. Designed to be easily navigated even by the computer-wary, this system communicates information on a person-to-person basis that greatly facilitates learning. The emotional response viewers experience as a result of these personalized anecdotes provides a longer retention of the historical themes and concepts the curatorial staff intended to explore. Folklorists were involved throughout the project's planning and implementation stages.

History museums have also been in the forefront of bringing "live folk artists" into the galleries to provide a more personalized and in-depth introduction to and understanding of the objects on display. Curators have learned that the direct experience with an object in a museum provides a more profound learning experience for the visitor than a mere reading of the written word. An authentic practitioner of the tradition explaining the construction and use of objects to a viewer goes even further, especially when the alternative is a static presentation with academic curatorial labels functioning as an obstructionist device between the object and the audience.

Although the use of folk artists in the museum is not without its problems (see Charlie Seemann's excellent article "Presenting the Live Folk Artist in the Museum" in Patricia Hall and Charlie Seemann, eds., *Folklife and Museums: Selected Readings* [Nashville: American Association for State and Local History, 1987], 59-66), folk artists can serve important and long-reaching roles not only in the education of the viewer (providing a memory instead of merely an experience) but also in broadening the constituency base of the museum by serving as an outreach vehicle to the target cultural group itself. Further, by examining which individuals the group itself values for their leadership roles or special services, a folklorist can learn more about the social phenomenon of the group and how it encourages and rewards the transmission of traditional skills and knowledge.

Although a museum can never recreate the past completely, knowledge of the values important to the group whose artifacts and expressive behaviors are being displayed is essential in presenting an accurate picture that details life as it was. Uncovering these values requires professional training in the field of folklore in order to make the correct distinctions among a myriad of cultural patterns and to be able to clarify and interpret these distinctions to viewers with greatly varied backgrounds.

Ethnic or Ethnographic Museums

The founding inspiration for many ethnic or ethnographic museums often had much to do with instilling or confirming a sense of pride for the target cultural group. Display of their artifacts and portrayal of their history served to validate their special importance vis-a-vis the nation as a whole as well as toward local history and often was a stimulus for a reexamination and a new appreciation of traditions and artifacts by the assimilationist second- and third-generation immigrants.

The often not-so-hidden agenda emphasizing group consciousness, however, has occasionally created somewhat incoherent combinations of popular culture and folklore in displays that purported to represent traditional materials alone. Even if the intent is to preserve a record of a (disappearing) culture through artifacts, it is still incumbent upon a folklorist to make the distinction between those objects that are authentic examples of material folk culture and those that were mass-produced or commercialized.

In the ethnographic museum, the emphasis is not on the isolated object per se but on the relationship of that object to other aspects of the culture as a whole. Thus, even objects that may have little inherent or intrinsic value are appropriate for exhibition if they lend meaning to larger themes. With this as a given, and with the corollary that even the most humble object exhibited in a museum becomes treasured and aestheticized simply by the fact of its placement in the gallery, the curatorial concept that serves as the original impetus for the display becomes especially important. Thus, the most successful of these displays or collections are those that have started with a strong thematic focus so that the artifacts can illuminate the overall meaning of the concept rather than commencing with artifacts related only superficially through their use by members of the given culture group and not illustrative of any particular thematic conceptualization.

An example of an exhibition that can positively examine a group's own self-identification, as well as explore the perception of that group by others, might be one dealing with a publicly celebrated yet culturally specific festival. The presentation might begin with a historical perspective on the celebration, to include the religious or cultural impetus (thus including an exploration into the belief system), the expressive manifestations of the observance in terms of both verbal and material culture, the change over time of the observance and its outward manifestations, and the perceptions by group members of the importance of the celebration in fostering individual leadership, group identification, education for the young, and other social-cultural values and meanings.

As with the historical examination of Native American baskets suggested earlier, this insider perspective could be balanced by a more formal, anthropological-sociological-folkloristic explanation of the events and their associated expressive manifestations. An ethnic museum might take this outsider's perspective one step further, perhaps by going beyond the academic interpretation to examining the perceptions of the celebration by nonparticipant, nonacademic onlookers. This in itself might be revalatory of ethnic prejudices (the knowledge of which can be helpful in taking positive steps to reduce these prejudices through intergroup education and clarification about the observance) but may also reveal a secondary yet equally important folkloristic focus: the exoteric view of the purposes, manifestations, and rationales for the celebration. Although this latter view may point up major misconceptions about the event, this exoteric folkloristic perspective is nevertheless a reality (albeit often subconscious) for the nonparticipant outsider. And, as it often shades intergroup interaction, it becomes a reality for the insider as well. Indeed, overtly examining dissonant perceptions is often a more faithful depiction of an integrated realilty than an exposition of only the most dominant voice.

An exhibition with this focus would likely include live performances, demonstrations of dances, hands-on workshops to create appropriate artifacts, video reminiscences by practitioners, and so forth. Beyond increasing the educational effectiveness of the exhibition, these supplementary events can serve as important marketing tools for the museum in increasing its audience base and augmenting public participation with and involvement in the institution.

Some ethnic museums have also seized the opportunity of exhibitions of this nature to involve local artists in a contemporary exploration of the folkloristic themes inherent in the observance. The creation of new altars or ofrendas by contemporary Mexican or Mexican-American artists as part of a traditional Day of the Dead exhibition, for example, underscores the continuing folkloristic tradition while also clarifying how new and contemporary elements are incorporated and become part of the cultural continuum.

The positive end results of an exhibition of this nature are a reconfirmation of the group identity (often a founding principle—even if unwritten—of museums of this type) as well as a potential reduction in intercultural friction caused by a misunderstanding of each other's folkloristic events and accompanying verbal and material cultural manifestations. Clarification of the distinction between who we are and who others think we are can be one of the most valuable interpretive lessons a museum can present. Further, through exhibitions of this nature, the museum is often able to become included as an active participant in the life of the community, and recognized as such, which broadens its audience base and may allow it to encourage the continuation of folkloristic behaviors—especially in the eyes of second- and third-generation immigrants—because of the perceived validation those behaviors have received from the local "official" cultural authority.

Living History, Open-Air, and Folklife Museums

The phenomenon of the attempted reconstruction of the past through a contemporary recreation—complete with staff in appropriate costumes, performing needed tasks with traditional tools and in a traditional manner, speaking appropriate dialects, and attempting an interpretation for the visitor with a disregard of subsequent historical events—can be a perfect laboratory for the exploration of folkloric themes. With museums of this nature, the present tends not to be considered as an element to aid in historical interpretation. Rather, earlier, different cultural patterns are described only in their own terms or in reference to even earlier expressive manifestations.

The essence of the living history or folklife museum is the celebration of ordinary people rather than the leaders or elite. It follows that the story that is told is not necessarily found in history texts, newspapers, or public records but instead is based on orally transmitted skills, beliefs, and assumptions and commonly held knowledge. Inscriptions in family Bibles, diaries, old photographs, letters, and reminiscences thus form the basis for personalizing and rounding out the displays that are presented.

The esoteric and private nature of this source material emphasizes the crucial need for intense folkloristic research. Again, a determination of the actual ways things were made, crops were sown, and calendrical rites of passage were observed holds equal importance with a determination of the values held by the group that can indicate the meaning and importance of a given action. Knowing that certain vegetables were planted in the dark of the moon exists in a vacuum without an understanding of what that action was expected to achieve. In large measure, folklore played a major role in decisions about every aspect of daily life and is reflected in tangible cultural patterns. Positive and respectful teamwork between folklorists, historians, and sociologists can elucidate not only the expressive behaviors actually manifest but their reasons for existence and importance within the group.

The more in-depth the examination becomes, however, the more clear it is that, although values may be shared and tasks may be handled similarly, individual variation within the group was the paramount reality and must therefore replace an emphasis on the "typical." Institutions such as Plimoth Plantation, which depict the lives of individual families with their distinct ways of handling life's traumas and delights, strive to more faithfully reveal avenues to a realistic understanding of the past. By immersing the visitor in the entire world of the past, the potential of creating the strongest sense of "life as it was" can be conveyed.

The importance of first-quality, professional folklore research cannot be stressed too highly for institutions of this type. Unless the correct historical and folkloristic details are provided to the first-person interpreter, it is only natural that, when pressed for answers by an inquisitive audience member, the interpreter will create the answers on the spot. This is not done maliciously but rather in good faith in an effort to respond to the audience and keep the show running. Nevertheless, contemporary folklore creation owing to assumptions and historical gaps must be forcefully guarded against at all times by museum and folklore professionals alike.

Living history museums often supplement their first-person recreations with separate interpretive centers, which try to place the historical depiction in context. As the first-person interpreters cannot be expected to provide information beyond that which they would have known, these centers, which are often physically distanced from the traditionally maintained areas, can help the visitor answer corollary questions, place the period depicted on a cultural/historical continuum, and provide a more academically oriented understanding of the period. Together, these complementary departments can be most effective in viewer education and understanding about the localized time period on display.

Science, Industrial, and Technological Museums

Although at first consideration it may seem that science museums and folkloristic studies might be mutually exclusive, there are in fact many innovative ways in which the latter can enhance the former. For example, exhibitions on medicine could include sections on traditional healing practices, folkloristic beliefs about the medicinal properties and relative effectiveness of certain herbs, chants, behaviors, and so forth. Displays featuring astronomical discoveries could include explorations into how human beings used to explain the origin of the stars, retellings of legends and tales associated with the constellations, and examininations of the symbolic value of eclipses in terms of expressive behaviors. Museums focusing on industry could add sections about traditional crafts, intergenerational transmission, and values regarding skills and competency. They could expand upon how economic, social, and cultural changes encouraged the transition from home craft to commercialized industry, and might also explore the revived interest in personalizing aspects of industry, from handmade furniture to customized automobiles.

Another tack could be an examination into the folklore components inherent in any industry, whether they be the stories about the "disappearing hitchhiker" of trucking lore (see Jan Harold Brunvand, *The Vanishing Hitchhiker: American Urban Legends and Their Meanings* [New York: Norton, 1981]), the jokes exchanged around the office water cooler, or the computer images and stories electronically transmitted by modem to different monitors across state lines.

Science and industrial museums, by focusing on state-of-the-art theories, inventions, and practices, may somewhat ironically be an exceptional way to underscore the notion that folklore and related expressive behaviors are ongoing and contemporary and are not only those things that happened in the distant past, created by those with little education and fewer cosmopolitan opportunities. Pioneering studies such as Michael Owens Jones's examination of organizational folklore can be utilized well in presenting the more human side of our complex, urbanized, often impersonal modern society; the public forum available to science museums can provide excellent opportunities for disseminating this important information.

Conclusion

This chapter is not intended to be an exhaustive survey either of different kinds of museums or of how folklore might be utilized therein. Variations of the museum types listed are numerous—from the historical house museum to the archaeology museum to the zoo/arboretum to the maritime museum, and on and on. Although the size, professional status, and governance of these institutions vary widely, museums do tend to share common concerns for the education of the audience in an enjoyable, nonthreatening way. Because of this, and because of the omnipotent nature of folklore itself, certain congruences appear to hold true across the board, which, if juxtaposed properly, can result in exciting educational displays disseminating primary research activities and eliciting positive and enthusiastic audience response.

1. An exploration of folkloristic issues as part of any museum exhibition can enhance the contextual information available to the viewer and can therefore promote increased comprehension of the artifacts on display.

2. Utilizing folklore resources to complement academic theories can enable the museum to concurrently present differing interpretations of the same artifact, experience, or event. This can, in turn, encourage a more democratized viewing of the exhibition, allowing for multiple perspectives that more clearly reflect the reality of the variation of individual experience.

3. When properly applied, folkloristic studies can emphasize the uniqueness of each human experience, focusing on distinctions and differences rather than "typical" similarities that may obfuscate or oversimplify the behavioral patterns being examined. The variety and specificity manifested in different expressive behaviors is fundamentally what being human is all about, and they should not be ignored in a misjudged attempt to "play down" to a "guesstimated" lowest-common-denominator audience education level.

4. The intrinsic popularity of exhibitions that include folkloristic themes or materials can enhance the museum's educational function with a positive recreational experience for the audience, and the museum can thus successfully compete for the audience's limited leisure time hours.

5. Supplementary cultural and educational events that may be utilized by the museum—such as enabling "live folk artists" to perform, sponsoring hands-on craft workshops, presenting films, slide shows, videos, etc.—can concurrently function as important marketing tools that can increase a museum's audience base within the community. Broadening the base of support can result in higher attendance, augmented membership figures, and additional publicity in a wider range of media outlets than perhaps habitually cover museum displays and ultimately may result in a more stable and secure financial base.

6. Because exhibitions of this nature tend to be nonthreatening, even though they may be presenting new and unusual material, museum visitors can become accustomed to looking and learning rather than immediately dismissing the unfamiliar. Over time, this can build a more sophisticated audience that is challenged by the new rather than intimidated by it.

7. The use of folk artifacts can often render larger themes more personal and comprehensible and can enhance public understanding of everything from technical processes to social frameworks. This can, in turn, often be used as a springboard to introduce more complex concepts and ideas to museum audiences.

An active and aggresssive folklore program can ultimately accrue positive results to almost any museum if it is handled wisely and professionally. Because of the large numbers (over seven thousand in the United States alone) and types of institutions, museums can serve as the perfect forum for an examination of folkloristic issues having an impact on the daily lives of us all, even if only on a subconscious level. To this end, museums and folklorists both would do well to continue to explore additional avenues for joint ventures and to promote these avenues as routes towards greater understanding of our history, our neighbors, and ourselves.

For Further Information

The best and most significant book on the different ways museums have treated products of folkloristic inquiry is Patricia Hall and Charlie Seemann, eds., *Folklore and Museums: Selected Readings* (Nashville: American Association for State and Local History, 1987). This includes my article, "Folk Art in the Fine Art Museum," pp. 67-75, as well as thirteen other articles and a comprehensive bibliography.

Several of the articles reprinted in *Folklore and Museums* concern the development of folklife holdings in museums or the growth of folk museums in the United States. Among these are Louis C. Jones and Candace T. Matelic,

"Folklife and Museums: How Far Have We Come Since the 1950s?" pp. 1-11; Robert Baron, "Folklife and the American Museum," pp. 12-26; and Howard Wight Marshall, "Folklife and the Rise of American Folk Museums," pp. 27-50. Another set of articles examines types of displays, the presentation of live artists, and applications of theory to practice. In "The Value in Things: Folklore and the Anthropological Museum Exhibit," pp. 99-107, M. Jane Young reviews the changing conception of museums and nature of exhibits as well as various interpretive and ethical issues.

For a discussion of the esoteric-exoteric concept, see William Hugh Jansen's article, "The Esoteric-Exoteric Factor in Folklore," originally published in *Fabula: Journal of Folktale Studies* 2 (1959): 205-11, and reprinted in *The Study of Folklore*, edited by Alan Dundes (Englewood Cliffs, N.J.: Prentice-Hall, 1965), 43-51. Patricia Hall summarizes his concept well in her article, "Applying Theory to Practice: Folklife and Today's History Museum," in the aforementioned anthology edited by Hall and Seemann.

Some other anthologies containing articles on folk art in museums are Ian M.G. Quimby and Scott T. Swank, ed., *Perspectives on American Folk Art* (New York: Norton, 1980); and John Michael Vlach and Simon J. Bronner ed., *Folk Art and Art Worlds* (Ann Arbor: UMI Research Press, 1986). On ethnological museums particularly, see Simon J. Bronner, "Object Lessons: The Work of Ethnological Museums and Collections," in *Accumulation and Display of Goods in America, 1880-1920* (New York: Norton, 1989), 217-54.

For discussions of the controversy between some museum curators and folklorists over the definition of folk art, see John Michael Vlach, "'Properly Speaking': The Need for Plain Talk about Folk Art," and Eugene W. Metcalf, Jr., "The Politics of the Past in American Folk Art History," in Vlach and Bronner *Folk Art and Art Worlds*, 13-26, and 27-50, respectively. See also John Michael Vlach, *Plain Painters: Making Sense of American Folk Art* (Washington: Smithsonian Institution Press, 1988).

Urban legends such as that of the mysteriously disappearing hitchhiker (who turns out to be a ghost) are examined by Jan Harold Brunvand in *The Vanishing Hitchiker* (New York: Norton, 1981), *The Choking Doberman* (New York: Norton, 1984), and *The Mexican Pet* (New York: Norton, 1986). Jones's examination of various aspects of organizational folklore can be found in numerous publications, some of which are "Works of Art, Art as Work, and the Arts of Working—Implications for the Study of Organizational Life," *Western Folklore* 43 (1984): 172-79; "Folklore in Organizational Life," *Folklore/Folklife* (Washington, D.C.: American Folklore Society, 1984), 14; "On Folklorists Studying Organizations: A Reply to Robert S. McCarl," *American Folklore Society Newsletter* 14:2 (Apr. 1985): 5-6, 8; "Aesthetics at Work: Art and Ambience in an Organization" (along with four other articles on symbolic behavior in organizations), in *Exploring Folk Art: Twenty Years of Thought on Craft, Work, and Aesthetics* (Ann Arbor: UMI Research Press, 1987), 133-57; "Making Work Art and Art Work: The Aesthetic Impulse in Organizations and Education," in Doug Blandy and Kristin Congdon, eds., *Art in a Democracy* (New York: Columbia Teachers College Press, 1987), 180-93; "Informal Organization and the Functions of Folklore in the Writings of Chester I. Barnard, CEO of the New Jersey Bell Telephone Company," *New Jersey Folklife* 13 (1988): 10-16; and "In Search of Meaning: Using Qualitative Methods in Research and Application," in Michael Owen Jones, Michael Dane Moore, and Richard Christopher Snyder, eds., *Inside Organizations: Understanding the Human Dimension* (Newbury Park, Calif.: Sage, 1988), 27-47.

3

Aiding the Homeless: Using Narratives in Diagnosis and Intervention

Marjorie Bard

The United Nations officially designated 1987 as the International Year of Shelter for the Homeless. Those involved in the fields of public and social policy released startling statistics concerning the ever-rising homeless population in this country. Although government officials noted the need for shelters, food, clothing, and services, they implemented widespread cutbacks in funding that adversely affected the homeless.

Why did the shocking statistics not serve to motivate the federal administration to aid the homeless? One reason might be that officeholders prefer funding military projects to human welfare programs. But also the numbers may have lacked impact because they were detached from identification with individuals in particular crises; there was no sense of immediacy. Stories about the personal experiences of the homeless are seldom elicited, documented, or analyzed. Even reporters seeking "human interest" material tend to focus on high visibility areas in which the hopelessly addicted and mentally ill loiter. Rarely has anyone interviewed in depth the immigrant families living in unheated and waterless garages, female single-parent families wandering from one mission to another, laid-off workers standing in welfare lines, jobless veterans camping under freeway bridges, and teen runaways banding together in substandard dwellings.

The phenomenon of homelessness continues into the 1990s. The results of the 1990 census reveal that homelessness is so prevalent that many living/sleeping places (shelters, gutted buildings, parks, and "tent cities") were not discovered by census takers. Therefore, even the highly visible homeless people in many major cities are not within the official population count. According to the U.S. Census Bureau's Post-Enumeration Survey, there are five million more people in the nation than were counted in the official census. The survey shows that California has an additional one million more people. We can properly deduce that the *hidden* homeless add significantly to that number of people.

In this chapter I discuss some of the applications of folklore and its study to understanding and aiding the homeless. Folklore can provide first-hand material indicating some of the causes of and possible solutions to homelessness. Sometimes the narrating of personal experience stories can serve as an interventionist strategy. It also can be used as a basis for social and political activism.

Stories and Folklore Methodology

The lack of qualitative research about the homeless can be traced to a pau-city of academicians trained in *fieldwork*. With few exceptions, social welfare providers, urban planners, psychologists, and sociologists utilize an office or mission setting for interviews. Seldom do they attempt to establish rapport with the homeless in *their* milieu: in alleys and malls, on sidewalks or cam-puses. If and when interviews occur, they involve the use of prepared ques-tions requiring brief, direct answers. Infrequently if ever do interviewers listen to hours-long, open-ended storytellings—as folklorists often do when they seek the manners of and meanings in aesthetic expression, traditional beliefs and customs, and symbolic behaviors.

Since the mid-1970s, folklorists have realized that people tell not just legends, jokes, and folk tales but also "personal experience narratives." Not generally known is that often people self-narrate, that is, they tell their stories (in some cases, frequently) to themselves long before they tell them to others. The process can be termed *idionarrating*, and the stories called *idionarratives*. This happens especially when an experience is deemed dramatic, traumatic, strange, particularly funny or sad, or socially important (which is the case for the homeless and victims of violence). Immediately (and for some time there-after), because the incident is so noteworthy, the memory bank reproduces the details to self—the "first audience." While "flashes" of the most alarm-ing or important components may be the initial outputs of the memory bank, what seems to happen is that we naturally form a story-mode of the incident as a replay-in-sequence; apparently we struggle with that aspect to "get it right." This internalized characterization appears to be a natural by-product of being human: biologically coded, culturally conditioned, and socially trained to make and tell stories. We daydream, of course, and daydreams are in a narra-tive mode; this storytelling is "self" narrating to "self." One researcher con-tends that we also narrate in our sleep: "Dreams are . . . plays which provide their own stage and their own scenery."[1]

Usually, we await the chance to tell someone else about a remarkable incident, but the experience may never be related to another: secrets are kept, an audience interferes with a "trial run," or the opportunity to tell the story just never seems to occur. A Vietnam veteran expressed it this way (on "60 Minutes," May 26, 1991): "It took seventeen and a half years for me to talk about Vietnam: two marriages, suicide attempts, drug overdoses, abuse of alcohol. The list goes on." As one of Barbara Myerhoff's informants said, "If no one listened, nevertheless the tale is told . . . to prove that there is existence, to tame the chaos of the world, to give meaning." [2] Hidden homeless women are constrained from telling about frightening or embarrassing situations for psychological and social reasons: not only have they lost personal belongings and position in life, but they are stigmatized for it.

While it is obvious that "secrets" can remain untold to others, the memory of an important event does not disappear: a replay exists for self as the sole audience. This solitary storying process may be a rehearsal: a recounting or rescripting of a scenario for deliberate purpose, such as trying to motivate oneself to speak out, attempting to ferret out the causes of the situation, or formulating a plan for the future. The communication of the experience to one or many can continue until a group with similar interests is formed that has the ability to influence others: one personalized story is interesting while fifty on the same topic are persuasive.

Sixteen years ago I began to collect personal narratives from women like myself who had been rendered indigent and homeless by abusive husbands. When my life changed abruptly a few years ago and I entered a graduate program in folklore studies, I came to realize that I had a collection of materials related to a significant societal problem and neglected population. I continued my research, seeking individuals who were not dependent on missions or settled in or near "Skid Rows," and concentrating on the homeless person who is literally undetectable by virtue of careful strategy. Most of the people with whom I talked had a routine—perhaps of mornings in a library, afternoons in a mall, and nights in a safe all-night facility such as an airline terminal, movie theater, or laundry. My success in establishing rapport and obtaining heretofore untold stories was based on my recall and emulation of behavior during my own period of homelessness. Techniques were flexible. Usually I dressed casually, carried two large bags, and looked like I was "just resting" on a bench, on a sofa in a mall restroom, or in a cafeteria. Women alone were the easiest to approach. Most of the time I placed small sandwiches between myself and a woman I suspected was homeless, began eating, and soon gestured toward the food. If she did not respond by helping herself, I started a conversation about something we might have in common—such as swollen ankles or arthritis. I always acted as if I were bored and in no hurry. Patience was usually rewarded with a traditional sharing of food and consequent sociability—

which generated the exchange of stories of personal experiences. I found that stories revealed personal, family, ethnic, religious, employment, aging, economic, service system, and political concerns. Not only were sources of homelessness uncovered, but storytellers often posited solutions to specific societal problems.

Subconscious Themes and Coping Mechanisms

The personal problems expressed by victims of homelessness are often ones that have been secrets. Victims of violence, for example, may find that stories emerge only after extensive private grief. Domestic violence, in particular, has become the source of many characterizations of events leading to homelessness. The severe stress related to prolonged physical and/or psychological abuse may be manifested in unconscious themes and coping mechanisms. I have heard such a disproportionate number of stories pertaining to supranormal visitations by an attacker who is identified as the real-life abuser that I cannot ignore the symbolic nature of the experience and the narratives. I refer to a phenomenon known in tradition and studied by folklorists as "hagging" (or being attacked by the "Old Hag").

A person who is hagged, witch-ridden, or attacked by the incubus or succubus is in a hypnagogic or "altered" state of consciousness just before actual sleep, or in the hypnopompic state prior to awakening. He or she senses a presence near the bed (or sofa); that apparition is almost always described as one that means to inflict harm. There is the feeling of a weight upon the chest and difficulty in breathing. The victim suffers from paralysis and an inability to cry out (see Hufford's research). Inherent in some of the victims' stories that I collected are subconscious concerns: sexual symbolism and references to archetypical imagery focusing on domestic life. Repeatedly victims told me that they had thought about these experiences many times before they had the nerve to tell others. They feared they would be disbelieved or considered mentally ill. Several women's narratives included comments about finally coming to terms with reality because of the uniquely strange and frightening experience, and indeed, some women have made a decision to leave an abuser immediately after such an episode. Adriana[3] (age 27, Los Angeles, California, 1986) refused to return to her home, choosing to believe that she could just "go" to Argentina (without money); however, she immediately became a "street person."

Last month I am in the hospital again and the social worker is trying to get me to call the shelter because Raoul has beaten me too much, and this time cut me with his switchblade. I don't want to leave him, since I am illegal and will be deported if I have no Raoul. . . .

I just find out I'm pregnant, and the baby must have his father. I lie in bed
. . . then God give me the sign. He makes Raoul come flying like a black cloud
into the window, which I see is full of sun. Raoul is changing shape, like the
clouds full of rain, and he is growing [larger] . . . and as he changes the shape he
is getting bigger until the big black cloud is over me, rumbling like the thunder.
Then the rain falls on me, but is Raoul lying on me, and he is so heavy that I no
can breathe. . . . I see his big switchblade moving in the cloud. It is Raoul and
the cloud all in one. The blade is coming at me and I no can move. . . .

God must then tell Raoul to leave me alone for I then can breathe and the
cloud is going out the window. But I am so weak from being afraid that I can
barely move, and for all day I pray. I know that I not to have this baby with
Raoul. I go back to mother and sisters in Argentina. Safer.

The family myth may also be an unconscious mechanism to escape
from reality. It masks unacceptable behavior. A shared belief that "nothing is wrong" in a family directs the individuals away from instead of
toward positive solutions. Glynis (age 44, Santa Monica, California, 1987)
disclosed how her ex-husband's family has avoided confrontation of important issues: "Listen, that Connors side of the family sticks together. It
always has. For generations, I guess. There's been troubles and the men
get into jail once in a while, but that's just because the men are real men.
The men are just going to be different; like they rule and rape and run
around and sometimes it's the woman who loses and gets put out with
zero. I did. I heard it from other women in the family. It's just that the
men have this mystique—isn't that the right word? We put up with it.
What else?"

Once recognized, however, as symptoms of dysfunction and as a
source of family disruption and individual homelessness, dubious assumptions can be challenged while behaviors are faced squarely for what
they really imply. New stories can emerge as therapeutic tools for establishing healthy family relationships.

Disclosing Concerns and Causes Through Narrating

When a woman knows that the only alternative to indigency and immediate homelessness is to remain with an abusive partner, there is a story
to be told regarding the reason. Cammy (age 33, Los Angeles, California, 1987) exposes a problem that is a direct result of well-meaning district attorneys and city attorneys who are slowly accepting a commitment
to prosecuting batterers. The male may be (properly) remanded to jail,
but the court system does not address the resultant lifestyle of the wife
(and children) who may be adversely affected:

I called the police several times when Howard beat me when he got drunk or
lost a job. I just wanted him to stop. But this last time they put him in jail and

kept him there. An attorney who works for the state wanted me to testify against him in court. Well, that means that Howard goes to County Jail for a while and comes out really angry and maybe can't ever get another job.

Everyone is real concerned that he gets help from AA and counseling for him hitting me. No one cares what happens to me. Who's going to pay the bills? A lady wanted me to call a shelter for battered women and get counseling. That's nice, but it doesn't get me a job and a place to live. I could be on the streets in a matter of days.

I said I wasn't going to testify against Howard, and the public defender said that was great 'cause they'd have to drop the case. Now the attorney for the state is angry with me and threatening to have me hauled into court to testify. He can jump in the lake. Unless someone offers *me* some way to better my life, then I have to stick with Howard.

Related to the economic entrapment that often results in homelessness is that of false beliefs concerning the Social Security and Medicare systems. Hilda (age 59, Los Angeles, California, 1986) says:

I was married for 29 years and never realized that I wasn't going to qualify for Medicare or anything when Stanley died. [He was self-employed and had not contributed sufficiently to any government or private plan.] I lived on our savings for about two years, and then I had to sell our house and move to a small apartment. I lived okay until I discovered that I couldn't pay for a minor operation. Boy, did it hit me hard that I was *poor*! . . . [Finally] I couldn't pay my rent. I was in a panic. Where could I go to live?

I packed up what I could take with me and went to the nearest mall and just sat for a while. I moved around so I wouldn't be conspicuous, and managed to eat and nap and use the department store's nice bathroom. I've been living from day to day like this for, oh, maybe two years now.

Oh, my God, it's awful, but what choice do I have? I won't go to any mission with a bunch of dirty street people and beggars who steal! I'd rather die first. . . . Thank God for the samples of perfume, shampoo, and stuff in the stores. I can always look nice. When a mall closes I'll go . . . sit in a hotel lobby. But I got to keep moving, 'cause I don't want anyone to think I haven't got any place to go.

Stories also reveal attitudes about contemporary business practices, especially those that are related to the enforced retirement of fully capable, longtime employees. Freddy Ramsey (Los Angeles, California, 1986) apparently regrets the disregard of his expertise (related to his age) more than his new status as poverty-stricken:

Getting old is a bitch, I'll tell you. I lost my job, I lost my wife, I lost my home. What is there to live for now that I spend my days in the park and my nights in a one room hole that is all I can afford. If my retirement check doesn't arrive on time and I miss one rent payment, I'll be on the street at night. I feel like I am homeless right now . . . it's just a matter of months, maybe days. Can't afford to do anything now that prices are rising so fast. I'm good and healthy, too.

So why did I get fired? Because I'm 71 and I'm considered too old to think. Bullshit! I could tell the young jerk that took my place that the wastebasket is full and he wouldn't even know what to do with it. The Great White Manager said all he needed was training. Well, I have the training and more. They'd rather spend money on years of training that jerk then keeping an expert.

Becoming a senior citizen does not always mean being forcibly retired from a good job. Many seniors become ill or disabled and cannot remain self-reliant. One alternative to a (usually expensive) nursing home is dependency on a third party who will provide necessary care while sharing quarters. Often, however, no suitable partner can be found, and seniors lose longtime living places. The result may be a day and night routine of wandering while attempting to pursue some type of personal interest that generates money. I met Frank Conroy in 1986 in the lobby of a downtown Los Angeles hotel where he was selling handmade cards.

This wheelchair is my daytime chair and my nighttime bed. I used to be able to change from it to a sofa in my living room and my bed at night, but now that I lost my apartment I just go wandering around from place to place and stay in the chair. I had to go on welfare last year for the first time in my life. I've always been—I guess I mean I think I was—able to get on by myself. I don't have any confidence any more. Now [at age 54] I don't have the job I could do at home [telephone sales] and I'm at the mercy of everyone. I don't want to go to a county run place for the down and outers—if there really is such a place. People kid me about being sent there. But so far no one has done it. I still have the ability to work and be useful. . . . If I could just get a roommate with some money.

Many men who have had successful careers become homeless because of one unforeseen circumstance. Most discover that the public does not believe that they were once productive and respected members of society—and can be again. At a 1987 Convention Center Franchise Show, Bobby Pearson of Salt Lake City was telling his story of the landslide effect of losing his business:

My life before I hit the streets? Hey, believe it; I was happily married, had a great business going, and never thought of losing everything. Everything hit the fan when I lost all my stock in a fire, the insurance wouldn't pay, and a bank manager who had ice in his veins wouldn't give me a loan to buy more. Heck, my family just vanished like the stock did. Now I don't even think of anything except revenge on that banker. I went to school with the sucker. Someone needs to straighten out bank loans for those of us who can't count on a thirty-year friendship. I had eighteen years of a great business behind me. Who else is going to give me a break? I'll eat the Salvation Army food, but I want an opportunity to get back on my feet. . . . I'm here looking for a business partner with money and no knowledge.

Women who have had successful careers and then experience a landslide syndrome have an even more difficult time persuading the public that they simply lack the opportunity to begin again. Susan Morrow owned a beauty parlor and dress shop in Beverly Hills (in the 1970s) until her partner took the funds from their joint bank account and disappeared.

You just wouldn't believe how I felt! I had to cancel my lease and try to coax my customers to a new location, and that was really impossible because I couldn't afford anything nice. I just went from bad to worse, and I moved to a crummy apartment and just cried for months. Then I tried to commit suicide—and couldn't even do that right. When I got back to the apartment—that very day when I left the hospital—I got mugged and all my money was in that purse. I thought about jumping off the roof and figured I'd probably just break every bone in my body and be a cripple, so I packed up my belongings and moved them into my car and parked it beside a park. Well, the view wasn't bad, and I was okay until a cop saw that my license tags weren't up to date and he called the tow truck while I was in the john and when I got back my car was gone. I've been trying to get someone to pay the money to get it from the impound people, but no agency will do that. In another few months I'll be getting Social Security checks, and the first thing I'm going to do is get a camper. No one is going to take that away from me! My home goes where I go.

I have discovered that many people who have become homeless live in cars. These vehicles may belong to them or be found abandoned. Rather than trying to find a boarded building or a willing roommate, homeless individuals may just try to upgrade the vehicle to a van, camper, or motor home. They feel a sense of self-reliance, value their privacy, and symbolically have a home from which they believe they cannot be evicted. One such lady, Dorothy Brown, keeps her old motor home parked on side streets in Santa Monica, California.

You know, sweetie, I am very grateful. I even put an announcement in the newspaper last month. You know, a prayer to St. Christopher. Oh, I know he isn't supposed to be the saint of travelers anymore, but I'll stick with the old ways. . . . I was kicked out of my house by my husband maybe ten years ago after I found that the guy was a bigamist. Can you beat that? I didn't know for six years that he had a wife up in Mendocino County. Then one day she showed up at our door with a gun, and he begged her to forgive him, and he told me to take off. Just like that.

Well, I didn't know what to do, being a woman with no job experience and a little heart problem. Just about the only thing I could do was to get in my car and hunt for a place to keep it. Lo and behold, I made friends with a nice old

gentleman who had a vacant lot next to his house and when the darling died he
left me some money. I decided that I was real happy with my ability to take my
place of residence with me, and I bought me this motor home. Now I go up and
down the coast and do flea markets. It's real nice, it is, and maybe some people
look at me as peculiar, but I don't want to rent some apartment in a middlin' area
and probably have to eventually share as the rents go higher. So I pay off the
same amount every month on this.

While some individuals like the idea of traveling, others do want to
"put down roots." Laura Botken (who roams the streets, parks, and alleys of Beverly Hills) dreams of a trailer park with a place for a garden. In
the middle of a conversation (in 1986) she began to recite this poem
(which I later asked for in written form):

> Got no money, got no home
> Don't want to have to roam.
> Get me some money, get me some land,
> Get me a man who'll take my hand.
> Put us with others in a shady spot,
> And we'll plant us some veggies on our lot.
> Don't want no rent, don't want no failure,
> Just give us a plot to put our trailer.

Some people must "pull up" roots. It has become commonplace for
families to be temporarily or permanently dissolved as one or both parents
leave in search of employment. Aside from the agony of leaving one's close
relatives, couples often discover that missions must separate males and fe-
males (for safety reasons). Arthur and Marie traveled from their recently
bankrupt family farmstead expecting that Los Angeles would provide opportunities unavailable in Nebraska. Arthur metaphorically refers to the Midwest as "one big 'for sale' sign" (1986):

We left the kids with a relative so we could get settled here. But there just isn't
anything we can do. I know that folks think farmers have no education or abilities, but I could work with any machinery, and I have three years of college
behind me. I was majoring in economics, but I guess that's a laugh. I couldn't
even make our farm—handed down for seven generations without any trouble—
pay off. I couldn't work it by myself and couldn't afford to hire men. My wife has
some nursing background, but she isn't licensed here, and it would take more
schooling for her to get one. We'd rather be back on the land, but we need jobs.
Everyone except the rich are starving in the Midwest; it's just one big "for sale"
or "auction" sign.
   We live in our car and eat at the missions, but this is a dead end. We can't
find a place where we can stay together—the two of us, you know—and I don't
even know when we'll see our kids again. How could we send for them and
where would they go to school? We don't have any address, and they need one to

go to school. Maybe if someone put me in touch with another family or two that are barely making it and need help with a business or farm . . . well, maybe we could pool our talents and manage all this better by working together.

Ted and Patricia Allan exemplify residents of small towns that have been decimated by plant and factory shutdowns and layoffs. They were sitting in a mall, talking (in 1987), when I overheard their conversation and introduced myself.

We're not homeless yet, but we sure do see it coming. The population in [small town in Kentucky] has shrunk from 6,300 to 2,700 in just three years. There's no work around any more since they closed the company that the town depended on, so people just moves on. It's a damn shame; it's a nice little town. We got good buildings boarded up, and the schools are hard put to keep teachers, so they probably will close next year. Then all the families with school-age kids will move away, and some of those parents own businesses. With no one to run the gas stations and food stores, who else will stay?
We come to L.A. to visit Patricia's relatives to see if we can find us a spot here, but this is awful. Smog, piles of nasty people, piles of cars honking at each other, and long lines in stores. I never thought I'd be looking at being homeless, but I can see it staring me in the face. I can't sell hardware and plumbing supplies to the collie lying on the sidewalk. I won't even be able to sell my house. Who'd buy it?

I have often heard references to "the city" as a source of personal and social problems that result in homelessness. Coralee Curtis (age 38, Los Angeles, California, 1986) expresses another city-related concern:

I just know that I would be able to pull myself together if I could just get away from the druggies and crazies who live in this city. You know what I'd like to do? Meet some nice rural family who need a tutor for their kids, or who would lead me to a teaching job in their community. I had a teaching credential once, and I really screwed up my life by marrying a drug addict who pulled me in with him. But I left him and now that I'm clean I really want to move to smog-free air and get a new life started. I don't know if I could reinstate my credential, but I was a good teacher, and some rural area probably wouldn't be as picky as Los Angeles. I may just start hitching until I get to some place that looks right.

Problem Solving Through Storytelling

As the preceding accounts imply, people dwell upon the situations and behaviors that affect them adversely, and these become the subject of storytelling. As one characterizes past and future scenarios to oneself through idionarrating, alternative plots evolve. Often a consequence of self-narrating is an intuitive feeling for the cause of and solution to a problem or a conscious and deliberate effort to evaluate a situation and formulate a resolution. In the minds of victims, then, may lie the innovative measures with which public and social planners can intervene to create positive policy and programs.

The "haggings" reported by victims of violence exemplify how self-narrating about these extraordinary experiences can be cathartic, act as a therapeutic tool in improving mental health, and support intervention in deleterious life events. A dissatisfied retiree has undoubtedly told himself over and over again how useful he could and should be in particular situations. The battered woman rendered homeless has probably reconstructed her situation with alternative scenarios many times, providing for better community services than are offered. Those who daydream (which is self-narrating) of opportunities are presenting interventions in daily activities by formulating more agreeable ones.

Narrating in interaction with interested others offers the opportunity to share one's problems and seek solutions through a continuous flow of information. Ron Tibbetts (age 36, Los Angeles, California, 1985) shares his ideas on alternatives to unemployment, loneliness, and homelessness:

This is such a waste of time, this waiting around for a job I know I won't get and going day to day without any real companionship. Sure, there are lots of bodies in this city, but no one to really share the good and bad times with and work towards something. What would really be great is to live and work with people you have something, well, special, with. You know what communes are like, and I don't mean that kind of living. I mean like a place where everyone has a place, but everyone works together to make a community out of what they have to offer.

Like I could help build houses, and that little gal Marylou over there, now, she knows how to do all kinds of craftwork, and Big Ben knows all about animal husbandry, for heaven's sake; he never stops talking about growing up on a Vermont farm. And that woman in line with the striped dress? She is real good at cooking just about anything out of nothing. She used to work as a restaurant cook, and if she had a chance she could create a restaurant all by herself.

It's a shame that we all sort of got stuck where we're wasting what we can do. By ourselves we can't do anything, but I'll bet we could together.

Many abused and homeless individuals have expressed the desirability of becoming part of self-sufficiency communities in which personal privacy is assured while all participate in creating homes, co-ops, cottage industries, businesses that benefit surrounding neighborhoods, and the sociability ensured through sharing experiences.

Initial movement toward such self-reliance and self-sufficient living is often found in storytelling sessions in support groups (e.g., victims' rights organizations). Synergistic behavior may evoke collaborative thought and action, intervention in system implementation, and the creation of new and more effective methods of operation.

Storytellings are also useful as strategic maneuvers to offset dysfunctional behaviors. In one instance, residents in a shelter for the homeless banded together with demands that would have caused the facility to close. One staff member acted as interventionist by sharing stories of her past as a homeless person to demonstrate both the personal and community need for the shelter. The residents, one by one, then symbolically responded with personalized stories, the result being a restoration of faith in the facility's positive place in their (and others') lives and a return to organizational equilibrium.

Narrating As Tactic and Strategy

Life experiences as told from a personal point of view can serve as a basis on which public and social planners create and implement innovative programming for the homeless. These personal experience narratives not only diagnose the ills of society, they also propose interventions in pre-crisis, mid-crisis, and after-crisis situations. Moreover, narrating can be employed effectively as tactic and strategy. This is because folklore is symbolic. It engages people, evoking strong emotions, visual imagery, and physical responses. Consider the following examples.

In the early 1980s, the city of Santa Monica, California, presented a proposal to demolish the Santa Monica pier. Hundreds of people attended a series of three community workshops to determine the fate of the historic pier and carousel. We sat at large tables, in the middle of each a model with movable parts upon which we could create the ideal pier. As stories unfolded, it became apparent that the pier was (and still is) utilized more by the very poor than one would have thought. Many accounts were told about how "as a young, poverty-stricken student (or architect, or immigrant), I used the pier as a place to meet friends, share adventures, eat cheap sandwiches, fish from," and so on. While no one at my table said she or he was homeless, one got the impression that the pier had been and still was being used as a haven by homeless people. No sooner did one story end than another began, interweaving new feelings, ideas, and experiences for consideration. The upshot was that such testimony—not through statistical data but through accounts of personal experience revealing the meanings and meaningfulness of associations with the pier—resulted in the city council's decision to restore the pier.

A second example: as the victim advocate for a city attorney's office in 1988, I was privy to the most intimate lifetales told by (usually female) victims of violence. Often a victim was reluctant to tell why she was afraid to testify, so I told a personal story of my own to exemplify how effective "sharing" could be. When a woman hesitatingly told of being "attacked" by what seemed to be a vaguely familiar figure emerging from a faint light to stand over her in bed and then lay upon her chest and press her breath away, I suspected a "hagging" episode, and I suggested that she might have been asleep and dreaming. "Oh, no!" she objected. "I know I was awake. No one will believe me. I'll be put in an institution for being crazy—and then my husband will go free." Immediately I told her stories of women who had been in the nearby shelter who reported much the same kind "attack," and of my exploration of this universal syndrome. The outcome was that she allowed me to relay all of this information to the prosecuting attorney without any prejudice to her testimony. Through such incidents as this, it eventually became policy to take these kinds of accounts and experiences seriously rather than dismissing them as irrelevant or indicative of diminished capacity.

Another example illustrates the use of narrating to defuse a situation and present alternative solutions. A three-day "1991 Veterans' Stand Down" had enormous attendence. More than one hundred men appeared at the building who were not preregistered, and therefore, unfortunately, could not avail themselves of the free meals, cots, and aid being offered. Many were disgruntled. On the second night I was about to leave when one man became abusive, threatening to assault the lone person at the door. I asked politely if I could do anything for the very angry vet. He outlined his grievances, mixed with numerous expletives, against the Veteran's Administration for ignoring his military-related injuries and therefore his compensation. I do not recall exactly how I got him to move away from the entrance, but I finally encouraged him to sit with me on a bench and tell me exactly what had happened in Vietnam, what injuries he had suffered, and why the VA had not given him benefits.

My statement that many veterans were not receiving proper benefits did not calm him. Then I remembered what I had been hearing since the day before: personal stories about how problems such as his had been solved. I told him a story about one of the registered vets inside who had resolved a similar situation with the assistance of a particular representative of the Vietnam Veterans of America Association. My story mollified the vet. He agreed to return the following day to talk to the representative outside of the building (since I was not in a position to promise him that he could enter). When I arrived the next morning, the vet was there to see if I would follow through. He was ready for a fight, and waited to see if I could get the representative to talk to him, which I did.

Often personal narratives have been instrumental not just in helping redress individual problems but in precipitating or advancing actual policy. Perhaps the most publicized example is the development of MADD (Mothers Against Drunk Driving) as an educational and political influence. Candy Lightner's frequent telling of her own family tragedy and loss propelled a grassroots movement against drunk driving. Similarly, regarding child support, lawmakers in some states have responded to a flood of personal stories from women who have experienced severe hardships, including homelessness, by enacting legislation that requires the garnishment of deliquent fathers' paychecks. In Los Angeles, the homeless who applied for General Relief were denied financial assistance because regulations required a home address. Because of the impact of many personal accounts of extreme distress collected by activists, there is no longer a requirement for identification or address to receive aid.

Certain principles regarding narrating, homelessness, research, and advocacy bear summarizing.

1. The individual must be respected as the primary source of knowledge when it comes to articulating the causes of (and possible solutions to) homelessness.

2. Methods need to be appropriate to the task. When interviewing the "hidden homeless" in particular, it is necessary to be flexible and patient and to utilize open-ended storytelling sessions.

3. Narratives about personal experiences can serve a researcher in diagnosing social ills; narrating can also be a tactic or strategy of intervention and change in interpersonal relations as well as in social policy.

4. The storying mode of human intrapersonal and interpersonal communication is the most promising method of "the art of persuasion by planning." This planning often begins with a rehearsal-to-self: the silent, private characterization of an event that has happened and is relevant, or is suggested by a prior occurrence and becomes the kernel for composing a new scenario.

5. Those trained in folklore studies are particularly skilled at eliciting people's stories, to listening to them, to taking them seriously, and to presenting them to others. Folklorists can become activists, not just documenters or advocates, by employing (or helping others utilize) narrating as a problem-solving strategy.

Conclusion

Public policy has not yet seen much impact from the startling quantitive data indicating a national homeless crisis. In addition to the noted highly visible homeless population, there are marginally invisible and completely hidden ones that include individuals who drift, seeking employment; hide in garages, cars, and tents; double up with relatives or friends; or attempt to blend into polite society by spending days and nights in malls, transportation terminals, hospital complexes, libraries, and churches. The highly visible have been the subject of occasional interest that highlights mental illness and chronic addiction. The marginally invisible and the totally hidden are neglected populations; little research has been pursued on them, and that only recently. Using the principles and methods of folklore fieldwork with emphasis on such concepts as stories and storytelling, I have been able to establish rapport with and interview in depth those whom others might not suspect are homeless. These individuals' stories—lucid accounts of unfortunate circumstances, unusual occurrences, and victimization by others or "the system"—can be analyzed as reflections of personal, social, and political concerns that provide valuable insights into the nature of human thought and behavior.

By addressing the behavioral, aesthetic, and traditional aspects of face-to-face interaction, folklorists are sensitive to the expression of attitudes, values, and concerns—which are communicated especially effectively in storytelling form. The intimate experiences that are characterized provide opportunities for self-discovery and assist in establishing immediate relationships, thus eliciting reciprocal communication. It is through this process, studied by folklorists, that the homeless individuals assess and express some of the causes of their plight. In similar fashion, they consciously or unconsciously posit solutions to problems, and in so doing invite intervention measures in the cycles perpetuating stress, abuse, unemployment, the neglect or disregard of skills, illness, system inadequacies, organizational crisis, and homelessness.

The value of using qualitative research to personalize quantitative studies is steadily gaining recognition by scholars in such fields as behavioral and organizational science, urban planning, psychiatry, nursing, and victimology. Conferences such as Myths, Symbols and Folklore: Expanding the Analysis of Organizations (cosponsored by the Folklore and Organizational Behavior faculty at UCLA in March of 1983) have brought new perspectives to interdisciplinary exchange. Further, coalitions currently forming in the private sector base their programming on the personal narratives of leading advocates, who stress the necessity of listening to those who have no voice in the sociopolitical arena so as to achieve a balance of power. Increasingly, folklorists are invited as speakers and workshop leaders—as I was at the 1987 Annual California Governor's Training Conference on Crime Victims. Like a growing number of folklorists, I have founded, and am director of, a not-for-profit organization the purpose of which is to put my folklore training to use in the interests of social change, in this case, helping veterans, victims of domestic violence, and other homeless people find homes, support, and a sense of community.

Notes

1. Norman Cameron, *Personality Development and Psychopathology* (Boston: Houghton, Mifflin, 1963), 15.
2. Barbara Myerhoff, *Number Our Days* (New York: Simon and Schuster, 1980), 30. See also Bruce Jackson, "The Perfect Informant," *Journal of American Folklore* 103 (1990): 400-416.
3. I have used pseudonyms throughout.

For Further Information

Some books on qualitative methods and principles of folklore fieldwork include Kenneth Goldstein, *A Guide for Field Workers in Folklore* (Hatboro, Penn.: Folklore Associates, 1964); Edward Ives, *The Tape-Recorded Interview: A Manual for Field Workers in Folklore and Oral History* (Knoxville: Univ. of Tennessee Press, 1980); and Robert A. Georges and Michael Owen Jones, *People Studying People: The Human Element in Fieldwork* (Berkeley and Los Angeles: Univ. of California Press, 1980).

Personal experience narratives have been of particular interest to folklore scholars as traditional forms of expressive behavior. Sandra Stahl focused her dissertation on the topic: "The Personal Narrative as a Folklore Genre" (Ph.D. dissertation, Indiana University, 1975). The special issue of *Journal of the Folklore Institute* 14 (1977) is devoted to this subject and includes an essay by Sandra K.D. Stahl: "The Personal Narrative as Folklore" (pp. 9-30). Some other works are Steven J. Zeitlin, "'An Alchemy of the Mind': The Family Courtship Story," *Western Folklore* 39:17-33; John A. Robinson, "Personal Narratives Reconsidered," *Journal of American Folklore* 94 (1981): 58-85; Susan Kalčik, "'Like Ann's Gynecologist or the Time I Was Almost Raped': Personal Narratives in Women's Rap Groups," *Journal of American Folklore* 88 (1975): 3-11; Stanley H. Brandes, "Family Misfortune Stories in American Folklore," *Journal of the Folklore Institute* 12(1975): 5-17; and William M. Clements, "Personal Narrative, the Interview Context, and the Question of Tradition," *Western Folklore* 39 (1980): 106-112.

Eleanor Wachs presents a link between urban (personal) crimes and victims' responses in "The Crime-Victim Narrative as a Folkloric Genre," *Journal of the Folklore Institute* 19 (1982): 17-29; and her discussion of the traditional components, style, and function of these stories is continued in *The Crime Victim Stories: New York City's Urban Folklore* (Bloomington: Indiana Univ. Press, 1988). In "Narrative Reactions to Brutal Murders," *Western Folklore* 49 (1990): 99-109, Amma A. Davis discusses what happens in a community faced with reactionary rumors, cautionary tales, "narrow escapes," accusations, stories about a rising crime rate, and an inept justice system. Of related interest is Bill Ellis, "Death By Folklore: Ostension, Contemporary Legend, and Murder," *Western Folklore* 48 (1989): 201-20.

For a discussion of the process of narrating between self-as-teller and self-as-audience (idionarrating), see Marjorie Bard's "Of Memories, Memorabilia, and Personal Narratives: Life Events in Introspect and Retrospect," *Folklore and Mythology Studies* 10 (Fall 1986): 42-51. See also Don Ward, "The Role of Narrative in Crisis-Situations: Personal and Cultural Identity," *Fabula: Journal of Folktale Studies* 31 (1990): 58-63. Of related interest is Barbara Myerhoff, "Telling One's Story," *Center Magazine* 13 (1980): 22-43.

For an exploration of the dynamics of storytelling between teller and listener, see the following articles by Robert A. Georges: "Toward an Understanding of Storytelling Events," *Journal of American Folklore* 82 (1969): 313-28; "Feedback and Response in Storytelling," *Western Folklore* 38 (1979): 104-10; and "Do Narrators Really Digress? A Reconsideration of 'Audience Asides' in Narrating," *Western Folklore* 40 (1981): 245-51.

Richard Bauman discusses the concept of sociability as related to storytelling in his article "The La Have Island General Store: Sociability and Verbal Art in a Nova Scotia Community," *Journal of American Folklore* 85 (1972): 330-43. See also Linda Humphrey's "Small Group Festive Gatherings," *Journal of the Folklore Institute* 16 (1979): 190-201.

In regard to the persuasiveness of stories and narrating, see Caren Siehl and Joanne Martin, "The Role of Symbolic Management: How Can Managers Effectively Transmit Organizational Culture?" in James G. Hunt, Dian-Marie Hosking, Chester A. Schriesheim, and Rosemary Stewart, eds., *Leaders and Managers: International Perspectives on Managerial Behavior and Leadership* (New York: Pergamon, 1984), 227-39. For an example of an essay advocating the learning of narrating skills for managerial effectiveness, see David M. Boje, "Learning Storytelling: Storytelling to Learn Management Skills," *Journal of Management Education* 15 (1991): 279-94.

The folkloristic point of view regarding the correlation between domestic abuse (and/or victimization) and homelessness is presented in "The American Dream Comes Home to Roost," *Women and Environments* (Fall 1987): 18-19, by Marjorie Bard, and also her book *Shadow Women: Homeless Women's Survival Stories* (Kansas City: Sheen and Ward, 1990). On the role of folklore studies in understanding and doing something about homelessness, see Marjorie Bard, "Domestic Abuse and the Homeless Woman: Paradigms in Personal Narratives for Organizational Strategists and Community Planners" (Ph.D. dissertation, University of California, Los Angeles, 1988).

Two of the more popular books on homelessness (by nonfolklorists) are Richard D. Bingham, Roy E. Green, and Sammis B. White, eds., *The Homeless in Contemporary Society*, (Newbury Park, Calif.: Sage, 1987), and Richard H. Ropers, *The Invisible Homeless: Losing the American Dream* (New York: Human Sciences Press, 1988).

A sampling of books and serial publications on "sustainable community" (self-sufficient and ecologically sound) include Kathryn McCamant and Charles Durrett, *Cohousing: A Contemporary Approach to Housing Ourselves* (Berkeley: Ten Speed, 1988); *The Community Land Trust Handbook* (Emmaus, Penn.: Institute for Community Economics in Massachusetts, 1982); Neder Khalili, *Ceramic Houses* (Claremont, Calif.: Geltafan Foundation, 1986); *The Networker*, a journal of the Cooperative Resources and Services Project (CRSP), Los Angeles, California; *In Context*, a quarterly publication of the Context Institute, Bainbridge Island, Washington; the newsletter distributed by H.O.M.E. (Homeworkers Organized for More Employment) in Orland, Maine, *This Time*, a quarterly written almost entirely in personal narratives regarding the building and progress of a self-sufficiency "town" since 1970.

The apparently universal phenomenon described as an attack by the "Old Hag" or as a "hagging" experience is examined at length by David Hufford in *The Terror That Comes in the Night: An Experience-Centered Study of Assault Traditions* (Philadelphia: Univ. of Pennsylvania Press, 1982). Hufford provides an extensive bibliography. In addition, a related phenomenon, witch-riding, is noted in Wayland D. Hand, ed., *Popular Beliefs and Superstitions From North Carolina*, 2 vols. (Durham: Duke Univ. Press, 1961-64). See also Shelley R. Adler, "Sudden Unexpected Nocturnal Death Syndrome Among Hmong Immigrants: Examining the Role of the 'Nightmare,'" *Journal of American Folklore* 104 (1991): 54-71; and Shelley R. Adler, "The Role of the Nightmare in Hmong Sudden Unexpected Nocturnal Death Syndrome: A Folkloristic Study of Belief and Health" (Ph.D. dissertation, University of California, Los Angeles, 1991).

For works on supranormal encounters, see Donald Ward's articles: "The Little Man Who Wasn't There: On the Perception of the Supranormal," *Fabula* 18 (1977): 212-25; and "The Return of the Dead Lover: Psychic Unity and Polygenesis Revisited," in Nikolai Burlakoff and Carl Lindahl, eds., *Folklore on Two Continents* (Bloomington, Ind.: Trickster, 1980), 310-17. Organizational folklore is a relatively new field of exploration, expanding folklorists' studies of occupational life. See, for example, "A Feeling for Form, as Illustrated by People at Work," "Aesthetics at Work: Art and Ambience in an Organization," "The Material Culture of Corporate Life," and "Preaching What We Practice: Pedagogical Techniques Regarding the Analysis of Objects in Organizations," which are chapters 7, 8, 10, and 11, respectively, in Michael Owen Jones, *Exploring Folk Art: Twenty Years of Thought on Craft, Work, and Aesthetics* (Ann Arbor: UMI Research Press, 1987). See also Michael Owen Jones, "Informal Organization and the Functions of Folklore in the Writings of Chester I. Barnard, CEO of New Jersey Bell Telephone Company," *New Jersey Folklife* 13 (1988): 10-16; Michael Owen Jones, "What If Stories Don't Tally with the Culture?" *Journal of Organizational Change Management* 4:3 (1991): 27-34; Michael Owen Jones, Michael Dane Moore, and Richard Christopher Snyder, eds., *Inside Organizations: Understanding the Human Dimension* (Newbury Park, Calif.: Sage, 1988); and David M. Boje, "The Storytelling Organization: A Study of Story Performance in an Office-Supply Firm," *Administrative Science Quarterly* 36 (1991): 106-26.

Aging and the interests and skills of senior citizens has been the subject of Roberta Krell's doctoral dissertation called "Folklore and the Elderly: Aging, Creativity, and Community" (University of California, Los Angeles, 1986).

4

Folklife, Cultural Conservation, and Environmental Planning

BENITA J. HOWELL

Environmental planning offers varied opportunities for folklorists and cultural anthropologists like me to use our knowledge of distinctive ethnic and regional subcultures, ethnographic research techniques, and the interpersonal skills cultivated through fieldwork to help resolve practical problems. Within the broad domain of environmental planning, cultural specialists contribute to various activities that may be grouped into two categories: cultural resource management and social impact assessment.

In order to protect resources, *cultural resource management* programs use archeological and architectural as well as folklife studies to inventory resources; determine their significance, i.e., their contribution to national, state, or local heritage; and compile thorough documentation of significant resources. Programs that not only protect but also interpret cultural heritage to the public may employ folklife specialists on short-term contracts or in permanent staff positions. Such positions offer opportunities to conduct research, prepare publications and exhibits, or organize festivals and similar events.

Interpretation of local and regional culture is a feature of many national and state parks, parkways, and recreation areas known primarily for their scenic and natural assets. Along the Blue Ridge Parkway in Virginia and North Carolina, historical exhibits and guidebooks, craft demonstrations, and occasional live music performances are popular with visitors. Cades Cove in the Great Smoky Mountains National Park features a tour of late nineteenth-century vernacular architecture and a working pioneer farm where costumed interpreters provide demonstrations of everyday activities. Jean Lafitte National Historical Park in southern Louisiana is a good example of the park created primarily to provide cultural interpretation. Jean Lafitte employs a number of folklorists on its permanent staff. Similar opportunities exist at the state level. In Tennessee, for example, folklorist

Bobby Fulcher has worked for the state Department of Conservation for well over ten years, exploring cultural history and locating folk artists and musicians in the vicinity of state parks in order to present them in park interpretive programs.

The natural resources in parks and recreation areas may be cultural resources as well. Environmental histories record not only natural events but also human impacts that have affected the resource base and modified the landscapes we see today. Cultural specialists who explore aspects of ethnoecology,[1] such as world views that value mastery or stewardship of resources or traditional knowledge and use of resources, augment the park naturalist's interpretation of natural history. Cultural knowledge can actually improve management of natural resources as well as add richness to their interpretation. By conducting ethnographic and ethnohistoric studies that reveal native knowledge and patterns of resource use, cultural specialists help natural scientists understand the role humans have played in shaping past and present ecosystems. Such knowledge of human impacts is critical to developing sound resource management plans for the future.

Cultural resource management is an ongoing activity on public lands where it is usually possible to conserve and interpret significant archeological sites and historic structures. But virtually all large-scale federally-funded development projects trigger a preliminary inventory of cultural resources and require mitigation of significant impacts before construction can proceed. In many cases, however, such as highway construction, it is impossible to save the physical resource. Thorough documentation before the site or structure is lost then becomes the only means of mitigation.

Social impact assessment, another aspect of the environmental studies that precede federally-funded development, may also incorporate folklife research. Social impact assessment attempts to determine how a proposed development, such as a new park or dam, might affect neighboring communities, both positively and negatively. By projecting likely effects in a way that permits calculating cost-benefit ratios, social impact assessment attempts to help decision-makers choose the most beneficial and least costly among alternative plans for proposed development projects. And economic costs and benefits, population changes, increased demand for public services, and the like, are the indicators most prominently featured in this kind of research because they are easily quantified.

Folklife studies can contribute to social impact assessment by helping planners appreciate community cohesion and its basis in common traditions and values. Fieldwork also uncovers local assessments of sociocultural costs and benefits and much information pertinent to "quality of life"—a dimension that social impact assessment is supposed to address but cannot easily quantify. Because citizens do act and react based on their perceptions, plan-

ners need to deal with these concerns whether or not they match the "factual" data obtained from other sources.

Potentially there are multiple niches for folklorists in environmental
planning, but folklife studies still are rare in this field. Archeologists and
architectural historians predominate in cultural resource management, as do
sociologists, demographers, and economists in social impact assessment. A
brief lesson in legislative history will explain why folklife has been marginal
to both kinds of environmental planning research and how "cultural conservation" with its realignment of priorities is helping to change this.

Legislative Frameworks Supporting Folklife
in Environmental Planning

Environmental planners are far more conscious than they were thirty years
ago that their work involves cultural as well as technical considerations. Federal legislation laid the groundwork for a series of changes that gradually
incorporated folklife research into environmental planning. As defined by
federal agency guidelines for translating legislative intent into action, cultural resource management initially was synonymous with historic preservation,
and social impact assessment implied strictly quantitative analyses of census
and econometric data. Thus these were the standard methods of accounting
for sociocultural factors in environmental planning. But ethnographic or folklife studies have gained ground as both historic preservation and social impact assessment have expanded their scope to address newly articulated
cultural conservation concerns.

Historic Preservation and Cultural Conservation

The National Historic Preservation Act of 1966 established the National
Register of Historic Places, creating state and local as well as federal programs to protect and preserve buildings, archeological sites, and historic districts. Oral histories, ethnography, and documentary research furnish the
information on cultural and historic context needed to support nominations
to the register and to develop interpretation of these properties for the public. Michael Ann Williams at Western Kentucky University is one of many
academically-based folklorists around the country who apply their expertise
on vernacular architecture in state historic preservation programs.

The American Folklife Preservation Act of 1976 was instrumental in
expanding the Historic Preservation Act's definition of cultural resources to
include living cultural expressions as well as archeological and architectural
resources. Support from the American Folklife Center (established by the

1976 legislation) and the Folk Arts Program at NEA has helped many folk-lorists transform state folk arts programs into comprehensive folklife centers that document, interpret, and present all aspects of traditional lifeways. Several of these are described in the introduction to this book. Through its own research projects, publications, and conferences, the American Folklife Center has been instrumental in articulating an expanded heritage protection agenda under the banner of *cultural conservation*—the principle that heritage protection should encompass encouragement and perpetuation of living cultural expressions as well as preservation of artifacts from the past.

In the course of reviewing and amending the Historic Preservation Act in 1980, Congress instructed the American Folklife Center and National Park Service to investigate means of extending cultural resource protections to "intangibles" as well as physical resources. Since that time the center has been quite visible in popularizing the term "cultural conservation" and the expanded mission of heritage protection it represents. The cultural conservation perspective is much needed in environmental planning. Prior to 1980, historic preservation programs effectively protected physical resources (sites, structures, and artifacts) that were threatened by development projects, but historic preservation funds supported ethnographic and ethnohistoric study of "intangibles" only to the extent that they furnished context for interpretation of specific sites or structures.

Cultural conservation is a multidisciplinary enterprise, and it unites academics, public sector practitioners, and concerned citizens. Various components of comprehensive cultural conservation are well established in programs supported by government and private agencies operating at local, state, and federal levels. Bobby Fulcher's work for the Tennessee Department of Conservation is just one example of the many existing programs that have been responsive to parts of the cultural conservation mission for some time.

As state, local, and privately-sponsored programs follow the American Folklife Center's lead, coordinating their activities and lobbying efforts to focus increased attention on cultural conservation, opportunities for folklorists to apply their skills to environmental planning will surely multiply. In spite of recent constraints on federal spending, cultural conservation is gaining recognition and support. For example, Senator Robert C. Byrd of West Virginia recently won congressional approval to include an Appalachian Culture Interpretive Center in the New River Gorge National Recreation Area in his state. The National Park Service is currently selecting interpretive themes for this facility in consultation with American Folklife Center staff and other cultural specialists.

At the state level, Massachusetts, New York, Illinois, and Pennsylvania all have initiated cultural park programs to preserve and interpret their industrial heritage. Folklorist Shalom Staub holds a position with the Pennsylvania Heritage Affairs Commission, helping to plan and coordinate a new state development initiative begun in 1989 to create a network of regional industrial heritage parks. These parks are intended to stimulate economic development—not just to preserve and interpret abandoned mills, mines, foundries, railroads and canals, but to help communities abandoned by heavy industry revitalize themselves, clean up their environments, and use well-planned cultural tourism to attract new employers as well as visitors.[2]

In 1989, the National Trust for Historic Preservation also began a three-year cultural tourism program, during which it will provide technical assistance to pilot projects in Indiana, Texas, Wisconsin, and Tennessee. The National Trust is supporting this effort in order to preserve historic places and stimulate creative approaches to interpretation and public education, but also to conserve neighborhoods and towns as wholesome environments for their residents, to aid local people in controlling the pace and nature of the development that affects them, and to ensure that economic and social benefits of tourism development accrue to local communities rather than outside corporate developers.

Social Impact Assessment and Cultural Conservation

The National Environmental Policy Act of 1969 (NEPA) set new standards requiring planners to assess anticipated impacts of development projects and consult the public in planning. It required planners to gather necessary background information, prepare environmental impact statements to summarize the anticipated costs and benefits of a range of alternative plans, and provide opportunities for the public to respond and contest the planners' data and conclusions, in court if necessary. These NEPA procedures were invoked whenever development projects involved federal agencies or significant federal funding. Among the diverse projects covered by these requirements were highway and dam construction, urban renewal, siting of defense and nuclear facilities, and establishment of new parks and recreation areas.

In principle, NEPA endorsed the goal of preserving the diverse strands in our national cultural heritage, but the regulations and guidelines agencies adopted to implement the legislation neglected this clause. Though guidelines varied among agencies, in general they dealt quite thoroughly with natural environment and resources and with the kinds of cultural resources already protected through historic preservation programs. Social impact assessment focused on anticipated demographic and economic impacts of development projects, factors for which quantitative data made calculation of the costs and benefits possible. This research drew heavily on existing statistical data sources rather than fieldwork in affected communities. It seldom acknowledged cultural "intangibles" whose value was not easily quantified.

Cultural conservation now offers justification for numbering threats to community life and values or "quality of life" among the factors to be considered in social impact assessment, just as it has expanded the scope of cultural heritage protection.[3] Greater sensitivity to cultural issues as well as specific resources should increase the possibility that environmental planning will promote rather than undermine long-term survival of still vital cultural traditions. Development projects affecting Native Americans helped to establish precedents for this expansion of social impact assessment.

Whereas economists, demographers, and sociologists made extensive use of readily available statistical summaries in compiling routine social impact assessments, cultural anthropologists often were asked to do ethnohistoric and ethnographic fieldwork when Native American and other ethnic communities were affected by development. Their work showed the utility of information generated from ethnographic studies and fieldwork contact, attended to an expanded range of sociocultural impacts, and made a strong case for timely, close consultation between planners and members of affected communities. Cultural factors may have assumed greater importance in these cases because pronounced cultural differences between planners and Native Americans made the need for cultural specialists on the impact assessment team obvious. More important, however, federal legislation explicitly acknowledged the special status and rights Native American tribes claim as once sovereign nations and set some special requirements for project planning.

The American Indian Religious Freedom Act of 1978 protects sacred places and associated resources (such as plants used in ritual), and it guarantees free exercise of religion. The need to comply with this legislation motivated the Bureau of Land Management to include an inventory of Paiute resources and sacred places in the environmental assessment done prior to construction of high-tension power transmission lines in southern Utah and northern Arizona. A team of cultural specialists led by anthropologist Richard Stoffle conducted this research.[4] Similarly, as part of its long-range planning cycle, the U.S. Forest Service must compile cultural resource inventories, including information about Native American sacred sites and resources. Recently, folklorist Barbara Reimensnyder worked with Cherokee elders to document sacred sites in the Pisgah and Nantahala National Forests so that these areas would be excluded from timber-cutting programs outlined in long-range plans being prepared for these forests.[5]

The National Park Service, in addition to fulfilling its responsibilities to protect sacred resources of Native Americans, is obliged to permit Native

Americans to continue traditional subsistence use of plant and wildlife resources in a number of national parks. This change in the customary policy
of "take only photographs, leave only footprints" was prompted by provi-
sions of the Alaska National Interest Lands Act of 1980, which created a
number of new parks and preserves. The principle of continuing subsistence use for Native Americans also has been extended to other parks in
Florida, Hawaii, and Minnesota.[6]

In order to determine and maintain sustainable levels of resource use,
park managers have employed anthropologists to compile "resource ethno-
graphies"—extensive information about past and present subsistence and
settlement patterns, demography, and social customs that might affect the
resource base. New responsibilities for managing parks' special relationships
with Native Americans prompted the National Park Service to create a small
Applied Cultural Anthropology Program distinct from its extensive historic
preservation activities, and Congress funded this program FY1991.

One hopes that increased attention to Native American cultural concerns in national parks will foster a climate in which park managers will
become more sensitive to the cultural conservation issues that affect other
neighboring communities as well. Trappers along the Ozark National Scenic
Riverways, for example, brought suit when the National Park Service attempted to rescind a prior understanding that they could continue to trap in
the area. Folklorist Erika Brady found that different values and behavior
standards also created friction between native Ozarkers and outsiders visiting the Riverways. If environmentalists from the city found trapping abhor-
rent, then so were trappers appalled and frustrated when skinny-dippers on
holiday obstructed their access to the river for livelihood.[7]

Because of his experiences conducting social impact assessments involving Native American tribes, Richard Stoffle was able to persuade the Department of Energy to fund folklife research in an assessment of potential
environmental impacts of a low-level radioactive waste storage facility proposed for Michigan. Folklife of non-Indian populations was accorded the
same importance as Native American archeological and ethnohistoric studies
in Stoffle's project design.[8] Marsha MacDowell, a folklorist based in the
traditional arts program at the Michigan State University Museum, managed
the subcontract for the folklife portion of the impact assessment. Almost a
dozen folklorists including Kurt Dewhurst did fieldwork in three Michigan
communities that were possible sites for the waste storage facility. When
hydrological studies eliminated two candidate sites from further consideration, the folklorists and anthropologists shifted their attention to identifying
the most significant of threatened resources in the remaining area so that
future planning could include measures to mitigate adverse impacts. Because the published report on this project in Michigan carefully spells out

the rationale and legal basis for social impact assessments to include folklife studies of non-Native Americans as well as Native American studies, this project is likely to serve as an important precedent for the future.

The project I describe in the next section of this chapter, a folklife survey of the Big South Fork National River and Recreation Area, has been cited as an example of ethnographic research in social impact assessment, but in fact it was conceived and funded as a component of cultural resource management.[9] As I describe the actual and potential contributions of folklife research to the overall Big South Fork project, bear in mind that in 1979 a huge gap still separated cultural resource management from social impact assessment. Logically, if not officially, the folklife survey potentially could contribute to social impact assessment as well as cultural resource management.

The Big South Fork Folklife Survey

The Big South Fork National River and Recreation Area, known to local residents as "the park," includes more than 110,000 acres of stream gorge and plateau uplands along the Big South Fork of the Cumberland River. It straddles the state line between McCreary County, Kentucky and Fentress and Scott counties in Tennessee. Aficionados of Appalachian music will recognize this as the homeland of Dee and Delta Hicks, Clyde Davenport, Virgil Anderson, and other artists introduced to a national public through folklorist Bobby Fulcher's recordings.[10]

Permanent white settlement did not occur in this area until the first quarter of the nineteenth century. For the most part, pioneers combined hunting with subsistence farming on the narrow bottomlands along the river and its tributaries. Exploitation of timber and coal resources was delayed until the Cincinnati Southern Railroad was completed across the Cumberland Plateau in 1880, but shortly after the turn of the century, Michigan industrialist Justus Stearns established the Stearns Coal and Lumber Company, headquartered at Stearns, Kentucky. This company built the Kentucky and Tennessee Railroad to link vast timber holdings in Tennessee with coal mines along the river and sawmills in the town of Stearns, near the junction with the Cincinnati Southern. A decade later, stockholders from Cincinnati and Middle Tennessee built another short line railroad, the Oneida and Western, in order to exploit coal and timber along its route between Oneida and Jamestown, Tennessee.

During the first quarter of this century, the Big South Fork region experienced population growth and prosperity as many farmers became industrial workers for the railroads, logging operations and sawmills, or coal mines. But the best and most easily exploited timber and coal resources were depleted even before the Great Depression began. World War II revived demand for coal and timber, but many families joined the stream of Appalachian migrants drawn to factory jobs in munitions plants and other war-related industries; from this area, many went to Muncie, Indiana. They were joined by family and friends during the 1950s as mines, logging camps, and sawmills near the Big South Fork ceased operations and the urban factories geared up to produce automobiles and other consumer goods. The Kentucky and Tennessee Railroad pulled up miles of track, and the Oneida and Western ceased operation. Old farming communities in the river gorge as well as the corporate mine and timber camps were abandoned, and the roads to them deteriorated. By the mid-1970s, fewer than forty households of year-round residents remained where once there had been dozens of communities. But many area residents still owned and used land that had belonged to their families for generations

Proposals for Regional Development

To counter the area's economic decline, local legislators tried repeatedly to win congressional approval for one or more hydroelectric dams that might draw industry to the region. In 1968 environmentalists first proposed designating the Big South Fork a wild and scenic river and enhancing its recreational potential. Despite the beauty of the river gorge, mining and clearcutting of the area had caused serious erosion and water pollution; abandoned farmsteads, railroads, and industrial sites dotted the landscape. Neglected country roads had become tracks for off-road vehicles bringing groups from nearby towns to hunt, fish, camp, and carouse along the river. Environmentalists hoped that federal purchase of the Big South Fork drainage would make it possible to correct these problems. [11]

The environmentalists' proposal came at a time when the general public's rising demand for clean, unspoiled natural environments coincided with increasing outdoor recreation, particularly among residents of the highly urbanized Eastern seaboard. Executive Order 11017 of 1962 had attempted to address both needs by establishing a new kind of land management unit, the National Recreation Area, which would make it possible to conserve or rehabilitate natural areas not quite of National Park caliber. Such areas would serve outdoor recreation needs more fully than federal lands set aside solely for conservation (parks) or managed for multiple extractive uses (forests or wildlife management areas). These recreation areas were to be located within a 250-mile driving distance of major cities. The Land and Water Conservation Act of 1965 provided funding for land acquisition by federal, state, or local agencies, with the stipulation that 85 percent of funds be spent to acquire lands in the eastern U.S, which had less extensive public lands than the west. Geographically, Appalachia was well situated to take advantage of these 1960s federal programs. Encouragement to do so came from the newly-formed Appalachian Regional Commission (a federally-funded planning consortium of Appalachian state governors), which advocated tourism and recreation as the most feasible route to economic development for isolated rural areas unlikely to attract business and industry.

Thus Congress called for preliminary feasibility studies and, based on favorable findings, authorized the Big South Fork National River and Recreation Area in 1974. The new recreation area was to be planned and constructed by the U.S. Army Corps of Engineers, the agency that already had investigated the feasibility of proposed dams on the Big South Fork. But as land was acquired from private owners, the National Park Service would assume responsibility for management of the area. This division of labor between agencies continued until 1991, when the National Park Service finally assumed full control of the project.

Sociocultural Research in Project Planning

By 1974, the Corps of Engineers had adopted environmental impact assessment guidelines in response to NEPA. A private contract research firm was hired to conduct these studies for Big South Fork, and arrangements were made for National Park Service archeologists to begin surveying cultural resources. Planners on the Corps of Engineers staff in Nashville coordinated the contractors' work and began preparing preliminary plans for development. Tightly scheduled site visits to the Big South Fork area did not give planners and contractors sufficient opportunity to assess local conditions, however. Their local contacts were with political and business leaders rather than a cross-section of ordinary citizens. The environmental impact statement was approved without formal challenge in 1976, even though both environmentalists and the local populace had concerns about social impacts that this document did not address.

When I began fieldwork for the folklife survey in the summer of 1979, I was surprised to learn how inadequate, from my perspective, social impact assessment for the Big South Fork project had been. Virtually no contact had been made with residents of the project area, in spite of the finding that they would bear the greatest burden of adverse impacts. During interviews and informal interaction with members of the folklife survey team, local residents volunteered many opinions and concerns about the recreation area. They countered our questions with many of their own, particularly questions about the land acquisition and relocation programs.[12]

As folklife researchers made initial contacts with all households inside the proposed boundaries, it became obvious that the Corps of Engineers was not communicating effectively with the people who would be displaced by the project. Some even seemed unaware that their homes were inside the proposed boundaries, although by the summer of 1979, Corps of Engineers appraisers were visiting each property and preparing purchase offers. Landowners could contest the fairness of the appraisal and recommended purchase price, but their land was subject to eminent domain—appropriation by the federal government to serve a purpose judged to be in the national interest.

A thorough resident survey conducted during social impact assessment might have laid the groundwork for a better managed land acquisition and relocation program. For example, with advance knowledge of land ownership patterns, some slight policy modifications might have been made. There was a homestead provision in the uniform federal land acquisition policy that permitted resident landowners to remain on their property for twenty-five years or until death. But among rural Appalachian families, elderly persons often deed over property to a child in return for support in old age. These children often have left the area to find work, so that they are absentee landowners, while their parents technically are tenants. Because no family member qualifies as a resident landowner, the homestead option is not available to the very households of elderly whom the policy seeks to shield from the difficulties and trauma of relocation.

The folklife survey report could only identify this problem and suggest that future projects investigate local land tenure practices and adjust the standard relocation policy if necessary. Folklife research was begun too late to contribute to social impact assessment, but then its sole official purpose was cultural resource management.

The Folklife Survey: Goals and Methods

In order to comply with NEPA and the National Historic Preservation Act, the Corps of Engineers had contracted with the National Park Service's Southeast Archeological Center for preliminary archeological surveys of the project area. In the course of this work, the archeologist heading the field team encountered many old-timers, learned something of regional history and traditions, and ultimately persuaded the Corps of Engineers to divert a small part of cultural resources funding ($50,000 of the $300,000 allocated for preliminary archeological surveys) to investigation of local history and folkways. The rationale for funding this research was contained in specific language of the enabling legislation Congress passed to establish the recreation area. This act called for conservation and interpretation of *cultural* in addition to archeological, historic, and natural resources.

In preparing a scope of work for the folklife survey, the archeologist specified goals that paralleled those of archeological resource management: identifying resources, determining their significance, assessing potential impacts of development, and making recommendations for mitigating adverse impacts. The technical report was to provide guidance for future interpretive programs on local history.

The Southeast Archeological Center contracted with the University of Kentucky Anthropology Department to undertake this project. I conducted eight months of fieldwork between July 1979 and March 1980, assisted by graduate students Susan Stonich Duda and Robert Tincher. We used standard historical sources and old photographs as well as ethnographic methods, including participant observation, informal and oral history interviewing, photography, and sound recording. Our investigations included a broad range of topics: vernacular architecture, cemeteries, foodways, folk medicine, subsistence farming practices, handcrafts and occupational skills, industrial development and social change, social customs, religion, lore, and music.

Both time and funds to explore the extensive range of cultural elements specified in the project scope of work were limited, so we needed to design an overall research agenda that established some priorities. Cultural or human ecology provided this framework, allowing us to focus on changing human adaptations to the Big South Fork environment. Continuities in folk tradition were evident between white pioneers, who adapted as subsistence farmers, foragers and hunters, and their descendants who became caught up in industrial exploitation of the region's timber and coal resources. No topic could be studied exhaustively, yet the technical report furnished a systematic overview of local culture and history, pointing to themes and topics that should be interpreted, establishing their significance, and identifying resources available for developing detailed interpretation.

Information contained in the folklife survey report has provided background for specific interpretive projects, such as a coal-mining museum complex located at Blue Heron, site of a large coal-processing tipple and mine camp operated by the Stearns Coal and Lumber Company. Many of the experts who shared their knowledge and experiences with us more than a decade ago have since died or become too infirm to be interviewed again. As the only source of information from these individuals, most of whom were considered by their peers to be the most knowledgeable about local traditions, the project's oral history archive, housed at the University of Kentucky M.I. King Library, remains an important interpretive resource. It includes contributions from several persons who were ninety or older when recorded, whose memories stretched back to the turn of the century. Thus the folklife survey was unquestionably useful in identifying significant resources for interpretation and at least laying the groundwork for thorough documentation.

A key aspect of the folklife survey scope of work was more difficult to address: how to mitigate adverse impacts the recreation area might have on folklife. If one assumed that traditional lifeways inevitably would disappear because of displacement of longtime residents and increasing tourism, then documentation would mitigate this loss, just as scale drawings and photographs mitigate the loss of a building about to be razed. But as fieldwork progressed, we found that our interest in traditional musicians and handicrafters sometimes rekindled their enthusiasm for old-time music or skills that their own children and grandchildren apparently appreciated less than we did.

If the National Park Service would develop and support interpretive activities as well as exhibits and printed matter, I reasoned, then cultural tourism might actually help to perpetuate traditional lifeways rather than threatening their survival. Accordingly, my recommendations for interpretation emphasized performances such as concerts, dances, and storytelling sessions; craft demonstrations, exhibitions, and sales opportunities; fairs and festivals. The Cultural Conservation report prepared by Loomis later designated such activities the "encouragement" aspect of cultural conservation. While funding curtailments during the past decade delayed Corps of Engineers and National Park Service plans for completing facilities and hiring interpretive staff, local governments and the private sector—working together in the Big South Fork Development Association—began privately sponsoring these cultural events.

Blue Heron and the Local Cultural Conservation Agenda

Local people were quick to recognize and cultivate opportunities for cultural tourism because, from their standpoint, their sacrifice of land, privacy, and their own traditional forms of recreation could be mitigated only by economic benefits—their original motive in seeking a federal project for the Big South Fork. Through fieldwork, the folklife survey team was placed in a position to identify impacts and suggest mitigations that our scope of work for cultural resource management did not anticipate and that the meager social impact assessment had not addressed.

Extended and frequent visits with "river people" as well as town elites, ordinary folk as well as officials and business leaders, exposed us to local concerns ranging from inadequate information and assistance with relocation to complaints that the low-impact recreation activities planned for Big South Fork (camping, canoeing and rafting, hiking and horseback riding) would do little to stimulate the depressed local economy. A sizable contingent of local people felt the recreation area was actually undermining their economic prospects by "locking up" coal and natural gas; they resented restrictions placed on their own preferred forms of recreation, hunting and off-road vehicle outings along the river.

In McCreary County, these economic concerns crystallized in public protest over the proposed location of a lodge to be built somewhere in the Kentucky end of the recreation area. Whatever aesthetic and engineering reasons the Corps of Engineers offered for siting this lodge at Bear Creek, Kentuckians only saw that this isolated location was practically in Tennessee and would require expensive road and utility construction. They believed McCreary County would pay for services to the lodge, while lodge visitors would drive south and spend most of their money in Tennessee. Furthermore, although the lodge site and the fate of the abandoned Blue Heron mine camp were in fact independent issues, McCreary Countians assumed that unless the lodge were located at Blue Heron, no development would occur there other than measures to protect the public from injury around open mine shafts and the ruins of industrial structures. Feasibility studies for the recreation area had proposed a coal mining interpretive center including reconstruction of the coal processing tipple, a tram bridge across the river, and part of the mine camp. An abandoned section of the Kentucky and Tennessee Railroad could be restored, permitting an excursion train to bring visitors six miles from Stearns through the scenic river gorge to the Blue Heron museum complex.

Local fears about socioeconomic impacts and desires for cultural interpretation coalesced around the Blue Heron issue. Having uncovered a wealth of occupational lore, personal experiences, memorabilia, and documentation in Stearns Company archives, I was able on technical grounds to make a strong recommendation that the interpretive center be built. Coal mining and the Stearns Company had been key elements in local history, and a rich, diverse resource base was available for interpreting that history to the public. But my recommendation also took into account local desires for an attraction that would draw tourists and tourist dollars. Retired coal miners and their families generally were skeptical that outdoor recreation would generate as much tourism revenue as planners projected. On the other hand, they were unanimously enthusiastic about a museum complex at Blue Heron that would celebrate their contribution to the region's history and draw tourists to their county.

In contrast to the overall Big South Fork planning process, which provided ordinary citizens only token opportunities to comment on polished "draft" documents, the Blue Heron complex engaged local citizens in key planning roles, beginning with a series of public workshops held at the Mc-

Creary County Library. Participants in these workshops enlisted many other local people in the project to share their memories and mementos—old photographs, scrapbooks, mining paraphernalia, and other artifacts of their personal experiences living and working at Blue Heron.

Instead of fully restoring the coal processing tipple, bridge, and other buildings in the camp at great cost, the planners took their cue from the naked steel structure of the abandoned tipple, erecting a number of "ghost structures"—open steel sheds that locate and outline the dimensions of buildings and duplicate their roof lines. These house appropriate graphic exhibits to interpret the company store, schoolhouse, church, and miners' homes. Each exhibit is accompanied by audio speakers, so that personal recollections and anecdotes allow the people who lived and worked at Blue Heron to share their own interpretations with visitors.

The Blue Heron Scenic Railway, which runs excursion trains from the town of Stearns to the site, operates as a private corporation, but the Corps of Engineers reconstructed bridges, trestles, and track through the recreation area and built a depot at the site. Through such cooperative ventures, constructive solutions are being found for economic issues that once engendered conflict and resentment of the recreation area.

The folklife survey research had still another application unforeseen in the scope of work. Because it organized a great deal of background information on local history and customs in one place, the report became useful orientation material for National Park Service employees newly assigned to Big South Fork. The report prepared them to answer many of the factual questions visitors might ask, but it also offered useful insights for management and public relations. Park Service employees trained in resource protection saw the scars of environmental abuse all around them in the form of acid runoff from strip mines, erosion caused by off-road vehicles and timbering, garbage dumps and mining spoils, poaching and pothunting. They could easily define their mission as saving the area from its former residents.

The folklife study report attempted to balance negative impressions and attitudes with more positive perspectives on local adaptation to the natural environment. For example, it described knowledge and use of medicinal plants, and the command of natural materials science employed in crafts and ordinary tasks of domestic production. In following the usual ethnographic practice of showing the "logic" behind cultural values and social customs, the report encouraged new employees unfamiliar with the area to shed some ethnocentric preconceptions about Appalachian people and adopt appropriate styles of interaction in dealings with their new neighbors.

The Big South Fork folklife survey came about almost by accident, through the actions of one archeologist. Since completing that project, I have taken advantage of opportunities to describe it to park managers at an international conference and in one of their professional publications.[13] I also supported efforts to secure a greater place for ethnographic studies in park planning and management by reviewing and commenting on drafts of revised policy guidelines which the National Park Service adopted in 1988, and by serving the following year on an advisory commission that evaluated research and resource management in national parks. Among other changes, the commission report recommended increased attention to cultural diversity in planning, resource management, and interpretation.[14]

Multiple Roles for Cultural Specialists in Environmental Planning

Whether in cultural resource management or social impact assessment, folklife applications potentially place cultural specialists in a number of different roles. The research role often predominates as in academic work, for example, when one conducts a "resource ethnography" in a national park. Other projects, including the Big South Fork folklife survey, are more complex because they involve multiple goals and actors (e.g., planners and other professionals in various government agencies, researchers from various disciplines handling various contract assignments, and diverse segments within local communities, such as town elites and "river people"). In such cases, conflict among parties is not uncommon, and the cultural specialist must negotiate other roles in addition to the relatively straightforward role of researcher.

Applied research often is a prelude to policy recommendations, so that the researcher becomes a consultant or advisor to the policy maker. Useful project reports must clearly outline implications or conclusions to be drawn from research findings and include recommendations as to appropriate courses of action. Managers often need advice about policy decisions before research and report writing is finished, as occurred when I was asked to investigate why the decision to build the Kentucky lodge at Bear Creek had aroused so much local opposition, or to indicate whether a mining museum complex at Blue Heron would be feasible and desirable.

Cultural specialists often adopt the role of liaison or culture broker to promote communication across the cultural barriers that tend to separate environmental professionals from at least some of the "affected publics" whose welfare they are obliged to consider. Though resource managers in the field are often in close contact with local people and can to some extent communicate local sentiment back to headquarters, they may be perceived as "the enemy" in confrontational situations; people may talk more frankly with independent contractors than "organization men." It is important to realize that environmental professionals belong to their own organizational subcultures; one must become familiar with these as well as with local folk cultures in order to be an effective liaison or communications facilitator.

Contractors feel a responsibility to help the agencies employing them publicize and explain their policies, as I did when I helped residents with questions about relocation obtain needed information or discussed the rationale for recently announced management policies. More important, contractors are in a position to report, and feel obligated to report, local reactions, concerns, and complaints in an effort to ensure that planners and resource managers give these opinions due consideration. In doing so, cultural specialists become advocates for local people who may have little other effective representation in the planning process. Balancing obligations to the people we study and the people who pay us can be ethically challenging. The codes of ethics endorsed by my professional organizations (Society for Applied Anthropology and American Anthropological Association) clearly assign my first responsibility to the people studied, not my employer; thus advocacy is appropriate in applied work, and it is often necessary to promote the goals of cultural conservation.

The Reagan era, with its reduced federal spending for domestic projects, brought about significant reduction in federal programs and greater local control over environmental planning. Increased citizen involvement and new local and state-level initiatives to stimulate recreation and cultural tourism mean that local governments and community organizations more often employ cultural specialists directly rather than dealing with those employed by state or federal agencies. Moving a step beyond the involvement of local people in the Blue Heron interpretive project, local cultural conservation programs that are supported by state humanities or arts councils typically make extensive use of participatory research and place responsibility for interpretive programming in local hands.

In collaborative research projects of this kind, cultural specialists assume new roles as consultants and facilitators who help community groups define and achieve their own goals, working with—rather than for—them. Thus folklorists who choose applied work in environmental planning in preference to academe may one day find themselves teaching American studies, fieldwork methods, and public programming skills to local apprentices eager to put all they learn to immediate use.

Notes

1. The concept of ethnoecology and appropriate field methods for its study are described in Donald L. Hardesty, *Ecological Anthropology* (New York: John Wiley, 1977). A classic ethnographic example of sociocultural construction

of the natural resource base is Roy Rappoport's *Pigs for the Ancestors* (New Haven: Yale Univ. Press, 1968).

2. Shalom Staub, "The Pennsylvania Heritage Parks Program: A Case Study," Presentation at the First National Cultural Conservation Conference, Library of Congress, May 16-19, 1991.

3. Ormond Loomis, coordinator, summarized findings and recommendations of the American Folklife Center survey of cultural conservation policy and programs in *Cultural Conservation: The Protection of Cultural Heritage in the United States* (Washington, D.C.: Library of Congress, 1983). Among its recommendations is the following: "increase the application of knowledge about community life and values to decision-making in environmental planning and design of impact mitigation projects" (p. 71).

4. Richard W. Stoffle, et al., "Southern Paiute Peoples' SIA Responses to Energy Proposals," in Charles C. Geisler, et al., eds., *Indian SIA: The Social Impact Assessment of Rapid Resource Development on Native Peoples* (Ann Arbor: University of Michigan, Natural Resources Sociology Monograph, no. 3, 1982), 107-34.

5. Barbara L. Reimensnyder, "Cherokee Sacred Sites in the Appalachians," in Benita J. Howell, ed., *Cultural Heritage Conservation in the American South* (Athens: Univ. of Georgia Press, Southern Anthropological Society Proceedings, no. 23), 107-17.

6. Muriel Crespi, "Cultural Anthropology and U.S. National Parks," *Anthropology Newsletter* 30 (Sept. 1989): 35.

7. Erika Brady, "Debatable Land: Frontier Versus Wilderness in the Ozark National Scenic Riverways," *Folklife Annual 88-89* (1989): 57.

8. Richard W. Stoffle, ed., *Cultural and Paleontological Effects of Siting a Low-Level Radioactive Waste Storage Facility in Michigan. Candidate Area Analysis Phase* (Ann Arbor: University of Michigan, Institute for Social Research, 1990).

9. This description of the Big South Fork Project draws upon an article I wrote for a National Park Service publication, "Folklife in Planning," *CRM Bulletin* 10 (Feb. 1987): 14-15, 29. *A Survey of Folklife Along the Big South Fork of the Cumberland River* (Knoxville: University of Tennessee, Department of Anthropology Publications, no. 30, 1981) is the full technical report on the project, including recommendations.

10. Recordings made and annotated by Bobby Fulcher include "Virgil Anderson . . . On the Tennessee Line," County 777; "Gettin' Up the Stairs. Traditional Music From the Cumberland Plateau," County 786; "Clyde Davenport. Clydeoscope," County 788; and Dee and Delta Hicks. Ballads and Banjo Music from the Tennessee Cumberland Plateau," County 789. All include notes by Fulcher and are available from County Records, P.O. Box 191, Floyd, VA 24091.

11. Benita J. Howell, "Mediating Environmental Policy Conflicts in Appalachian Communities," in *Environment in Appalachia. Proceedings from the 1989 Conference on Appalachia* (Lexington: University of Kentucky, Appalachian Center, 1990), 99-105, further describes conflict between environmentalists' goals for the recreation area and those of Big South Fork residents.

12. I wrote the article "Folklife Research in Environmental Planning," in William Millsap, ed., *Applied Social Science for Environmental Planning*, (Boulder: Westview Press, Social Impact Assessment Series, no. 10, 1984), 127-39, early in

1980, before "cultural conservation" had emerged as a convenient label for the potential applications I identified during my Big South Fork fieldwork experience.

13. Before contributing to the *CRM Bulletin* special issue on ethnography (see note 9), I participated in an international conference sponsored by the National Park Service and attended by policy makers from all levels of its bureaucracy. My paper was later published as "The Anthropologist as Advocate for Local Interests in National Park Planning," in *International Perspectives on Cultural Parks* (U. S. National Park Service and Colorado State Museum, 1989), 275-80.

14. The National Parks and Conservation Association formed this advisory panel and published its report and recommendations: NPCA Commission on Research and Resource Management Policy in the National Park System, *National Parks: From Vignettes to a Global View* (Washington, D.C.: NPCA, 1989). I describe how this commission dealt with cultural factors in ecosystems management in "Reconfiguring the Cultural Mission of the National Park Service," in Mary Hufford, ed., *Reconfiguring the Cultural Mission: Issues and Case Studies in Cultural Conservation*, (Urbana: Univ. of Illinois Press, forthcoming).

For Further Information

The federal government's commitment to cultural resource management derives from historic preservation legislation stretching back in time to the Antiquities Act of 1906. An excellent current overview of cultural resource management from an archeologist's perspective is Don D. Fowler, "Cultural Resources Management," *Advances in Archaeological Method and Theory* 5 (1982): 1-49. Ormond Loomis, coordinator, *Cultural Conservation: The Protection of Cultural Heritage in the United States* (Washington, D.C.: Library of Congress, 1983), provides a concise introduction to federal, state, and local cultural resource management efforts and references case studies, technical literature, and essays that evaluate effects of the federal program in place before 1980, e.g., Henry Glassie, "Archaeology and Folklore: Common Anxieties, Common Hopes," in Leland Ferguson, ed., *Historical Archaeology and the Importance of Material Things* (Lansing, Mich.: Society for Historical Archaeology Special Publications, no. 2, 1977), 23-25; Alan Jabbour, "Folklife and Cultural Preservation," in Robert E. Stipe, ed., *New Directions in Rural Preservation* (Washington, D.C.: National Park Service, 1981), 43-50; and Ronald W. Johnson, "The Historian and Cultural Resource Management," *The Public Historian* 3 (1981): 43-51. For an introduction to the role of landscape protection in National Park Service treatment of rural historic districts and a useful bibliography, see Robert Z. Melnick, *Cultural Landscapes: Rural Historic Districts in the National Park System* (Washington, D.C.: National Park Service, 1984). Michael Ann Williams, "The Realm of the Tangible: A Folklorist's Role in Architectural Documentation and Preservation," in Burt Feintuch, ed., *The Conservation of Culture: Folklorists and the Public Sector* (Lexington: Univ. Press of Kentucky, 1988), 196-205, describes her involvement in state historic preservaton programs. Ormond Loomis discusses the process through which historic preservation and folklife programs came to share common cultural conservation goals in "Links between Historic Preservation and Folk Cultural Programs," in Feintuch, *Conservation of Culture*, 183-95. For a brief account of American Folklife Center research projects involving cooperation with federal land management agencies, see Carl Fleischhauer, "Cultural Conservation and Government Planning," in Benita J. Howell, ed., *Cultural Heritage Conservation in the American South* (Athens: Univ. of Georgia Press, Southern Anthropological Society Proceedings, no. 23), 118-24.

Contributors to Roy S. Dickens and Carole E. Hill, eds., *Cultural Resources: Planning and Management* (Boulder: Westview Press, Social Impact Assessment Series, no. 2, 1978), address the need for attention to living cultures and intangible resources, describe various difficulties of doing contract research, and discuss treatment of cultural resources in social impact assessment. See especially Sue-Ellen Jacobs, "Experiences in Social Impact Assessment: The Anthropologists and the Agencies," 98-126; and C.P. Wolf, "The Cultural Impact Statement," 178-93. My article, "Implications of the Cultural Conservation Report for Social Impact Assessment," *Human Organization* 42:346-50, cites examples of ethnographic studies used in conjunction with social impact assessment. For a good general introduction to standard social impact assessment procedures, consult Kristi Branch, et al., *Guide to Social Assessment: A Framework for Assessing Social Change* (Boulder: Westview Press Social Impact Assessment Series, no. 11, 1984). Also useful is Kurt Finsterbusch and C.P. Wolf *Methodology of Social Impact Assessment*, 2nd ed. (Stroudsburg, Penn.: Hutchinson, Ross, 1981).

For case examples of the relationship between cultural knowledge or use of natural resources and conservation, see Jeffrey A. McNeely and David Pitt, eds., *Culture and Conservation: The Human Dimension in Environmental Planning* (Dover, N.H.: Croon Helm, 1985); Jonathon Berger and John Walter Sinton, *Water, Earth, and Fire: Land-Use and Environmental Planning in the New Jersey Pine Barrens* (Baltimore: Johns Hopkins Univ. Press, 1985); and Mary Hufford, *One Space, Many Places. Folklife and Land Use in New Jersey's Pinelands National Reserve* (Washington, D.C.: American Folklife Center, Publications, no. 15, 1986). "Resource ethnography" is described in Muriel Crespi, "The Ethnography of Alaska Resource Use," *CRM Bulletin* 10 (Feb. 1987): 24-25. Other articles in that issue of *CRM Bulletin* present other interesting applications of ethnography. The December 1987 issue of *Courier, Newsmagazine of the National Park Service* on park relations with Native Americans includes articles on continuing use of subsistence resources, one by park superintendent Mack Shaver, the other by Andrew Balluta, a Dena'ina park ranger who assisted anthropologist Linda Ellana with the resource ethnography for Lake Clark National Park and Preserve. By identifying and protecting culturally important natural resources that are threatened by development, planners can safeguard the cultural traditions that depend on these resources. Steps have been taken to conserve the African-American basketry tradition of coastal South Carolina by protecting sweetgrass habitat from resort development; this work is described by Dale Rosengarten, "'Bulrush Is Silver, Sweetgrass Is Gold': The Enduring Art of Sea Grass Basketry," *Folklife Annual 88-89* (1989): 148-64. A similar case of protecting sedges important for Pomo basketry is described by Richard N. Lerner, "Preserving Plants for Pomos," in Robert M. Wulff and Shirley J. Fiske, eds., *Anthropological Praxis: Translating Knowledge into Action* (Boulder: Westview Press, 1987), 212-22.

Charles C. Geisler, et al., eds., *Indian SIA: The Social Impact Assessment of Rapid Resource Development on Native Peoples* (Ann Arbor: University of Michigan, Natural Resources Sociology Monograph, no. 3, 1982), includes numerous case studies illustrating uses of cultural research and consultation with communities to identify and mitigate adverse impacts of development projects. Richard W. Stoffle, ed., *Cultural and Paleontological Effects of Siting a Low-Level Radioactive Waste Storage Facility in Michigan. Candidate Area Analysis Phase.* (Ann Arbor: University of Michigan Institute for Social Research, 1990) cites previous environmental planning studies that have incorporated ethnohistorical or ethnographic research.

In assessing how development will affect quality of life, a community's perceptions of risk are probably more significant than experts' objective measures of risk. A special issue of *Practicing Anthropology* edited by Amy K. Wolfe, "Anthropology in Environmental Risk Studies," *PA* 10(3-4), explores uses of ethnographic community studies in risk assessment. Another aspect of environmental planning not discussed in this chapter is housing design. With prior knowledge of cultural preferences, activity patterns, and social interaction, architects can design culturally appropriate housing. For articles ilustrating how folklife and ethnographic research are applied in housing design, see Setha M. Low and Erve Chambers, eds., *Housing, Culture, and Design: A Comparative Perspective* (Philadelphia: Univ. of Pennsylvania Press, 1989).

The final section of this chapter alludes to several features of applied social science: multiple roles with potential for role conflict, knowledge utilization and policy relevance of applied research, and issues of ethics. Each topic is discussed in John van Willigen's *Applied Anthropology: An Introduction* (South Hadley, Mass.: Bergin and Garvey, 1986). The Society for Applied Anthropology Code of Ethics and discussion of it appear on pp. 41-53 of van Willigen's text. The policy relevance of applied research is the theme of Erve Chambers, *Applied Anthropology: A Practical Guide* (Englewood Cliffs, N.J.: Prentice-Hall, 1986).

PART II

Improving the Quality of Life

5

Folklore and Medicine

DAVID J. HUFFORD

In the conventional view, folk medical beliefs and practices are a cultural vestige influencing only isolated populations in the United States and new immigrants from less developed countries. Such a notion stems from the idea that folklore itself consists largely of obsolete information and ways of doing things from past times. This conventional idea of the prevalence and nature of folk medicine is quite inaccurate.

"Folk medicine" refers to those health-related beliefs and practices that have a traditional existence alongside an official, politically dominant system of medicine. Of course, "official" is a term rooted in context. It is used here to refer to the position of "M.D. medicine" within a governmental system of regulation (accreditation, licensure, the Surgeon General, departments of health, and so forth). The "unofficial" traditions are sometimes further subdivided according to their mode of dissemination, with those primarily in oral circulation being classed as "folk" and those with a heavy reliance on print being called "popular." This distinction has some practical importance. For example, folk medicine in oral tradition tends to have group and regional affinities, such as Mexican-American *curanderismo*. Traditions that utilize mass media are more national, as in health foods or charismatic healing. However, all modern traditions are affected by and to some extent disseminated through mass media, and *all* medical traditions in the pluralistic cultural environment of the United States affect one another deeply and constantly. Health food beliefs have developed from traditions of folk herbalism, Pennsylvania German powwow doctors have been influenced by both Puerto Rican spiritism and by chiropractic, and New Age healers explicitly seek out and adopt the practices of Native American shamans. For purposes of applied folklore the folk-popular distinction is of secondary importance, so I shall use the term "folk medicine" in its broadest application.

To many, the term "folk medicine" conjures up images of isolated, uneducated, ethnic populations who depend on traditional beliefs and practices because they have no medical alternatives or cannot be persuaded to use them. If this stereotype were accurate, then folklore applications to medical practice would be limited to a few easily recognized situations involving a limited number of patients. However, in fifteen years of research and teaching in a medical school, I have found that the stereotype is a gross error that frequently interferes with the delivery of good health care. The following case, typical of many from my fieldwork, will help to illustrate the problems with the stereotype.

A Case

Mr. B. is a middle-aged, white businessman. His medical history and demographic characteristics are quite typical of middle-class urban and suburban patients.

"In July I was diagnosed as having a hiatal hernia, which was not relieved by several different treatments. . . . Over the next year and a half I got sicker and had more and more attacks [this condition can cause severe chest pain]. In desperation I went to another doctor. . . . This doctor did a biliary drainage test . . . and he suggested [gall bladder] removal. . . .

They removed the gall bladder and performed an exploratory—the surgeon put his finger through the hole in the diaphragm. . . . However, I did not improve. In fact, the attacks occurred even more frequently. I went back to the internist and he said that if I [continued to get worse] they'd have to operate. . . .

[At that point Mr. B.'s wife heard about a local prayer-for-healing group that was about to hold a large meeting locally.] I agreed to go although I hadn't been involved in any healing group before. I kind of took Oral Roberts as a joke. . . . Friday morning before the evening service I became very sick and left work. . . . At the service I felt a little uneasy, but I became more at ease because the service was sedate, well done. . . . I got in the healing line . . . [and one of the ministers] laid his hands on my head and prayed for the Lord Jesus to heal me. I didn't feel anything.

[Later] on the way to my car I thought, "I wonder if I got healed? How are you supposed to feel?" . . . Then suddenly, I felt like high voltage touched me on my head and I had a feeling that I can only describe as like bubbling, boiling water rolling to my fingertips and back up. . . . And I felt the presence of God right there on the street. . . . I knew I had been healed.

[Mr. B.'s wife also believed he had been healed; after a night of prayer they decided also that he should return to his physician.] I told him what had happened, somewhat cautiously. . . . He listened intently, smiled and said, "You had a mental experience, like a mental high—you can go right back to where you were in a few weeks." I said to him, "Can this hernia close?" And he said,

"No way." I said, "Could I have another upper GI series [X-rays]?" He said, "Sure."

. . . I had the series the next morning. The following morning he called and said, "I can't explain it, but the X-rays are perfectly normal."

That was over ten years ago. Mr. B. has required no further treatment for hernia and has been symptom-free ever since. He has also become a strong believer and participant in this form of healing, and he continues to use medical treatment for himself and his family—simultaneously with prayer—whenever any of them is seriously ill.

This case illustrates many common features of contemporary folk medicine: Mr. B. is part of the American cultural "mainstream;" he tried folk healing after "all else had failed"; the healing approach had a major spiritual component; improvement was associated with sensations of energy and other powerful subjective elements; and his use of folk medicine did not occur *instead* of conventional care nor did it subsequently replace medical care but was instead *added to* it. And, while this case cannot be claimed to "prove" healing miracles, the patient's beliefs are easily understood as rational.[1]

The Prevalence of Folk Medicine

Just how representative is the case of Mr. B.? A 1984 study indicates that 13 percent of cancer patients at the University of Pennsylvania Cancer Center were also using one or more folk medical treatments for their disease.[2] Contrary to stereotype, however, these patients were largely white and well educated. In the spring of 1986, the firm of Louis Harris and Associates carried out a national survey under contract with the Department of Health and Human Services. According to the Executive Summary of this survey, the investigators not only confirmed earlier reports regarding the simultaneous use of various treatments for cancer, but they also discovered that nearly 30 percent of the general population will probably use folk alternatives for their illnesses. Although the researchers found no single set of demographic variables with which to predict who would do what, college graduates do seem more likely than others to use folk medicine.

Often folk medicine has been said to be without therapeutic value, at most having some psychological benefits in relieving anxiety. But in 1976 a study published in *Cancer Treatment Reports* indicated that among 3,000 plants used as folk medical treatments of cancer 52.4 percent of the genera and 19.9 percent of the species are now known to have antitumor activity.[3] This is about twice the rate resulting from chance, as random screening of plant samples previously carried out by the National Cancer Institute demonstrates. To cite

another example, the current recommendations for increased fiber and reduced animal fats in the diet to reduce the risk of several diseases has been a
major element of folk belief since the last century, if not before. But as recently as the mid-1970s these beliefs were derided in medical journals.

These examples could easily be multiplied many times. Clearly, some
longstanding assumptions about folk medicine must be reconsidered and reassessed. From pharmacology to patient behavior, health professionals need to
know more about the traditions of their patients if they are to serve them well.
Drawing on my experience in instructing doctors, nurses, and others in the
health care professions, I present below some of the concepts about folklore in
medicine that these practitioners have found helpful. Although I write to folklorists about how their methods and insights can be utilized in the medical
field, I also aim some comments directly at health professionals for whom
folklore has much to offer.

Folklore Studies and Health

I first became interested in the application of folklore studies to medical education, practice, and research while I was a graduate student in folklore at the
University of Pennsylvania in the late 1960s. My doctoral dissertation, entitled
"Folklore Studies and Health" (1974), developed this concept as a broad area
including, but not restricted to, folk medicine. For example, traditional foodways and folk religion are directly pertinent to health and health behavior, and
folk narrative is a central topic in the study of the ways that people perceive
and describe their health histories. While my medical work is set in this broad
context, here I shall concentrate on those aspects of the subject traditionally
understood as comprising folk medicine.

I have always considered "folklore studies and health" to be a primary
example of "applied folklore." My definition of applied folklore is simply
the application of concepts, methods, and materials from academic folklore
studies to the solution of practical problems. This places applied folklore in
the same relationship to basic folklore research as is engineering to the
basic natural sciences. This analogy is useful in indicating that the distinction is not merely between research and application, or between the academic and the public sectors. There is in fact research in engineering;
moreover, basic scientists occasionally create practical inventions in the
course of their experiments. Similarly folklore studies and health involves
its own kinds of inquiry, and basic folklore research often serves practical as
well as "theoretical" ends.

Pursuing folklore studies and health, I became a member of the Behavioral Science Department of the Penn State College of Medicine at the Mil-

ton S. Hershey Medical Center in 1974. A brief description of my applied work since that time will serve to suggest the range of folklore/medicine applications that are possible, and the demand that exists for them. My primary teaching at the College of Medicine involves a behavioral science unit that I have developed entitled "Social and Cultural Aspects of Health" that is taken by all first-year students. The unit emphasizes the patient's point of view and is heavily illustrated with cases in which folklore is prominent. In addition to my teaching of medical students, I have made a variety of other health applications of folklore materials, including the teaching of residents, the presentation of both clinical and grand rounds, and clinical consultation. Outside the Medical Center I have taught, for the past several years, courses in folk medicine for nursing graduate students and social gerontology students at the University of Pennsylvania where I have adjunct appointments in Folklore and Folklife, Nursing, and Social Gerontology. I have made presentations on folk medicine and folk belief for a variety of medical and multidisciplinary continuing education programs, especially dealing with the needs and behavior of cancer patients. In 1987 and 1988 I prepared three major reports on folk medicine and alternative cancer treatments at the invitation of the Congressional Office of Technology Assessment as a part of their project concerning the evaluation of unorthodox cancer treatments. These reports were based on videotapes, case studies, printed materials, and other data in the Medical Ethnography Collection of the Penn State College of Medicine, founded in 1983, over which I serve as academic director.

Folk Medicine, Belief Systems, and World View

Unfortunately, folk medicine has generally been conceived both by academics and health professionals as consisting of sets of healing recipes, the efficacy and behavioral impact of which could be individually measured by reference to current medical criteria. Modern folklore theory, however, recognizes that such beliefs and practices exist within larger, organized systems of cultural materials, health belief systems. Furthermore, these systems include sets of values, attitudes, and expectations partly taught by culture and partly developed by the individual through unique life experiences that challenge these culturally provided "world views." The question, "Why do you believe that works?" cannot be answered purely on the basis of observations about a healing practice itself, but must include its cultural context. For example, the belief in the efficacy of ginseng as a universally effective tonic is associated with a high valuation of age and experience, characteristics of wise healers as exemplified by traditional herbalists. The belief is further supported by the current status of the Oriental healing traditions from which the use of ginseng was learned by Westerners. That status includes the observation that many Oriental health ideas (including the properties of ginseng) are today receiving serious medical scrutiny.[4] In North America, beliefs about ginseng often benefit from a common idea, usually found in a Christian framework, that God would not have placed us in a world that did not contain remedies to match all problems. Associated with this belief is a common skepticism about harsh chemicals and "high-tech" treatments, and the expectation that natural healing is safe by definition. This latter idea is related to the popular conception of natural healing materials as more like food than medicine, thus connoting a nurturant mechanism in contrast to the combative images associated with many modern medical treatments. In a given clinical encounter the belief in the usefulness of ginseng may have little direct relevance, but several of these related issues may have great importance, for example, difficulty in accepting the authority of a relatively young physician, noncompliance or undercompliance with prescription regimens, and ignorance of the potential risks of many natural healing methods (e.g., liver toxicity with some herbs, protein malnutrition with some diets).

Each of the ideas just described may be different in any given case. For example, for some patients the belief in natural remedies may be supported by an evolutionary theory that includes such concepts as "diseases of civilization" with no explicit religious component. Thus, health belief systems must be understood in both their individual forms, as represented by single, real patients, and in the idealized, cultural forms that help in the analysis of overall social interactions, such as the affinity of a particular set of beliefs for specific social groups. If this distinction is not made, and individual health systems are assumed to mirror cultural trends, the result is stereotyping that interferes with good care.

It is, therefore, generally the case that individual folk medical beliefs are practically impossible to understand in isolation. Nor do they provide a useful starting point for examining the interaction of modern medicine and folk tradition.

The Logic of Folk Medicine

To understand the prevalence of folk medicine in North America it is necessary to contrast the way that it operates among those raised within a traditional folk healing system and those who are brought to it by circumstances later in life, very often serious illness.

Highly prominent folk medicine systems identified with particular "folk groups" have served as the model for studies of folk medicine, resulting in the stereotypical notion of "their" medicine as opposed to "our" medicine. However, even within those groups for whom a folk medical system is dominant, there exists a variety of alternatives. For example, chiropractic, the health food movement, and the folk medicines of neighboring groups are all quite salient for both Christian Scientists and those Mexican-Americans who utilize *curanderismo*. Furthermore, true folk medical dominance is rare in North America. More frequently folk medicine constitutes a set of alternative influences and options that coexist with the modern, official medical system, varying in prominence according to context. This is well illustrated by the case of Mr. B., given above, who had no interest in any form of folk medicine until faced with a crisis in which official medicine was unable to provide adequate help. At that point he experimented with an alternative approach, and his beliefs and practices have been permanently changed as a result. In other words, the health culture of the United States is basically pluralistic, and the routes through the various possible resources by a given individual constitute a "hierarchy of resort." This concept is very useful for the analysis of the ways in which individuals sort through their options in a rational order. However, if one assumes that clinical encounters are the fundamental form of health behavior, an assumption encouraged by the medical model, analysis yields a deceptively simple hierarchical picture. It is true, for example, that many patients go to their family doctor for back pain but subsequently may try a chiropractor if the M.D.'s treatments yield no satisfactory result; or Christian Scientists *in extremis* may consult a surgeon. However, the health resources of most people include a wide variety of home treatment (and prevention) strategies that are utilized far more often than any kind of healer, that are likely to continue in use during regimens prescribed by healers, and that involve beliefs that shape the manner in which a healer's advice is followed. Even for those for whom a single health system is dominant, it is rare not to find a variety of health resources used, in different orders, for different problems, and at different stages of those problems.

I have just described the process by which an individual works her or his way through a hierarchy of health options as "rational." I use that term advisedly, and whenever I discuss health systems I begin by noting that most of them (from conventional medicine to psychic healing to homeopathy to herbalism) are rational systems of thought. Immediately I encounter an argument to the effect that this cannot be because such and such a system is *not correct*. Whether or not this judgment of correctness is right is not relevant. "Rational" simply means based on the coherent use of human reason. Reasoning, including formal deductive logic, cannot guarantee truth. If assumptions, criteria for the admission of evidence, and observations differ, then the same kind of reasoning may lead to very different conclusions.

The importance of recognizing the rationality of a system of ideas is that it gives people with different viewpoints a common ground for discussion. A surgeon and a folk healer can rather easily be brought to understand the logic of each other's thought if each will listen to a straightforward description of the assumptions and observations involved. This understanding can lead to a reasonable discussion that can work to the advantage of each, and even more importantly to the advantage of a patient who may be seeking help simultaneously from both. Because emotions tend to be so strong in such discussions, it may be necessary for a third party to help communicate the "straightforward description," for example a medical folklorist or anthropologist, or the patient in the middle. But it is still not that complicated a task to accomplish.

Two crucial points here are worth reiterating. First, it is not that folk medical systems have *their own logic*, as is often suggested. It is the *same* logic that is used in other kinds of reasoning including medicine, granting that not all individuals are equally adept at reasoning or reason the same in all situations. For example, emotion occasionally overwhelms reason regardless of the individual's cognitive skills. But this is as true of official thought as of folk tradition. It is differences in initial assumptions (e.g., that God can heal miraculously or that "natural" treatments are better than "artificial" ones), the selection and ordering of one's authorities (e.g., intuition or scripture as opposed to—or in addition to—scientific journals and textbooks), and criteria for evidence that set any particular folk medical system apart from official medicine. The most important single difference in criteria for evidence is that folk tradition highly values the patient's *experience*, i.e., subjective evidence, while official medicine is much more comfortable with objective evidence, especially that obtained through technological assessment. A major consequence of this is that folk medical practice tends to be in closer touch with the patient's feelings about health and disease. This is often referred to as a focus on *illness* as opposed to *disease*.

The second point is that the result of a rational discussion based on an understanding of another's health system as logically ordered does not necessarily result in agreement about which beliefs are true. Neither does it suggest that health care professionals should stop short of making the strongest case possible for the best current medical knowledge and practice. But the data indicate that regardless of good medical arguments a substantial number of patients will persist in refusing some aspects of recommended treatment and in adding folk medical treatments outside the clinic or hospital. The choice is not between requiring 100 percent compliance and permitting freedom to patients. The choice is between knowing when folk medicine is important in a case and not knowing. If the health care team knows of pertinent beliefs and practices, then there is an opportunity to assess and discuss them with the patient. Otherwise the implications of those beliefs and practices, for better or for worse, will remain inaccessible to medical intervention. The possible nature of such intervention is outlined in the following section.

Dealing with Folk Medicine in the Clinic

Frequently folk medical beliefs in the clinical setting are viewed primarily as obstacles to compliance. For example, many health care professionals phrase the primary question regarding folk medicine as follows: "How can we get patients to give up those health practices and beliefs that are not in accord with medicine or, failing that, how can we get them to follow medical advice regardless of those beliefs and practices?" This response derives largely from the stereotypical assumption that folk medicine is found mostly among poorly educated, culturally marginal individuals. From this perspective the problem is simply one of education and acculturation. However, the discovery of the prevalence of folk medicine among *all* segments of society indicates that merely informing the patient that medicine does not share a belief is no guarantee that the belief will be given up. Neither does the nonmedical status of a health belief logically mean that it *should* be given up. I teach instead that the problem is much more complex:

   • First, physicians must become aware of their patients' "unorthodox" (in medical terms) beliefs and practices, and this is difficult because patients usually conceal them from physicians.

   • Having become aware of a patient's beliefs and practices, the physician must determine whether they actually constitute a risk, either a direct risk (as in liver toxicity in infants being given certain herbal preparations) or the risk of conflict with medical advice (as in a belief that medical treatment indicates a lack of faith and is therefore an impediment to healing through prayer).

   • If there is no risk, the beliefs and practices must be considered among the patient's health resources, and must remain of interest because these resources readily change over time, and their medical implications may also change.

   • If there are risks involved, the patient's commitment to the practices and beliefs must be assessed and compared to his or her commitment to medical treatment.

• If the commitment is relatively light, medical arguments alone may accomplish the desired effect.

• If commitment is relatively strong, the physician must engage in a process of negotiation between the medical framework and the framework of the patient. This final step requires eliciting from the patient the exact nature of the practice or belief in question and its place within the patient's health system. This necessitates some understanding of ethnographic interviewing methods, or a willingness to draw upon non-medical experts for consultation (ranging from faith healers to herbalists to scholars such as folklorists and anthropologists).

In some cases this negotiation leads to full compliance, but very often it does not. The ultimate goal is to maximize the delivery of good medical care, to minimize the medical risks identified in the folk medical belief and practice, and to create a cooperative doctor-patient relationship. The negotiation may be as simple as the following: discovering that an Hispanic patient believes in the ancient hot-cold balance theory of disease and treatment; that the penicillin prescribed for a bacterial infection was initially accepted because the disease was classified as "cold" and penicillin is considered "hot"; however, if the penicillin causes diarrhea then the patient may stop taking it because this is a "hot" disorder. Merely explaining the mechanism by which penicillin is known to produce this side effect and insisting that the medicine be continued can end discussion, but it is not likely to result in actual compliance. However, if the explanation is accompanied by the suggestion that the "heat" of the penicillin be balanced by taking it with fruit juice which is considered "cold," full compliance may be obtained together with a much better relationship between doctor and patient. The patient need not think that the doctor shares the hot-cold beliefs. It is enough that the doctor is aware of them, respects the patient's cultural heritage, and sees ways in which the two approaches may be kept from conflicting.

Other cases may be much more complicated and may require a compromise involving less than full delivery of preferred medical treatment and less than complete reduction of risk in the patient's practice. However, if the only alternative to this is constant, hidden noncompliance or complete loss of the patient to medical care, such a negotiated middle ground is clearly desirable. Also, this kind of accommodation has been known to add to medical knowledge, as when Jehovah's Witnesses have refused blood transfusions while simultaneously accepting the idea of surgery. This has resulted in major developments in reducing the amount of blood needed for many surgical procedures.

Furthermore, the negotiation process itself is important beyond its direct impact on the management of *a particular case*. It provides the best

Figure 5.1. Decision Tree

A clinical decision tree for dealing with clinically important patient involvement in alternative health practices and beliefs.

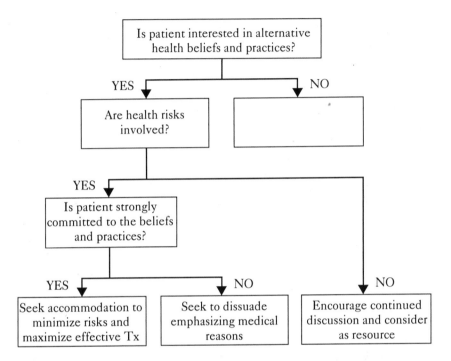

opportunity for doctors and nurses to become familiar with the beliefs and practices of the local patient population, and the functions of those beliefs and practices in the case of specific diseases. No textbook can ever give all of this information, and it is not feasible to have a designated cultural specialist on every health care team. Therefore, the first role of the folklorist in the medical process is one of education, with clinical consultation an important second function.

This discussion of folk medicine in the clinic illustrates several points about folklore studies and health. First, not only must material and methods of use to the physician be taught, they must be taught together with the specifics of their application. I teach the process described above in the form of a clinical decision tree (figure 5.1).

Each of the steps in this algorithm is accompanied by a list of actions to be taken or information to be acquired. For example, the first step, becoming aware of a patient's beliefs and practices, includes the following: (1) familiarize yourself with the health systems of your area; (2) "give permission" for patients to raise unconventional health topics in the clinic; (3)

listen for "nondisclosing cues," cautious efforts to raise the subject of folk medicine while minimizing the disclosure of personal beliefs (as in "I have a friend who believes that . . . "); (4) explicitly reopen this subject with patients whenever they are faced with a serious health problem of their own or in their family, because these are the times at which they are most likely to seek (and be offered) additional or alternative health resources.

Although I have referred primarily to physicians throughout my article, all members of the health care team can and should be involved in this process. In fact, many patients are much more willing to share this information with practically anyone other than the doctor, because they reasonably perceive the physician as most likely to be very negative about medically unorthodox beliefs and practices.

Conclusion

I have described folk medical belief systems as rational, although I have granted that they may conflict with official medical care. I have also outlined a negotiation process that includes the possibility that the accommodation of patient beliefs and folk medical practices may involve some risk and may interfere with medically indicated treatment. This is not intended to suggest a medical relativism in which any practice is acceptable if the patient believes in it. It is instead intended to be practical, acknowledging that a long history of efforts by official medicine to eliminate the influence of folk medicine indicates that this is not an achievable goal. The study of folk medicine also helps one to understand *why* it is so persistent. Despite the very broad authority that our society has granted to the medical profession it is clear that official medicine does not and cannot provide *everything* needed to deal with sickness, suffering, and death. No matter how many professional resources are developed and added, from social work to counseling and so forth, such official efforts never serve all needs. It is out of this social fact, the inability of official culture and authority to provide for all contingencies, that folklore has always grown. Viewed in this way the situation may be seen as less adversarial. Official medicine has always been surrounded by additional community health resources, which is good because by itself it cannot fulfill such functions as explaining the meaning of suffering or providing all of the support that a chronically disabled person requires.

The ultimate goal of folklore applied to health care, then, is to help official medicine to recognize its cultural location within the community and to discover the means for interacting as effectively as possible with those additional resources with which it coexists. In this way conflict, with its attendant costs, can be minimized and the positive aspects of both official and folk medicine can be enhanced. This can be done without asking the physician to become an ethnographer or attempting to bring into official medicine everything that helps sick people.

Folklorists, of course, are not the only academics with an interest in the cultural and social aspects of health care. The discipline of folklore, however, does have certain unique features relevant to medical applications. First, although folklore research is carried on all over the world in many different populations, American folklorists have a strong tradition of working with "local" populations. Therefore, the central subject matter of folk medicine for folklorists involves the major American patient populations, unlike medical anthropology, for example, that has a much greater emphasis on Third World cultures. However, folk medical research shares with medical anthropology an ethnographic approach; that is, its primary methods involve rich and complex descriptions of actual behavior using a great variety of techniques, from interviewing to participant observation to photographic documentation. Quantitative and numerical methods are also used, but they do not dominate as in medical sociology. Therefore, the descriptions are readily applied to an understanding of clinical situations, whereas the more heavily quantitative descriptions characteristic of medical sociology are often more easily used for public health purposes. Folklore studies also has a tradition of combining humanities and social science perspectives. This allows the folkloristic study of folk medicine to be broadly interdisciplinary and to include insights ranging from history and philosophy to epidemiology and psychobiology. But in the last analysis, perhaps folklore's greatest advantage in this kind of work is its strong populist orientation. That is, cast into a clinical situation all of a folklorist's training immediately suggests questions aimed at understanding the patient's point of view and describing it in the most sympathetic manner possible. This is a central part of the discipline's intellectual history and development: the assumption that ordinary people tend to be underestimated and that their knowledge tends to be discredited by authorities. The folklorist seeks to understand that overlooked knowledge, especially by learning the traditional idioms and modes of thought from which it arises. This does not make the folklorist a critic or adversary of medicine, but it does make her or him an informed advocate of the patient, one who has the intellectual tools necessary to render physicians and patients mutually intelligible.

Notes

1. For a detailed analysis of this patient's reasoning and possible alternative medical explanations, see Hufford "Contemporary Folk Medicine," in Norman

Gevitz', ed., *Unorthodox Medicine in America* (Baltimore: Johns Hopkins Univ. Press, 1988), 228-64.

2. Barrie R. Cassileth, Edward J. Lusk, Thomas B. Strouse, and Brenda J. Bodenheimer, "Contemporary Unorthodox Treatments in Cancer Medicine: A Study of Patients, Treatments, and Practitioners," *Annals of Internal Medicine* 101 (1984):105-12.

3. R.W. Spjut and R.E. Perdue, Jr., "Plant Folklore: A Tool for Predicting Sources of Antitumor Activity?" *Cancer Treatment Rep.* 60 (1976): 979.

4. Walter L. Lewis and Memory P.F. Elvin-Lewis, *Medical Botany: Plants Affecting Man's Health* (New York: Wiley and Sons, 1977).

For Further Information

The Nature of Illness

Folk medicine intimately reflects patients' perceptions of sickness, and since the mid-1970s the literature has reflected an increased concern about those perceptions and the factors that shape them. The difference between professional and lay views is explored by Leon Eisenberg, in "Disease and Illness: Distinctions Between Professional and Popular Ideas of Sickness," *Culture, Medicine and Psychiatry* 1 (1977): 9-23, and in 1976 Elihu M. Gerson provided a new analysis of the significance of that difference in "The Social Character of Illness: Deviance or Politics?" *Social Science and Medicine* 10 (1976): 219-24. Eric Cassell, "The Nature of Suffering and the Goals of Medicine," *The New England Journal of Medicine* 306 (1982): 639-45, discusses a major source of the professional/patient difference, while David Hufford, "The Love of God's Mysterious Will: Suffering and the Popular Theology of Healing," *Listening*, 22 (1987): 225-39, discusses the medical implications of two different views of suffering commonly found in folk medicine.

Alan Harwood ed., *Ethnicity and Health Care* (Cambridge: Harvard Univ. Press, 1981), provides an excellent introduction to the relationship of ethnicity and health, including warnings against the equation of folk medicine and ethnicity.

Introductions to Folk Medicine and Specific Systems

There are only a few brief introductions to folk medicine in general available. Don Yoder's "Folk Medicine" in Richard M. Dorson, ed., *Folklore and Folklife: An Introduction* (Chicago: Univ. of Chicago Press, 1972), 191-215, and David Hufford's "Folk Healers" in Richard M. Dorson, ed., *Handbook of American Folklore* (Bloomington: Indiana Univ. Press, 1983), 306-13, are complementary treatments written from the folklorist's point of view. Irwin Press's "Urban Folk Medicine: A Functional Overview," *American Anthropologist* 80 (1978): 71-84, illustrates the anthropologist's focus on Third World populations, providing an international context for the definition of folk medicine.

Norman Gevitz, ed., *Unorthodox Medicine in America* (Baltimore: Johns Hopkins Univ. Press, 1988), is a collection of articles on the most historically important folk medical traditions in the United States including botanical medicine, water-cure, Christian Science, homeopathy, osteopathy, chiropractic, and Divine Healing. My own chapter, "Contemporary Folk Medicine" (pp. 228-64), is a relatively detailed introduction to modern American folk medicine that includes case examples and a discussion of major concepts in the study of folk medicine.

Arthur Kleinman, *Patients and Healers in the Context of Culture: An Exploration of the Borderland between Anthropology, Medicine, and Psychiatry* (Berkeley: Univ. of California Press, 1980) analyzes the entire cultural context of healing, using field materials from Taiwan. Cecil G. Helman, " 'Feed a Cold, Starve a Fever' — Folk Models of Infection in an English Suburban Community, and Their Relationship to Medical Treatment," *Culture, Medicine and Psychiatry* 2 (1978): 107-37, describes the folk health beliefs of a middle-class, English patient population, exploring the manner in which this tradition and official medical thought often reinforce each other.

Wayland D. Hand was one of the great comparative scholars of folk medicine. *American Folk Medicine: A Symposium* (Berkeley: Univ. of California Press, 1976), which he edited, contains essays on a great variety of topics ranging from Native American medical systems to ancient and medieval beliefs about disease and healing, all written by participants in the international conference on folk medicine that he organized at UCLA in 1973. It is a good introduction to the breadth of folk medicine scholarship. Wayland D. Hand, *Magical Medicine: The Folkloric Component of Medicine in the Folk Belief, Custom, and Ritual of the Peoples of Europe and America* (Berkeley: Univ. of California Press, 1980) offers a great variety of specific folk medical beliefs studied in historical and comparative detail.

Edward Spicer, ed., *Ethnic Medicine in the Southwest* (Tucson, 1981) is a helpful set of descriptions of the folk medical systems of several groups in the southwestern United States, including Mexican-American, Native American, and "Anglo" groups.

Most folk medical systems have a major spiritual dimension, and religious healing is a highly significant part of American folk medicine. David Edwin Harrell, Jr., *All Things Are Possible: The Healing and Charismatic Revivals in Modern America* (Bloomington: Indiana Univ. Press, 1975), is an excellent discussion of the major Protestant healing movements in twentieth-century America.

My own "Christian Religious Healing," *Journal of Operational Psychiatry* 8 (1977): 22-27, and "The Love of God's Mysterious Will: Suffering and the Popular Theology of Healing" (cited above) analyze the differences between the approaches to religious healing that are most likely to interfere with medical care and those that are more likely to accommodate such care while helping the patient to cope with illness. My "Ste. Anne de Beaupre: Roman Catholic Pilgrimage and Healing," *Western Folklore* 44 (1985): 194-207, describes one major aspect of Roman Catholic healing traditions in the United States.

Michael Owen Jones's *Why Faith Healing?* (Ottawa: National Museum of Man, Canadian Centre for Folk Culture Studies Paper No. 5; 1972) is an excellent field study of one particular magico-religious healer functioning in an isolated rural setting (in Newfoundland, Canada). Jones examines one aspect of the tradition, that of some consequences of narrating on attitude, along with the process of how notions of appropriate therapy alter with conceptions of the nature of illness, in his article "Doing What, With Which, and To Whom: The Relationship of Case History Accounts to Curing," in Wayland D. Hand, ed., *American Folk Medicine: A Symposium* (Berkeley and Los Angeles: Univ. of California Press, 1976), 301-14.

Curanderismo, the folk healing tradition of Mexican-Americans, is one of the better studied folk medicines found in the United States, The best introduction to the subject is Robert T. Trotter II and Juan Antonio Chavira, *Curanderismo: Mexican American Folk Healing* (Athens: The Univ. of Georgia Press, 1981).

"Holistic healing" is, in a sense, the major folk medical system of modern, middle-class Americans. Arthur C. Hastings, James Fadiman, and James S. Gordon, eds., *Health for the Whole Person* (Boulder, Colorado: Westview Press, 1981) provides the best overview of this developing tradition written from *within* the holistic perspective. Phyllis H. Mattson, *Holistic Health in Perspective* (Palo Alto, Calif.: Mayfield Publishing Co., 1982) is a sympathetic but scholarly description and analysis of the movement.

Finally, for a study of traditional, Appalachian beliefs and practices in conflict with clinics in a northern city, see Ellen J. Stekert, "Focus for Conflict: Southern Mountain Medical Beliefs in Detroit," in Ellen J. Stekert and Américo Paredes, eds., *The Urban Experience and Folk Tradition* (Austin and London: Univ. of Texas Press, 1971), 95-136.

The Prevalence of Folk Medicine

The prevalence of folk medicine's influence has been consistently underestimated, and only a few studies have recently begun to offer hard, empirical data on the subject. The first and best of these is Barrie R. Cassileth, Edward J. Lusk, Thomas B. Strouse, and Brenda J. Bodenheimer, "Contemporary Unorthodox Treatments in Cancer Medicine: A Study of Patients, Treatments, and Practitioners," *Annals of Internal Medicine* 101 (1984): 105-12.

On the related subject of what most patients do before consulting a physician, Kathryn Dean's "Self-Care Responses to Illness: A Selected Review," *Social Science and Medicine* 15A (1981): 673-87, provides an excellent literature review.

Lola Romanucci-Ross's article "The Hierarchy of Resort in Curative Practices: The Admiralty Islands, Melanesia," *Journal of Health and Social Behavior* 10 (1969): 201-9 describes the hierarchical sorting by which people move through their health resources. This is also a crucial idea for the interpretation of information on prevalence. This concept is discussed in detail in the context of American folk medicine, with several examples, in my own "Contemporary Folk Medicine" cited above.

For some recent theses and dissertations on folk medicine, with implications regarding the prevalence of folk medicine as well as some of the topics dealt with below, see Philip Dwyer, "Herbalism and Ritual: Folk Medical Practices Among Asian Immigrants in Southern California" (Ph.D. dissertation, University of California, Los Angeles, 1987); Maria Teresa Valenzuela, "Awareness of Folk Medicine Practices of the Mexican-American: A Survey of School Nurses" (M.S. thesis, Texas Woman's University, 1985); Teresa F. Keeler, "Narrating, Attitudes, and Health: The Effects of Recounting Pregnancy and

Childbirth Experiences on the Well-Being of the Participants" (Ph.D. dissertation, University of California, Los Angeles, 1984); Sondra B. Thiederman, "The Use of Opium By Women in Nineteenth-Century Britain" (Ph.D. diss., University of California, Los Angeles, 1984); Beatrice A. Roeder, "Chicano Folk Medicine from Los Angeles, California" (Ph.D. diss., University of California, Los Angeles, 1984); and Barbara L. Reimensnyder, "Powwowing in Union County: A Study of Pennsylvania German Folk Medicine in Context" (Ph.D. dissertation, University of Pennsylvania, 1982).

Cooperative Interaction Between Modern and Folk Medicine

Although rare in most American health settings, around the world there have been a number of efforts made to develop cooperative relationships between modern health care teams and folk practitioners. R.H. Bannerman's "WHO's Program," *World Health* (1977): 76-77, describes such an initiative made by the World Health Organization.

One of the few systems found in the United States with which this kind of effort has been made is Puerto Rican spiritism. The following two articles are descriptions of this cooperation by two scholars who have actually been involved in this application, Vivian Garrison in the northeastern United States and Joan Koss in Puerto Rico: Vivian Garrison, "Folk Healing Systems as Elements in the Community Support Systems of Psychiatric Patients," in U. Rueveni, R. Speck and J. Speck, eds., *Innovative Interventions: Healing Human Systems* (New York: Human Sciences Press, 1982), 58-95; and Joan Koss, "The Therapist-Spiritist Training Project in Puerto Rico: An Experiment to Relate the Traditional Healing System to the Public Health System," *Social Science and Medicine* 14B (1980): 255-66.

Clinical Impacts of Folk Medicine

More common than programs to link folk healers with medical teams have been efforts to teach health care providers to recognize folk medicine and other cultural components in the management of individual cases. Ray Brown, Mario Ramirez, and E. Fuller Torrey, "Could the Hangup Be Medical Folklore?" *Patient Care* (Sept. 30, 1972): 61-75, was an early indication of physicians' growing awareness of the clinical importance of folk medicine. Arthur Kleinman, Leon Eisenberg, and Byron Good, "Culture, Illness and Care: Clinical Lessons from Anthropologic and Cross-Cultural Research" *Annals of Internal Medicine* 88 (1978): 251-58, is a good general introduction to this from the cross-cultural orientation.

My own (David J. Hufford) *American Healing Systems: An Introduction and Exploration* (Hershey, Penn.: Medical Ethnography Collection of the George T. Harrell Library, 1984) is an overview of major elements involved in the clinical negotiation of folk medical concerns, from the viewpoints both of providers and of patients. Printed in looseleaf format for use at a public conference held at the University of Pennsylvania in 1984, the booklet has since been used at several medical schools and nursing programs. My "Folklore Studies and Health" *Practicing Anthropology* 7, nos. 1 and 2 (1985): 23-25, is an introduction to the medical application of folk medicine studies written primarily for folklore and anthropology graduate students.

The following describe folk medical systems associated with specific ethnic groups and discuss their clinical importance: Lillian Comas-Diaz, "Ethnicity and Treatment: Puerto Rican Espiritismo and Psychotherapy," *American Journal of Orthopsychiatry* 51, no. 4, (1981): 636-45; Alan Harwood, "The Hot-Cold Theory of Disease: Implications for Treatment of Puerto Rican Patients," *Journal of the American Medical Association* 216 (1971): 1153-58; Loudell F. Snow, "Folk Medical Beliefs and Their Implications for Care of Patients: A Review Based on Studies Among Black Americans," *Annals of Internal Medicine* 81 (1974): 82-96; Margaret M. Clark, ed., *Cross-Cultural Medicine*, a special issue of *The Western Journal of Medicine* 139 (1983): 806-938, which deals with several different groups.

The Risks of Folk Medicine

Although it has long been assumed that folk medical practice constitutes a major direct risk to patient health, there has not been much empirical confirmation of this idea. In fact, current studies suggest that direct health risks may be relatively uncommon. However, they do exist and it is obviously important to understand them. Allen L. Brown, Steve Whaley, and Watson C. Arnold, "Acute Bicarbonate Intoxication From a Folk Remedy," *American Journal of Diseases of Children* 135 (1981): 965; and C.H. Gold, "Acute Renal Failure from Herbal and Patent Remedies in Blacks," *Clinical Nephrology* 14 (1980): 128-34, document specific cases of injury caused by folk medical practices.

Conflict with medical care is a more likely clinical problem with folk medicine than direct physical risk, and conflict is generally something which can be ameliorated (or completely removed) through informed negotiation. Lois Hoffman's article, "Problem Patient: The Christian Scientist," *Medical Economics* 33 (Dec. 1956): 265-83, reprinted in E. Gartly Jaco, ed., *Patients, Physicians and Illness* (New York: Free Press, 1958), 279-83, is a well-known illustration of clinical problems in one of the few cases in which successful negotiation is rarely possible.

The Efficacy of Folk Medicine

Harder to document than risk, although obviously important, is the matter of the efficacy of folk medicine. Walter L. Lewis and Memory P.F. Elvin-Lewis, *Medical Botany: Plants Affecting Man's Health* (New York: Wiley and Sons, 1977), is an indispensable introduction to those herbal folk medicines now known to be effective. The issues involved in new research on the subject are well introduced by Edward M. Croom, Jr., in his "Documenting and Evaluating Herbal Remedies," *Economic Botany* 37 (1983): 13-27. "Plant Folklore: A Tool for Predicting Sources of Antitumor Activity?" *Cancer Treatment Report* 60 (1976): 979, by R.W. Spjut and R.E. Perdue, Jr., presents research on the efficacy of folk herbal cancer treatments.

The possible efficacy of folk medicine is more frequently taken seriously in connection with herbal treatments than with "magico-religious" practices, although the latter are of even greater importance in folk medical traditions around the world. Jerome D. Frank, a psychiatrist from Johns Hopkins University, has pioneered efforts to develop a medical model for understanding the apparent success of healing practices that do not involve any physical "medicine." His "The Faith That Heals," *The Johns Hopkins Medical Journal* 137 (1975): 127-31, gives a brief overview of his theories. *Persuasion and Healing: A Comparative Study of Psychotherapy* (rev. ed., New York: Schocken Books, 1974) is his very influential book on this subject.

Not all medical researchers have concluded that such successes are best understood through the medical model. *The Miracles*, a book by H. Richard Casdorph, M.D. (Plainfield, N.J.: Logos International, 1976), documents several cases of what he concludes were genuine miracles in the literal sense. In a similar vein Rex Gardner, M.D., in "Miracles of Healing in Anglo-Celtic Northumbria as Recorded by the Venerable Bede and His Contemporaries: A Reappraisal in the Light of Twentieth Century Experience," *British Medical Journal* (1983): 1927-32, argues that while miracles as such may not be capable of scientific proof, it is often evident that a belief in them is rational and well supported by empirical evidence.

The efficacy of folk medicine is part of a larger question, namely, whether folk tradition contains substantial amounts of valid knowledge not currently known to science, or whether it is merely a repository of obsolete notions. My book, *The Terror That Comes in the Night: An Experience-Centered Study of Supernatural Assault Traditions* (Philadelphia: Univ. of Pennsylvania Press, 1982), addresses this issue by comparing medical and folk knowledge of sleep paralysis. Evidence from many cultures indicates that while folk and medical traditions of this state overlap to some extent, both bodies of knowledge contain unique information, and folk tradition contains some very surprising and accurate knowledge about the *experience* itself.

6

Democratizing Art Therapy

KRISTIN G. CONGDON

In October of 1975, I found myself faced with a new job and a new challenge. I was to teach art classes to women inmates in the Milwaukee County Jail in Milwaukee, Wisconsin. Although educational programs in prisons are now plentiful (in quantity if not quality), at that time there was only one other similar jail program, in Pittsburgh. The Pittsburgh program was stated to be therapeutic in design, while our program emphasized an educational approach. Working in a jail, as opposed to a prison, is more difficult in several aspects. The population is diverse in terms of crimes, the restrictions on materials and other environmental controls are often greater, and the tension is usually greater. Inmates are awaiting trials and sentences, and the unknown is worrisome.

Armed with a master's degree in art education and experience teaching art to inner-city elementary school students in Fort Wayne, Indiana, I began by feeling rather directionless. I questioned myself: What do I, a middle-class art teacher, have to offer lower-economic-class women imprisoned in a maximum security jail? Likewise, what benefits could come from creating and studying art for these women at this time in their lives? These were not new questions for me. I had asked them as a public school teacher, and I was to ask them again and again as I taught art in museums, community centers, mental health treatment facilities, and recreational settings. The answers seemed to vary according to the population and the setting. Later, as a university professor, I would encourage my art education and art therapy students to ask these questions of themselves. The answers to these questions, in the jail setting, came from a combination of an understanding of culture-based aesthetics, lower-class perspectives, jail culture, and the inmates' needs and abilities to find ways to break out of their present despair. Since I worked exclusively with women inmates, I knew the additional programming had to be oriented toward women's cultural perspectives.

As I began my two and a half years working in the jail, the women inmates became my teachers. They were a diverse group of individuals, but the majority of them were economically very poor, were women of color, and had very little academic schooling. They had children, responsibilities, and a lot of past failures. A few were "in" for murder, some for shoplifting, and many for prostitution.

These women were eager to learn (when faced with an interesting, reasonable challenge); they were extremely supportive of each other, and they were, for the most part, extraordinarily creative (not necessarily always with their art work, but they could see possibilities for increasing their freedom in an incredibly stark and unwelcome environment where I more often saw only bars). They had great humor, and fantastic stories to tell, which, it turned out, were often quite true. They were concerned about their children and their family responsibilities. Repeatedly they told me that they dreamed of being traditional mothers, living quiet, stable lives. Their choice of artistic activities reflected that dream and traditional female values.

Most of these woman were at a crisis point in their lives. Like the Chinese ideograph for crisis that conveys two meanings—that of danger and that of opportunity—it was a time when attention could be diverted toward change. But it was only through an understanding of their cultural perspectives that I was able to help facilitate a therapeutic (or some might say educational) environment where empowerment might take place.

As I presented my lessons, I learned to listen carefully to the women inmates, and I began to ask questions. As my classes grew in size beyond my ability to work individually with new attendees, I began to hire more experienced students to teach newcomers. The money earned was placed directly into their commissary funds. My goals in many respects became more identifiably therapeutic than educational, although there is no confusion in my mind that that which is therapeutic is also educational.

What became important to my students was success, reflected in the completion of a satisfactory project and the ability to communicate an idea or obtaining knowledge to be able to teach a skill when the need presented itself. Students became impressed by their own abilities to reflect on their individual and group identities. They began to recognize and further define their aesthetic tastes and to envision more knowledgeable and assertive ways to present themselves artistically. It became clear to them that art was a means of communication. Usually this form of communication was to reinforce or change a creator's identity or to send a message of love and caring to a bewildered child living with a relative or in a foster home.

Griselda Pollock points out that women speak from a different historical perspective than men. Their art reflects a negotiation of their place in a particular historical moment and their need either to struggle against given definitions and ideologies of femininity or the necessity to bring themselves more comfortably within that role.[1] My students saw themselves as "bad women" who had not been able to become (or accept) their given roles as homemakers, dependable and responsible mothers, and good wives. Choosing to work in traditional ways helped them remake connections to these roles. Embroidery, sewing, crocheting, and knitting were personally satisfying for these women at this time in their lives. This work made connections to their lives. Harmony Hammond theorizes that "connecting was the function and meaning of women's traditional art, and it is still consistently a function of feminist art today."[2]

My students' expressions were not always ones that agreed with my aesthetic tastes or life values. For example, when they dried a banana peel from their evening meal on the radiator, rolled it into a joint, and passed it around the room, simulating past experiences with marijuana, I was not amused. The smell alone in a poorly ventilated room was overwhelming, not to mention the health hazard to everyone, including unborn children. But I did understand the activity and enjoyed the creativity behind it.

Neither was the art work always consistent with my cultural values and tastes. While I wear very little jewelry, most of the women were thrilled when I brought in bright beads and fibers, which they knotted and shaped into headbands, chokers, and necklaces. My choices of neutrally colored wool yarns for knitting, crocheting, and weaving were not well received; requests were quickly made for bright colors, variegated yarns, and choices of polyesters over natural fibers. The shine of the polyester yarn pleased the majority of women, and its ease of washing also made it more reasonable. The practicality of the materials and art forms was an integral part of their aesthetic preferences. Furthermore, my efforts to encourage drawings and the creation of wallhangings was met with a great lack of enthusiasm. Consistently, these students wanted to make traditional (yet fashionable) objects to wear or use in the home. If these creative products were not designed for themselves, they were made for a family member, most often a child.

Talking, sharing, and reflecting became very important during our classes. I had not planned for this kind of discussion in the beginning, but I found it to occur naturally as an extension of the art activities. This was a time when the women interacted positively, stopping to help each other, but working to fulfill their individual goals on a particular piece. Working time was limited, so it was precious. The rules, generated by the sheriffs and correctional officers, were very rigid and always acknowledged peacefully. The room was very warm and smoky; the record player played quietly; and the discussions began. Many scholars have written about the development of camaraderie and friendship that occurs in a sewing group. Historically, the quilting bee or sewing group allowed its participants a time and a space to visit and create social bonds without betraying their family responsibilities. It also was (and continues to be) a time when women engaged in the meditative activities of moving a needle in a repetitive manner, thereby creating a sense of calm, of order and control, and of working toward an attainable goal.

The dialogue was important talk. It was a clarifying and sharing, which flowed easily with a small amount of direction from me. Often it began by reflecting on one's work: a crocheted pair of slippers for a daughter; a necklace to wear to court to show the judge what a particular inmate was doing with her time; a suggestive halter top fashioned to draw attention. Discussion evolved into topics about hierarchies in prostitution, the oppression and/or benefits of pimps, responsibilities to family, cultural differences and race relationships, the meaning of being poor, and choices for change. Values were being clarified, choices were being made, and lives were being justified and reshaped.

Although I had little knowledge of art therapy at that time, I soon realized that much of the group process in the jail sessions could have been the result of well-applied art therapy theory. Years later, after having immersed myself in this body of knowledge, I came away with some relevant theories that were enhanced through my background in folklore. Though much of art therapy depends on those aspects of human nature and artistic ability that are identifiable as universal, my jail experiences, as well as experiences with other varying populations and settings thereafter, taught me that cultural differences (especially those of race, class, and gender) must also be noted, enjoyed, and developed in order to work effectively with groups of people from differing backgrounds.

Overview of Art Therapy

The fields of art therapy and art education are often linked, much to the disdain of many professionals who want separate identities. Indeed, these disciplines overlap in many respects because both facilitate art experiences and both are concerned with the well-being of the individual. Furthermore, art educators work with specialized populations, and many art therapists believe that they can be effective with nonlabeled or so-called normal people.

Folkloric fieldwork and methodologies, however, have been more readily accepted in art education literature than in art therapy, probably because of the easily supportable interest in cultural pluralism espoused in multicultural educational materials. Although art education has a long way to go in fully appreciating and utilizing the work of folklorists to its benefit, the field of art therapy tends to be less well developed in terms of its cultural recognitions. Whereas educators at least attempt to develop curriculum around diverse populations, those in the mental health fields have often not responded to cultural differences due, in part, to the input of the more traditional, inflexible approaches of the hard sciences.

To ignore the artistic and cultural expressions of a pluralistic society works against the fundamental principles of democracy in which a wide variety of expressions are valid. It tends to alienate and devalue people who are not a part of the established art world. This myopic approach to art and culture contributes to the existence of a mentally ill society in which some people are not allowed the give-and-take necessary to healthy social well-being.

Besides being so closely linked with art education, art therapy has not been an easy profession to define for a number of other reasons.[3] The first reason may be its relative newness as an academic field of study. Almost fifty years ago, the application of art therapy began with Margaret Naumberg's use of art as a tool in her psychotherapy sessions. She believed that art could release messages from the unconscious through symbolic speech. In keeping with her times, the works of Freud and Jung influenced her greatly. For Naumberg, this tool could be used by any psychologist regardless of previous training in art. The aesthetic result was of no consequence; only the psychoanalytic interpretation was important.

There are other art therapists such as Edith Kramer who also utilize psychoanalytic theory yet stress the need for aesthetically pleasing results, feeling that there is a relationship between mental wellness and well-integrated, well-designed works of art. Theorists disagree on how important it is to talk about and reflect on a work of art. Joan Erickson feels it is unnecessary (we should learn from working with art materials in a safe atmosphere free from the verbal analysis of the traditional therapist), and Janie Rhyne, who builds on gestalt experiences, feels it is necessary to talk about the process and the product. Some art therapists work with individuals, like Naumberg does, and others, like Kramer, Rhyne, and Hanna Yaxa Kwiatkowska, who work with families, engage more than one person at a time in artistic expression.

Some theories suggest that art therapy be used in ways other than to uncover unconscious messages. The developmental approach is most often used with children who are mentally or physically delayed to help them move through the so-called normal stages of artistic development, which are hypothesized to be part of normal human growth. Each theoretical approach, including developmental art therapy, is more or less based on the idea that all healthy human beings have universally identifiable ways of communicating. Although art therapists are becoming more cautious about stating that all knotholes in trees signify the sexual abuse of the artist, or that all faces scribbled over are done so in anger at the represented figure, little work has been done to recognize the differences in cultural symbology, both visual and verbal, in therapeutic settings. A lack of this kind of understanding could readily trigger grave misunderstandings.

If art therapists were to study folklore theory using knowledge about folk beliefs, folk speech and folk art, their attempts at communication with culturally different clients could be improved. Water may signify one thing to a group of people who know the dangers of an ocean and have an entirely different meaning to those who live in the desert. Likewise, colors do not necessarily have universal meanings but may vary from group to group and even among individuals.

A Folkloric Approach to Art Therapy

By and large, most leading art therapists start their sessions by having their clients engage in a freeing-up exercise, usually the creation of a scribble that may then be spoken about as representative of particular emotions or may be further drawn on to represent an object seen within the lines.[4] Art therapists frequently begin with chalk or pastels on large sheets of paper. These are materials that are often used by so-called fine artists, and the free-flowing use of line is the kind of expression encouraged by instructors in art schools.

While I found paper, pencils, paints, and pastels of interest to a few of my students in the jail setting, most of these women vehemently objected to touching them, stating that they had no talent. (Most art therapists say they seldom get that kind of response after the first drawing.) On the other hand, art materials that were traditionally used in these women's communities, cloth and fibers, were embraced with a quick recognition of identity. Everyone knew people who made clothes or crocheted afghans, and they were admired individuals.

Beginning with materials and art forms that were understood and seen as useful helped them develop an awareness of who they were. Underclass women still employ sewing skills when they can; they still need to make do with what is available to them; and the activity of sewing or otherwise creating with fibers has a long tradition of association with the values to which these women adhere. They wanted to be good wives and mothers; they wanted homes and middle-class lives, and fiberwork, for them, was a part of that dream.

In the academic art world, there continues to be a strong hierarchical value system that says that objects made with fibers are less worthy than those made with paint; and those objects that hang on walls have more aesthetic potential than those that are worn or used in some other physically utilitarian way. The study of folklore could contribute to changing these beliefs and expand on the art facilitator's awareness of the therapeutic function of a variety of art materials and art forms. In his work, *Chain Carvers: Old Men Crafting Meaning*, Simon Bronner tells us about how southern Indiana carvers used this activity therapeutically to help them adjust to difficult changes in their lives. Patricia Cooper and Norma Buferd, in their 1978 book, *The Quilters*, beautifully demonstrate how quilting reflects an individual's expression of how she sees the world.[5] One can find evidence throughout folklore literature of how traditional art helps to provide an individual with a sense of place, identity, community, and history. It functions to express values, creating stability and giving direction.

There is also folkloric evidence that the repetitive motions involved in activities such as basketry or quilting can help to calm and soothe. As already noted, these processes can be a retreat to solitude, to ordering and reordering the world, and the product can be the physical evidence that substantiates one's individual existence.

Art therapists can also benefit from the study of folklore by understanding the meanings behind folk speech. A cultural phrase may be easily misinterpreted if one does not have a grounding in minority or underclass language styles. In *The Challenge for Mental Health: Minorities and Their World Views* (Austin: Hogg Foundation, 1983), Richard A. English stated that "to ignore or fail to understand and consciously recognize the world views of minorities is to engage unwittingly or otherwise in a form of cultural oppression. When mental health practitioners fail to take into account world views of minorities, or in the absence of doing so, substitutes their own views (especially when they differ from their clients), they are likely to impute negative traits to their clients and to contribute to the high drop-out rates of minority clients in mental health services" (p. 23). The more we are able to encourage and understand language, both verbal and visual, from the creator's world view, the better chance we have of working effectively with that person.

Folklorists and others are beginning to make it clear that not only are there cultural-based aesthetics, but inside group members repeatedly speak about their creations with specific language choices reflective of what they see as important and pleasing. For example, Afro-American artists often refer to "having visions," and Afro-American quiltmakers repeatedly say that "the colors have to hit each other just right," which refers to the placement of bright, complementary colors next to each other to effect an offbeat pattern.[6] The term "fancy" can indicate either a positive or a negative reaction to an art work, depending on one's cultural values. There are differences in language which reflect ethnic, religious, environmental, technical, and generational identities.[7]

My jail students referred to their best creations as "rags." So often was this term used that when a fashion show was organized, the program was named and advertized to outsiders as the "Rag Show." The term "rag" may have been employed to affirm the black or minority position of "them" against the dominant Anglo society, much as the term "bad" (pronounced "baaadd") is used in Afro-American narrative tales to mean good.[8] Language is a powerful tool. Words, phrases, and dialects have the ability to affirm one's position and dignity in an often unjust and difficult world. Verbal and nonverbal language, and a variety of other artistic expressions, can teach us much about the creative powers, world views, and human needs of varying cultural groups.

One particular art activity that was undertaken in the jail illustrates how a certain cultural world view was expressed. After I had been working in the jail for about a year, overcrowding and the need for remodeling split the women into two groups. About half were sent to the Franklin House of Corrections just south of Milwaukee. This facility was a medium security work farm for men. The Franklin women inmates occupied a different kind of setting, that of dormitory living rather than separate locked cells for each person. Furthermore, with approval, inmates could work on projects during the times when I was not there. This new arrangement, I believe, gave my students a new kind of freedom. Although I worked hard not to stifle their expressions, the lack of my constant presence while they worked no doubt encouraged more freedom.

We had been given tubs full of men's old jeans, the official uniform for this setting. It was the correctional officers' hope that the new women inmates would want to conservatively and appropriately mend the rips and tears. As my students had been using the sewing machine to make new clothes and had been embroidering on all kinds of apparel, they readily took to redesigning the denim. Long and short skirts were fashioned as well as halter tops, hats, vests, and headbands. They then began to embellish them with embroidery.

The majority of these women were "in" for prostitution, and their newly made wardrobes began to reflect their roles as seductresses. When I came for class, they would model their new clothes for me and tell me about the outfits that had gone out with the inmates on work or childcare day-releases. The slits on the skirts were high, and the halter tops showed lots of midriff and breast. Suggestive embroidered statements such as "the best part's inside" or dollar signs appropriately placed were common. Street names such as "Monique" and "Honey" or names reflecting geographical areas such as "Mississippi" were often used. (Most inmates had several names they used in an effort to protect themselves.) Sometimes female figures in suggestive poses were depicted. When modeled, the tight-fitting clothes enhanced the proper stance of the hooker.

Although the correctional officers thought I should put a stop to this type of creativity, I refused. I was pleased to have the opportunity to talk to my students about who they were when they wore these clothes, who could view them when they were worn, and what spaces they would chose to wear them in. We discussed other kinds of clothes and images that felt good to them, and choices they might want to make about their identities. My position in these experiences was not to place my values and judgments on them; rather it was to help them clarify their own perspectives and directions. Unfortunately, since the correctional officers did not approve, our seemingly endless source of denim material was taken away. Still, during that time the creative process and product within a particular cultural context was used effectively to communicate, validate, change, and enhance the lives of these women.

Conclusion

The field of art therapy could greatly benefit from the utilization of folklore studies in both its theory and practice. In this chapter, I have described three interlocking ways in which folklore knowledge can be useful to the art therapist:

1. The recognition and utilization of art materials, artistic forms, and symbolism that comes from the participant's traditional culture can assist in engaging and interesting the individual and validating his or her identity as having positive, creative aspects on which predetermined change can be built.

2. Recognizing and understanding how language or folk speech can be used by a participant and how it can assist the art facilitator in understanding the artist's world view, value system, and functions of artistic expression, thereby affecting better communication in therapeutic settings.

3. These forms of recognition can contribute to a respectful consideration of the participants' art and work to further the mental health of a community by building on the creative strengths of our pluralistic society, rather than using therapeutic settings to inadvertently engage in systems of oppression. The use of folkloric understandings in the theory and practice of art therapy can help lead to the democratization of art encouraging more active participation in our society by all of its citizens.

If art therapists expand in this direction, they can assume a leadership role in reacquainting the mental health field with the original intent and purpose of community mental health efforts: building on the strengths and expressions of existing natural support systems in a community and encouraging and developing mental health rather than treating mental illness. In the case of the women inmates who redesigned the men's jeans, they learned to build on:

- their knowledge of who they were and who they wanted to become (especially as women in our society);
- the incredible richness of their visual and verbal communities;
- the strong commitment to mutual group support they shared; and
- the ability to communicate and create in the most horrible of settings.

Folklore can contribute to the ability of both mental health professionals and educators to work within the perspectives of varying cultural groups. Culturally sensitive professionals who benefit from this process will be more effective in building on strengths and empowering groups by facilitating individual and cultural communication that respects personal history, identity, and the viability of the people with whom they are working.

An Afterword

It has been almost fifteen years since I began my work in the Milwaukee County Jail. Since that time I have helped to facilitate many more arts programs in diverse settings including AIDS support groups, alcoholism treatment centers, and groups such as Orlando Fights Back (which brings people together to fight drugs in high-risk neighborhoods). As director of the Community Arts Program at the University of Central Florida, I have worked to teach students not only the theory but also the practice of the lessons outlined in this chapter.

In the Community Arts Program we try to emphasize *learning* from cultural groups with which one does not centrally belong, before one attempts to teach. We try to get students to see that a single way of behaving (doing art, organizing a group, speaking about an idea) is not adequate. We require all Community Arts students to spend time in existing programs working with populations which will get them away from the university setting and its (often single-minded) perception of knowledge. Not only are students advised to pay careful attention to the cultural values and norms of a particular community, they are sometimes asked to create new communities whereby all participants will be strengthened by the bond. For example, we have an ongoing journal writing class that takes place in an identified community setting each semester, such as a women's long-term substance abuse treatment center or an independent living facility for people who are physically disabled. University students and community students (usually enrolled as noncredit students) come together for the journal class as peers. They are charged with the responsibility not only to learn the class material but also to communicate with classmates to ensure that they function as a cooperative group. Since we recognize that students often learn as much from their classmates as from the professor, we try to capitalize on this. The community setting alone gives university students another perspective; the hosting students often demand —by virtue of who they are—changes in learning styles, organization of materials, and curricular input.

We also work with community organizations who ask for assistance but do not wish to have university leadership. Such an organization is the Preserve the Eatonville Community (P.E.C.). Located in one of the oldest black incorporated townships in the country, it is the birthplace of novelist and folklore collector Zora Neale Hurston. The president of P.E.C., Mrs. N.Y. Nathiri, is currently finalizing the third "Zora Neale Hurston Festival of the Arts and Humanities," which takes place each January in Eatonville. This is a community effort that includes assistance from businesses as well as academe. The University of Central Florida cooperates by making available resources such as information and assistance regarding grants, instructional resource expertise, and academic consultation on scholarship issues. P.E.C. now has a museum, an ongoing lecture series, a traveling exhibit, publications, and curricular materials for the public schools as well as plans for many other projects and endeavors. Students are able to facilitate these projects, but the focus of the efforts is centered in Eatonville, and rightly so.

Another example of how Community Arts works with varying cultures and community groups is our (informal) partnership with Orlando Fights Back, a federally funded project that targets two "at-risk" communities each year to fight drugs through community organizational efforts. These projects are often accomplished through the use of the arts. For example, under the direction of the Orlando Fights Back and another treatment center (and sometimes with the help of Community Arts students), high school students from these areas develop improvisational groups to perform in their communities to help youth deal with troubling problems. The identity of the content issues is determined by the group (actors and audience), and the solutions come from anyone and everyone who cares to participate.

There are other examples illustrating how the arts, folklore, and community organizational efforts help this program to assist substance abusers. One Community Arts student, who now works for this organization, spent three semesters working on an art curriculum that would help substance abusers in treatment move through the twelve steps of recovery visually, engaging individuals and groups in art processes and products. It is intended to help those who learn better by working with art materials, unlike other programs, which typically rely solely on verbal practices, and it has been extremely successful in a variety of inpatient and outpatient settings. Community Arts is currently working with Orlando Fights Back to develop a mentorship project that will place "at-risk" youth who are talented and interested in the arts with an identified artist or art group in the community. This will, it is hoped, give both parties a chance to see the world a little differently, enhancing possibilities to recognize and redefine individual and cultural practices.

What the women inmates in the Milwaukee County Jail taught me about artistic practices, modes of communication, historical needs, environmental dictates, and fundamental issues of race, class, and gender are not lost in the theory and practice of the project in which I now work. Every effort is made to attend to folkloric sensitivities and to utilize defensible cultural practices toward agreed-upon goals. We work toward the development and maintenance of mental health (as opposed to the focus on treating mental illness) through the strengths and practices of community cultures. In this way, the practice of art therapy is redefined and expanded to integrate community perspectives and varying cultural methodologies.

Notes

1. See Griselda Pollock, "Women, Art and Ideology: Questions for Feminist Art Historians," in Hilary Robinson, ed., *Visibly Female: Feminism and Art Today* (New York: Universe Books, 1988), 203-21.

2. See Harmony Hammond, *Wrappings: Essays on Feminism, Art, and the Martial Arts* (New York: Mussman Bruce, 1984).

3. See Elinor Ulman, Edith Kramer, and Hanna Yaxa Kwiatkowska, *Art Therapy in the United States* (Craftsbury Common, Vt.: Art Therapy Publications, 1977), where they discuss why art therapy's professional territory is likely to remain inconclusive.

4. Art therapists generally refer to those with whom they work as clients or patients. I refer to the women inmates I worked with as students throughout this chapter partly because the program I worked in was an educational one and I was hired as a teacher. However, given a choice, I would still refer to them as students because educational programs are more often approached in healthy, normalized ways, whereas therapy assumes a problem or illness of some kind. It would have been far more difficult for me to attract participants to my program had it been identified as a therapy session. Despite the differences in terminology, the reader should keep in mind that the students I refer to here did engage in art activities that had therapeutic results.

5. See also the films "Quilts in Women's Lives" and "Hearts and Hands," both produced by Pat Fererro; and Pat Ferrero, Elaine Hedges, and Julie Silber, *Hearts and Hands: The Influence of Women and Quilts on American Society* (San Fran-

cisco: Quilt Digest Press, 1987); and Patricia Mainardi, "Quilts: The Great American Art," in Norma Broude and Mary D. Garrards, eds., *Feminism and Art History: Questioning the Litany* (New York: Harper and Row, 1982), 330-46.

6. See Maude Southwell Wahlman, "Africanisms in Afro-American Vision-ary Arts," in *Baking in the Sun: Visionary Images from the South* (Lafayette: University Art Museum, University of Southwestern Louisiana, 1987), 28-43.

7. See Kristin G. Congdon, "The Meaning and Use of Folk Speech in Art Criticism," *Studies in Art Education* 27 (1986): 140-48.

8. See William R. Ferris, "Vision in Afro-American Folk Art: The Sculpture of James Thomas," *Journal of American Folklore* 88 (1975): 115-31.

For Further Information

Several works will give the reader a foundation in the field of art therapy: Florence Cane, *The Artist in Each of Us* (rev. ed., Craftsbury Common, Vt.: Art Therapy Publications, 1983 [1951]); Edith Kramer, *Art As Therapy With Children* (New York: Schocken Books, 1971); Margaret Naumberg, *Psychoneurotic Art: Its Function in Psychotherapy* (New York: Grune and Stratton, 1953); Rawley A. Silver, *Developing Cognitive and Creative Skills Through Art: Programs for Children with Communication Disorders or Learning Disabilities* (Baltimore: University Park Press, 1978); Hanna Yaxa Kwiatkowska, *Family Therapy and Evaluation Through Art* (Springfield: Charles C. Thomas, 1978); and Elinor Ulman, Edith Dramer, and Hanna Yaxa Kwiatkowska, *Art Therapy in the United States* (Craftsbury Common, Vt.: Art Therapy Publications, 1977).

Much used anthologies in the field are Elinor Ulman and Penny Dachinger, eds., *Art Therapy in Theory and Practice* (New York: Schocken, 1975); and Elinor Ulman and Claire A. Levy, eds., *Art Therapy Viewpoints* (New York: Schocken, 1980).

For a good discussion on defining art education and art therapy, see Sandra Packard and Frances E. Anderson, "A Shared Identity Crisis: Art Education and Art Therapy," *American Journal of Art Therapy* 16 (Oct. 1976): 21-28.

Several art educators write about how art should be studied in a democratic, pluralistic society. Doug Blandy and Kristin G. Congdon, eds., *Art in a Democracy*, (New York: Columbia Teachers College Press, 1987), contains articles on the artistic expressions of women, occupational groups, children, and others who are often overlooked or devalued in our diverse society. For information on how folk speech can be used in art educational settings, see Kristin G. Congdon, "The Meaning and Use of Folk Speech in Art Criticism," *Studies in Art Education* 27 (1986): 140-48. A good example of how folk speech can be related to Afro-American art can be found in Maude Southwell Wahlman, "Africanisms in Afro-American Visionary Arts," *Baking in the Sun: Visionary Images from the South* (Lafayette: University Art Museum, University of Southwestern Louisiana, 1987), 28-43. See also Susan S. Arpad, "'Pretty Much to Ourselves': Midwestern Women Naming Experience Through Domestic Arts," in Marilyn Ferris Motz and Pat Browne, eds., *Making the American Home: Middle-class Women and Domestic Material Culture 1840-1940* (Bowling Green, Oh.: Bowling Green State University Popular Press, 1988), 11-26. For an overview of the literature on folk art in educational settings, see Kristin G. Congdon, "Educators and Class-rooms," in Simon J. Bronner, ed., *American Folk Art: A Guide to Sources* (New York: Garland, 1984), 241-54.

Little has been written on how folk art can be therapeutic or used in thera-peutic settings. Two of the best works in this area to date are Simon J. Bronner, *Chain Carvers: Old Men Crafting Meaning* (Lexington: Univ. Press of Kentucky, 1986); and Patricia Cooper and Norma Bradley Buferd, *The Quilters* (Garden City, N.Y.: Anchor Press/Doubleday, 1978). For information on how art educa-tion should relate to mental health goals, see Kristin G. Congdon and David C. Congdon, "A Systemic Approach to Art Education and Mental Health," *Visual Arts Research* 12:2 (1986): 73-79.

An excellent article on how mental health has failed ethnic groups is Rich-ard A. English, *The Challenge for Mental Health: Minorities and Their World Views*, Second Annual Robert L. Sutherland Lecture, University of Texas at Austin, Nov. 3, 1983 (Austin: Hogg Foundation). The reader may be interested in some background on the initial plans for mental health centers. For this information, see Arthur Blum, "Community Assessment," in *Proceedings of Community Mental Health: Program Development and Evaluation* (Cleveland: School of Applied Social Sciences, Case Western Reserve University, 1971), 2-20.

For descriptions of firsthand experiences in teaching art in the Milwaukee County Jail, the reader may wish to refer to Kristin G. Congdon, "Art Education in a Jail Setting: A Personal Perspective," *Art Education* 37 (1984): 10-11.

7

Designing Public Spaces for People's Symbolic Uses

Sara Selene Faulds

For more than a century, ethnographers have chronicled and interpreted planned and spontaneous ritual performances, parades, cultural and culinary festivals, dramas, and other community events. While this research continues, the focus has expanded to include in more detail the settings that serve as stage or backdrop for these public performances—including the buildings, environments, and situations in which expressive or symbolic behavior is manifested.

Design Dynamics of Public Space

We engage in behaviors in our public environments that invest spaces and forms with special meanings. We manipulate public spaces to express ourselves creatively, to perform for others, to disseminate and encourage our group culture and lifestyle, to better our quality of life, and to provide ourselves with a sense of identity. A rich and multifaceted approach to urban design and planning can result when urban designers take into account these patterns of behavior in their projects. The key is to develop methods that incorporate the study of people's expressive behavior into a design and usage program. Such an approach can provide a sense of dignity, delight, and magic to our public environments.

Responses to the Urban Form

Our everyday uses of spaces and forms quite often are very different from the idealized uses and behaviors envisioned by architects, developers, and planning departments. How people actually use a space, the emotional and cultural needs we expect our public spaces to serve, and the symbolic actions we perform both spontaneously and in our public rituals are all important design elements when creating public places. Too often design and construction leads not to a satisfying and enjoyable experience but rather to the creation of environments that produce feelings of frustration and hostility.

Many scholars of the urban experience contend that the form and ambience of public spaces have a direct bearing on personal competence—either supporting or inhibiting our effectiveness as human beings. For example, C.M. Deasy in *Design for Human Affairs* ([New York: Wiley and Sons, 1947], 45) points out that the settings we use help or hinder us in a social and psychological sense in three major ways:

1. They influence the stress we experience in accomplishing our group or personal goals.
2. They influence the form and nature of our social contacts.
3. They influence our feelings of identity and self worth.

It has been suggested that our environments are often seen as extensions of ourselves. When our public places are less than they should be, we feel ourselves to be made in some way ugly, small, and without dignity. Unfortunately, too often public places are created more as an afterthought to development and less as a place owned by the people for their own uses and needs.

Issues and Trends in Architecture and Urban Planning

Interest in neighborhood development and design issues has grown over the last decade. Planners, designers, developers, and governmental agencies are experiencing new demands on their talents. In many cities people are working to bring back the former vitality and excitement of their downtown areas. In suburban areas, the issue of "slow growth" is paramount. People are concerned with both a real and a perceived lessening of their quality of life, and members of local governmental bodies are beginning to feel the consequences as their constituencies vote their concerns. A people-oriented, user-directed approach to these development issues is urgently needed.

It takes courage and commitment by local governments to implement an emphasis on community needs and desires in development. The whole planning and design process has to be opened up for public input, review, and acceptance in order to proceed. Decision-making becomes a shared responsibility among politicians, planners, and local residents and merchants. However, sharing responsibility also empowers, and, as such, most governmental bodies steer away from such an orientation.

Santa Monica, California, is one local government that made a commitment to involve its citizens in the decision-making and planning process throughout most of the 1980s and, to a great extent, the 1990s. From 1981 to 1986, neighborhood consensus was required before a project could be built;

this policy is still nominally pursued. Outreach to the community was a prerequisite. Good design and amenities for pedestrians were emphasized.

"Community consensus" has also become an important concept for some planners as a way of helping guide neighborhoods through the often distressing and confusing process of development. But attempts to build consensus often fall short. Too few urban planners are trained in techniques of mediation, leadership, and public workshop facilitation. Planning schools need to teach the kinds of "people skills" typical of ethnography, such as interviewing, active listening, prioritizing, and recognizing the emotional content, symbolism, and dynamics of interaction and negotiation. Consensus building also requires understanding the importance that tradition, community culture, public ceremonies, and expressions of creativity assume in people's uses of public places.

Some architecture and planning schools have sporadically included courses in their curricula providing a general awareness of other cultures and giving an idea of the variety of ways people relate spatially to their environment. Students learn that there are similarities as well as differences in people's uses of public places, their interactions with others within such spaces, and the ways in which they respond to the built environment. Students are—or should be—exposed to such issues as the social dynamics involved in settlement patterns; the special meanings to the community of building shapes, architectural detailing, and the positioning of buildings; the communal use of spaces; and the nature and role of performance arts.

A recent trend in the field of architecture has been the "Post Modern Movement," which, in part, advocates the inclusion of architectural icons and forms from the past in current projects. It is assumed that these architectural details hold inherent interest, meanings, and value for today's populace. By incorporating them into contemporary buildings or designed spaces architectures sought to humanize the structures, encouraging positive responses to these artifacts in the neighborhood. However, there rarely is sufficient research on a neighborhood's history and its traditions, the living context that has grown up around the built environment, or the lifestyles of the residents to create truly symbolic buildings or community spaces.

Behavior-Based Design

What makes a public space work? In part, it begins to work when designers look at the specific context in which the project will reside—the built environment, local customs, and lifestyles. From this contextual look they can then determine the appropriate width of sidewalks, the proportion of window frontage to walls, the ratio of retail and restaurant concerns per block, the most manageable route for foot traffic, the best crowd control techniques, the amount and type of lighting, and where parking is located, its cost and the number of parking spaces available. However, while these factors figure strongly into user-oriented concerns, there is much more to the issue of a well-designed public space than numbers and ratios.

The uses people make of specific types of environments at different times of the day and of the week, the kinds of activities they engage in, and the many manifestations of expressive and symbolic behavior that take place in the public arena are all important elements to be considered if we are to achieve a truly "behavior-based design." Typical questions within this expanded perspective are the following:

   • Will these spaces be used solely for the functions intended? Could they also be used for other, unplanned-for activities; if so, what type of additional uses could effectively take place here?

   • Based on experience with similar kinds of spaces, are there further enhancements to the space and its flexibility of uses that might be made through design, street furniture, landscaping, or other amenities?

   • Would such elements allow for greater opportunities of communication, exhibition, cultural and creative expressions, and improvement of one's skills to occur?

Using a Behavior-Based Design Methodology

By using a behavior-based design methodology, we begin to understand what is really occurring in our streets and on our sidewalks, in public recreation and entertainment areas, and at shopping malls and in parks and civic and cultural areas. We also learn how people respond to these varied public environments. It is to the ethnographer, possessing the required expertise, methodology, and interest in traditional and symbolic behavior, that local governments and neighborhood groups are beginning to turn.

My experience may help clarify ways in which those trained in ethnographic studies can apply their skills to urban planning and design issues. Much of my field research has been done in two adjoining cities, Santa Monica and Venice, California; specifically along their boardwalk and beach bike path. The site is a large, multifaceted public space and covers much of the beachfront of these two neighboring cities. It has provided extremely rich research material on people's behaviors in public spaces and on subsequent urban design principles. In addition, my experiences as vice-chair of the Santa Monica Architectural Review Board, as a member of the Executive Board of the Third Street Development Corporation (TSDC), and as a liaison to the Santa Monica Arts Commission have given me many opportunities to extrapolate specific design principles from the research data and apply them to other public areas in Santa Monica.

The TSDC worked with city leaders and staff to define a new role and importance for the Third Street Outdoor Pedestrian Shopping Mall. Several public workshops were held to help people discover for themselves the types of land uses, public activities, and commercial emphases they wanted encouraged in the revitalization program for their mall. As a facilitator for the community workshops, I was asked to help residents and merchants identify their individual visions for the mall, to translate these ideas into a visual and verbal presentation, and to arrive at a group consensus for action. From these community workshops, a decision was reached that the mall should fill the role of a cultural and entertainment nub for Santa Monica and the surrounding region, incorporating such elements as live theater, movies houses, jazz clubs, a museum, perhaps a children's theater, restaurants with outdoor seating, book stores, retail shops related to the arts, and artists' studios. There was also much discussion of the need to recognize the great variety of ethnic and cultural groups in the city and to highlight some of their traditions.

As a member of the Architectural Review Board, I was able to champion the need to pay attention to neighborhood context, including street facades, landscaping, design articulation, pedestrian amenities, and the local architectural aesthetics and character of the community. I have also been asked to act as a community resource person, providing insights derived from my research and acting as an advocate for behavior-based design programs before city council and the planning commission.

Santa Monica also encouraged public participation in the design and development process for the Santa Monica pier and its beachfront. The project included the designing and placement of beach furniture and viewing areas; the creation of a children's playground; the upgrading of the bike path and boardwalk; and the placement of public art. Again, public workshops were convened and people were asked to consider the types of events and variety of activities they wanted to encourage on the pier. This meant that items ranging from a band shell and oceanography museum to the upgrading of the pin ball games and bumper cars were considered. I participated as a facilitator and local resource in this process, guiding the public in its consideration of all possibilities and working through issues of trade-offs and priorities to develop consensus for action.

Another example of the public being asked to look to its own actions and preferences for public elements in the built environment was the Arts Commission Conference on Art in Public Places. A public design charrette for the beautification of Wilshire Boulevard emanated from this conference, eliciting public opinion and support of design concepts to symbolize this street (and the city in general) through new types of street furniture (bus benches, trash cans, and newspaper stands), the planting of trees and other landscaping, lighting, pavement treatment, and public art in all future development on Wilshire Boulevard. The coordinating committee sponsoring this event worked with the participants to explore the relationship between symbolism and culture, lifestyle, tradition, history, and neighborhood context in making public spaces unique and special places. In developing the scope of the project, we brought together community residents, merchants, local artists, craftspeople, and city officials.

Applying Folklore Methods to Behavior-Based Design

As suggested earlier, there are various skills, kinds of knowledge, and research tools that folklorists can apply to some of the problems of urban design. They share several of these with other ethnographers; some may be unique, however.

Fieldwork Techniques

A major data-gathering technique in ethnography is that of "participant-observation." The researcher not only tries to observe all that is being said, done, and implied within a specific context but also participates in the activities under study to better understand motivations, constraints, and interactions. Participant observation is also useful in urban planning and design situations to help understand how people are utilizing their spaces and why they are doing what they do. The researcher experiences some of the same feelings in these places as the "natives" do, sensing what facilitates or impedes interaction, becoming aware of the possibilities for or inhibitors to creative expression, and discovering opportunities for or hindrances to using spaces for a variety of planned and spontaneous activities.

Concepts

Folklorists have evolved numerous concepts in order to isolate expressive forms and processes as well as interpret them. They recognize that "festive events" and "festive behavior" can be manifested both in large, formal occasions and in small group or individual festive gatherings. It is because people do engage in small-scale, everyday events and impromptu activities that attention to flexibility in design is so important.

Folklorists also recognize the prevalence of personal and secular rituals as well as public, social, and religious events all taking place in the public forum. They understand that people have the need to express themselves and the urge to create things of aesthetic value. Additionally, they are keenly aware of the role context plays in the form and content of public creative expressions. Thus, they are uniquely qualified to help urban designers develop public spaces that provide a maximum of flexibility of uses.

Orientation and Emphasis

It has often been remarked that folklorists study people's everyday activities. Certainly folklorists are less interested in major movements, elite art forms, or the products of mass production and the mass media than are scholars in other disciplines. Instead, they focus on a group's traditions, and on the beliefs, customs, rituals, and stories in everyday life that are generated in and have an effect on individuals' interactions. One result is an emphasis on communication, performance, and sociability.

I have discovered several large "behavior settings" along the Santa Monica and Venice beachfront. These behavior settings encompass stretches of the boardwalk, the beach, and the bike path. Within these aggregate spaces appear to be smaller, more specific behavior settings or backdrops that are manipulated by groups and individuals to service their creative performances and other activities. These smaller areas include portions of the built environment used on an ad-hoc basis as "stages" by street vendors, mimes, musicians, public speakers, and aspiring actors. They include as well the many outdoor eating areas where people congregate to watch the passing show and perhaps put on an impromptu "performance" of their own. The steps of apartments fronting on the boardwalk are often used as viewing stands, while the pavilions along the bike path are "homesteaded" by groups engaged in many different activities, from playing music to giving massages; the grassy areas everywhere are commandeered for a multitude of outdoor activities many of which are playful, celebratory, festive, or ritualistic in nature. Other behavior setting elements include the facades of buildings with their unique design features, bright colors, and murals; public benches; the palm trees; and even the look and behavior of the crowd itself as it promenades up and down the Boardwalk.

Ascertaining Behavior Patterns in Public Spaces and Places

Using the aforementioned research techniques and concepts, I have delineated a few basic behavior patterns that people engage in while using public spaces as behavior settings. Once noted, these seem neither mysterious nor surprising, but their ramifications for design nevertheless remain profound.

• People like to dress distinctly when out in public, to be seen and to express their own style and creativity.

• Individuals like to entertain others and to be entertained: to act, tell stories, play, make music, and improve their skills in public places.

• People also enjoy having the opportunity to take a passive role in public, to serve as an audience, watching an ongoing, ever-changing show. Even in the role of audience, however, they often manage to perform, whether for a larger audience or simply for friends with whom they joke and kid, tell stories about personal experiences, sing, or play musical instruments. Interestingly, from the point of view of a person riding a bike along the bike path, for instance, performer and audience are both part of a larger performance whole, to be viewed, appreciated, and then passed by as the next piece of public theater comes into focus.

• Visitors to places like Venice Beach come deliberately to witness, experience, and be part of a certain group of activities, to mingle with particular groups of people, and to see specific events and behavior. It is the activities and ambience of the place that draws them.

• People form groups, develop subcultures, perform ritualized activities, engage in celebrations, and create imaginative performances and crafts in public spaces, just as they do within their own homes and within their own support networks, and for similar reasons.

Discovering and interpreting these behavior patterns is not always easy. To see how activities are connected and why they are meaningful requires both practice and the use of appropriate methods for assessing what is going on as well as guarding against imposing one's own values, attitudes, and beliefs.

Ad-Hoc Ownership of Public Environments

For several days in 1984, Santa Monica and Venice experienced a hard-hitting winter storm that tore away a third of Santa Monica's pier, uprooted beach structures from their moorings, carried out to sea an enormous amount of beach sand, and exposed many old pilings. People spontaneously created special places within this new environment. They used pilings uncovered from previous piers as seating places and as quiet, protected spots to view the ocean, the sunset, and the people on the bike path and boardwalk. They also used them as places for picnics, to meet friends, and to meditate.

A public restroom that had come loose from its foundation and floated a small distance away served as a platform from which to watch activities and view the scenery, both oceanside and on the boardwalk. It was also used as a private, out-of-the-stream-of-activity place where couples and friends could go to be alone. Special nooks and crannies were discovered, the whole structure becoming a piece of public furniture. A lifeguard station, which had also come unstuck, was similarly used.

Informal and impromptu uses of places and pieces of the built environment, encompassing both mundane, everyday activities and the ritualized or ceremonial uses individuals and groups put their environments to, provide excellent data regarding the needs and desires of people using public spaces. When individuals feel free to make of their environments what they will, performing the activities they wish to in them, then such spaces can truly be considered to belong to the public. Situations that allow for the greatest amount of flexibility of uses also provide the best answers regarding people's spatial priorities and their varied needs in using public places.

Conclusion

"The designer who is seriously concerned with the questions of human effectiveness must widen the scope of his interests to include a complex new set of human factors," writes Deasy in *Design for Human Affairs*. "If personal motivation and group interaction are elements that affect our competence as human beings, the designer has a clear responsibility to create environments that will do as much as an environment can do to recognize and accommodate these factors" (p. 14).

Folklorists have much to offer to the planning and design of our cities, especially our public areas, through their research and their attention to such expressive activities as performance, rituals, ceremonies, community traditions and creative self-expression. Armed with their research findings, folklorists have a major role to play in developing urban environments that invite people to them, and that allow for many different types of active and passive, formal and informal activities to occur. They can help to create places where people feel comfortable just passing through, casually using the space, or becoming active participants there.

Folklorists are already bringing their research skills to the studies of such behavior-based design issues as:
  • Performance activities in public places,
  • Audience roles and reactions within a performance context,
  • Group and individual ceremonies, rituals, customs, and other interactive behaviors,
  • Expressions of creativity and the motivations and rewards that call these expressions into being,
  • The role of aesthetics in our lives,
  • Play and leisure activities,

• Creation and dissemination of group and individual cultures and lifestyles.

Folklorists can also assist urban designers, local governments, and neighborhood residents in developing a thorough approach to the behavior-based design process by bringing their skills and expertise to the following important areas of community involvement:

• Recognizing and understanding people's uses of the built environment and their psychological and emotional responses to it.

• Serving as community facilitator and resource, helping people discover their vision for their neighborhood, to arrive at a group consensus for action, and to deal with development possibilities and alternatives.

• Being a leader, generating and crystalizing support for neighborhood context, history, and quality of life issues in any changes to the built environment, emphasizing the importance of community design values and aesthetics, and insisting on accommodating community expressive behaviors.

• Acting as advocate for action and involvement, and serving as mediator in the sometimes volatile situation that results from proposed changes.

In *People and Places: Experiencing, Using, and Changing the Built Environment* (Englewood Cliffs, N.J.: Prentice Hall, 1978), Jay Farbstein and Min Kantrowitz nicely sum up the need for a humanistic and behavior-based design approach in their discussion of the dynamics involved in creating urban projects that are fulfilling and satisfying on many levels. "Since places contain activity, define movement, invite feeling, and respond to change" they write, "making places means making experiences" (p. 180). Folklorists, in particular, have the tools to uncover the nature, meanings, and functions of those activities and movements, and hence of helping design public spaces that will best serve personal use and symbolism.

For Further Information

In 1980, the New York Folklore Society sponsored the Urban Folklore Conference. Exciting and thought-provoking, the conference focused on many creative forms of public expression. Local street performers, for example, told conferees of their individual reasons for performing in the public arena, the skills and techniques used, and the joys and tribulations experienced. Since then, folklorists have worked specifically on issues of the city's built environment and its impact on people's behavior and creative expression. Some of these issues were addressed, for example, in a conference directed by Michael Owen Jones at UCLA in 1982 called Aesthetic Expression in the City: Art, Folk Art, and Popular Culture. A particularly interesting review of research problems and prospects is Barbara Kirshenblatt-Gimblett's "The Future of Folklore Studies in America: The Urban Frontier," *Folklore Forum* 16 (1983): 175-234.

For some of the concepts and data-gathering techniques in folklore studies, see Alan Dundes, ed., *The Study of Folklore* (Englewood Cliffs, N.J.: Prentice-Hall, 1965); Jan Harold Brunvand, *The Study of American Folklore: An Introduction*, 2nd ed. (New York: Norton, 1979); Simon J. Bronner, *American Folklore Studies: An Intellectual History* (Lawrence: Univ. Press of Kansas, 1986); Richard M. Dorson, ed., *Folklore and Folklife: An Introduction* (Chicago: Univ. of Chicago Press, 1972); Richard M. Dorson, ed., *Handbook of American Folklore* (Bloomington: Indiana Univ. Press, 1983); Elliott Oring, ed., *Folk Groups and Folklore Genres* (Logan: Utah State Univ. Press, 1986); and Barre Toelken, *The Dynamics of Folklore* (Boston: Houghton Mifflin, 1979).

On qualitative research, see Michael Owen Jones, "Using Qualitative Methods in Research and Application," in Michael Owen Jones, Michael Dane Moore, and Richard Christopher Snyder, eds., *Inside Organizations: Understanding the Human Dimension* (Newbury Park, Calif.: Sage, 1988), 31-47. Personal experience stories are addressed by Sandra K. Stahl in "The Personal Narrative as Folklore," *Journal of the Folklore Institute* 14 (1977): 9-30, and by other articles in the same issue. See Linda T. Humphrey, "Small Group Festive Gatherings," *Journal of the Folklore Institute* 16 (1979): 190-201, for information about festivals and SGFGs.

Architectural writings that I mention in my article include C.M. Deasy, *Design for Human Affairs* (New York: Wiley and Sons, 1974), a key work in behavior-based design offering a humanistic approach to design and development; and Jay Farbstein and Min Kantrowitz, *People in Places: Experiencing, Using, and Changing the Built Environment* (Englewood Cliffs, N.J.: Prentice Hall, 1978), a user-oriented and experiential approach to designing the built environment.

A Pattern Language by Christopher Alexander, Sara Ishikawa, and Murray Silverstein, with Max Jacobson (New York: Oxford Univ. Press, 1977), looks at the many patterns that make up the way we use our homes, the public facades of buildings, and our community spaces; it establishes succinct behavior patterns to be used in design, from the placement of the bed in the bedroom to the design of a neighborhood street.

Other methodological works include Roger G. Barker, *Ecological Psychology: Concepts and Methods for Studying the Environment of Human Behavior* (Stanford: Stanford Univ. Press, 1968); Robert A. Georges and Michael O. Jones, *People Studying People: The Human Elements in Fieldwork* (Berkeley and Los Angeles: Univ. of California Press, 1980); Edward T. Hall, *Beyond Culture* (Garden City, N.Y.: Anchor, Doubleday, 1976); Michael Owen Jones, *Exploring Folk Art: Twenty Years of Thought on Craft, Work, and Aesthetics* (Ann Arbor: UMI Research Press, 1987); and Jon Lang, Charles Burnette, Walter Moleski, and David Vachon, ed., *Designing for Human Behavior: Architecture and the Behavioral Sciences* (Stroudsburg, Penn.: Dowden, Hutchinson and Ross, 1974).

In *A New Theory of Urban Design* (New York and Oxford: Oxford Univ. Press, 1987), Christopher Alexander, Hajo Neis, Artemis Anninou, and Ingrid King demonstrate how each increment of construction in the city can and must be designed in such a way as to "heal the city." Mark Girouard discusses the many uses of public spaces such as squares, plazas, and markets throughout history along with the reasons for their development and growth as well as the changes in architecture and the built environment to accommodate the evolving uses of these public spaces; see *Cities and People: A Social and Architectural History* (New Haven and London: Yale Univ. Press, 1985). For other background materials, see Nathan Glazer and Mark Lilla, eds., *The Public Face of Architecture: Civic Culture and Public Spaces* (New York: Free Press, Macmillan, 1987); Jane Jacobs, *The Death and Life of Great American Cities* (New York: Vintage, Random, 1961); Kevin Lynch, *The Image of the City* (Cambridge: MIT Press, 1960); Kevin Lynch, *What Time Is This Place?* (Cambridge: MIT Press, 1972); and Constance Perin, *Everything in Its Place: Social Order and Land Use in America* (Princeton, N.J.: Princeton Univ. Press, 1977).

Those interested in a more behavioral approach to architectural design and urban planning might examine Clovis Heimsath, *Behavioral Architecture: Toward an Accountable Design Process* (New York: McGraw-Hill, 1977); Christian Norberg-Schulz, *Existence, Space and Architecture* (New York: Praeger, 1971); Constance Perin, *With Man in Mind: An Interdisciplinary Prospectus for Environmental Design* (Cambridge: MIT Press, 1970); and Robert Sommer, *Personal Space: The Behavioral Basis of Design* (Englewood Cliffs, N.J.: Prentice-Hall, 1969).

I also want to mention some folklore studies. In "Tending Bar at Brown's: Occupational Roles as Artistic Performance," *Western Folklore* 35 (1976): 93-107, Michael J. Bell examines the development and performance of public creative expressions and the process as they become self-conscious actions; he explores the way in which individuals work at perfecting these performances for public consumption and the motivations and rewards for doing so. In "L.A. Add-ons and Re-dos: Renovation in Folk Art and Architectural Design," in Ian M.G. Quimby and Scott Swank, eds., *Perspectives on American Folk Art* (New York: Norton, 1980), 325-63, Michael Owen Jones investigates homeowner conceptions and uses of space, with ramifications for architectural design. See also Henry Glassie and Betty-Jo Glassie, "The Implications of Folkloristic Thought for Historic Zoning Ordinances," in Dick Sweterlitsch, ed., *Papers on Applied Folklore* (Bloomington, Ind.: Folklore Forum Bibliographic and Special Studies, No. 8, 1971), 31-37.

Finally I would mention two works that consider some specific ritualistic behavior. One is Lyn Lofland's *A World of Strangers: Order and Action in Urban Public Space* (New York: Basic Books, 1973), which shows how we take great effort to make spaces our own, and how we tend to homestead places, developing "home territories" away from home. Lofland's is an individualistic approach to behavior in the city, including people's personal networks, the underlying structures of social situations, privatizing public space, and developing skills to "use the city." The other publication is my article, "'The Spaces in Which We Live': The Role of Folkloristics in the Urban Design Process," *Folklore and Mythology Studies* 5 (1981): 48-59. In it I focus on the design of living spaces and the importance of looking at the personal, idiosyncratic uses of space. I emphasize the personal rituals we develop and act out in our homes, the psychological importance of being able to engage in our personal ritual performances, and the interactive role our living spaces have with these rituals. Finally, I consider the need for flexible spaces which invite such environment-oriented rituals to occur.

8

A Folklorist's Approach to Organizational Behavior (OB) and Organization Development (OD)

Michael Owen Jones

Recently the friend of a disgruntled employee at a financial institution gave me a document from work. It is an interoffice memorandum from "The Management Advisory Committee" addressed to "All Employees." The memo's subject is "Creating a More Professional Environment."

"In an effort to provide the Firm with consistency and a professional atmosphere, we are in the process of developing a Policy Manual," reads the first sentence. "In advance of your receipt of the manual in its entirety, certain sections will be sent to you as they are developed. The following are some current guidelines aimed at improving our environment."

Then follow several rules and regulations, each one preceded by ellipses. The first reads:

. . . Other than nameplates (where already installed), office doors should be left free of all signs and decorations. This does not include the standard "Do Not Disturb" sign distributed to all supervisory personnel.

In one paragraph after another, the memo instructs employees to turn off lights, calculators, and typewriters, to obtain covers for equipment, to close doors on covered shelves or covered bins, and to keep common areas clean. The next admonition is

. . . All work areas have been provided with bulletin boards for your use. Art and personal items should be displayed within the work area and not outside of, or on top of, the work area.

Next, it admonishes employees:

. . . Birthday celebrations are to be held outside of the office. If held during the lunch hour, they must be restricted to one hour. Although "in-house" luncheons are not permitted, desserts (cakes, etc.) may be brought in and placed in a common area; however, singing of birthday songs, sending of singing telegrams or other outside entertainment services or congregating in large groups is not permitted.

In the unlikely event that employees still feel festive on occasion, especially during winter holidays, the Management Advisory Committee decrees:

. . . Decorations (holiday, birthday, etc.) are not allowed anywhere in the office. However, at year-end (December 15 through December 31) all previously listed restrictions will be ignored. Note: For safety reasons, only artificial trees may be used, and no electric decorations of any kind will be allowed.

A second interoffice memo from the Management Advisory Committee dated the same day sets forth two pages of guidelines for a dress code.

These memos did not improve morale, which was already low. They did not diminish absenteeism or reduce the turnover rate, both of which were high, nor did they increase people's professionalism and effectiveness in their jobs. Quite the contrary.

In explaining what went wrong, a specialist in organizational behavior might point out that, among other things, employees were not being treated as responsible adults, they were not allowed to participate in decisions affecting their work lives, and they had no sense of "ownership" in the organization of which they were supposed to think of themselves as representatives. The specialist would probably question aspects of organizational structure, the human resources function, and leadership.

A folklorist likely would note that these employees are being denied some forms of symbolic communication and interaction that are fundamental to being human. They must work in an impersonal, institutionalized environment. They cannot surround themselves with personal items, mementos, photos, photocopier lore, cartoons or comic strips, and other objects helping them deal with tensions, release pent-up frustrations, and cope with the job on the one hand, and seek reverie and inspiration on the other. Because their dress is restricted, they have little opportunity to express themselves in unique and individual ways and no prospects for a sense of "folk costume" evolving as a badge of distinctiveness or source of identity.

Their impulse to celebrate has been curtailed. Rather than occurring spontaneously at the moment that people feel joyous, as it does in the "natural state," the urge to celebrate has been relegated to a particular place, time of day, and season of the year.

One can predict that there will be no joking except for "gallows humor," little storytelling, and none of the social routines and rituals usually generated when people interact on a cordial basis or organize informally (e.g., food-sharing, playfulness, kidding, cooperative work effort). There *will* develop, however, uncomplimentary nicknames, negative sayings and traditional expressions, a preoccupation with "beating the system," and other expressive behavior with themes of antagonism, hostility, and demoralization.

In this chapter I describe ways of utilizing concepts and approaches from folklore research to better understand behavior in organizations and to help bring about change benefitting individual participants as well as the organization as a whole. First, however, some background to several concepts and trends.

Organizational Behavior and Occupational Folklore

Defined simply as "the study of why people behave the way they do in organizations,"[1] organizational behavior (OB) draws on such disciplines as psychology, sociology, social psychology, political science, and economics. Many specialists in OB teach in university departments of behavioral and organizational science, which are usually in schools of public policy, administration, and industrial and labor relations. Some are independent consultants who advise government agencies, school districts, hospitals, businesses, charities, and similar institutions. Others find employment in various units of organizations, particularly those concerned with communications, training, or employee relations and human resource development.

OB specialists examine individual behavior in organizations, developing or applying hypotheses about perception, personality, learning, motivation, and creativity. They investigate such aspects of group behavior as inter-group tensions and interaction, how groups develop a collective identity and common ways of doing things, and a group's effects on individuals' attitudes and behavior. They consider various kinds of organizational structure, including authority and responsibility relationships, job design, and reward systems. Finally, specialists in OB examine organizational processes such as leadership, strategy, communication, coordination, and decision-making.

Only recently have OB specialists begun to realize that most behavior in organizations, as in other social settings, is traditional and symbolic. "Imagine going to work in an organization devoid of symbols. Only tangible, explicit, instrumental objects would exist," writes Richard L. Daft.[2] "This organization would have no retirement dinners, no stories or anecdotes, no myths about the company's past, no annual picnic, no catchy phrases . . . , no Christmas turkeys. . . . The organization texture would be reduced to a mechanical system, nearing machine perfection, yielding goods and services with robot-like efficiency," he continues.

"An organization designer's dream? More likely a nightmare," writes Daft, for "an organization without symbols would be unworkable for human beings. . . . Employees receive a wide range of cues from symbolic elements of organization. Symbols help employees interpret and understand the organization and their role in it by providing information about status, power, commitment, motivation, control, values and norms."

What Daft calls "symbols" is largely folklore. Lacking customs, social routines, rituals, specialized language, and examples in their work group of what to do and how, people would be unable to function well—if at all. In addition, stories, ceremonies, rites of passage, festive events, joking, play, and other expressive behavior provide a basis for interaction and communication. Depending on its context and content, folklore may instruct, persuade, entertain, help an individual cope, reinforce factionalism, protect personal integrity and promote self-esteem, or stimulate bonding and a sense of community.

Folklorists have long studied occupational lore. Beginning early in this century they assembled collections of songs, tales, and beliefs of cowboys, sailors, lumberjacks, miners, and oil field workers. The 1970s saw great strides forward in broadening the range of expressive forms, vocational identities, and research questions. Folklorists investigated, for example, occupational role as artistic performance, initiation rituals among smokejumpers as ritualized communication, the pervasiveness of photocopier lore in modern offices, the functions of beliefs of commercial fishermen, the themes and ambience in industrial factory lore in the North and a hosiery mill in the South, and rodeo as symbolic performance.

Publications in organization studies and administrative science on expressive behavior in the 1970s paralleled the folklore literature on occupational lore. Among these were essays on stories managers tell, formal structure as myth and ceremony, leadership as a "language game," symbols and patterns in organizational settings, and "myths" in organizations.

In 1980, two works appeared that seemed to cross disciplinary boundaries. Thomas C. Dandridge, Ian Mitroff, and William F. Joyce published an article in *Academy of Management Review* entitled "Organizational Symbolism: A Topic to Expand Organizational Analysis." This seminal essay introduced organization behavioralists to expressive forms and research questions similar to those dealt with in folklore studies (without referring to "folklore" or citing folklorists' works).

The authors' list of "types of symbols," for example, brings to mind one of the textbooks in folklore studies, Jan Harold Brunvand's *The Study of American Folklore: An Introduction*. Dandridge, Mitroff, and Joyce identify "verbal symbols" (myth, legends, stories, slogans, creeds, jokes, rumors, names) similar to Brunvand's category of "verbal folklore." Their list of "actions" (ritualistic special acts, parties, rites of passage, meals, breaks, starting the day) is not unlike Brunvand's section on "partly verbal folklore." Their nomenclature "material symbols" (status symbols, awards, company badges, pins) is analogous to Brunvand's "non-verbal folklore."

Many of the research problems that Dandridge, Mitroff, and Joyce discuss overlap those in folklore studies. "Questions arise," they write, "as to the origin of stories, how they reflect the present organization, and how they participate in subsequent growth or stabilization." Are there industry-wide "symbols" (i.e., legends, rituals, jargon), they ask; are certain individuals more influential in initiating or modifying them; and what happens to these forms of expressive behavior during organizational change? What are the effects of an organization's "symbol system" on the social environment, and vice versa?

Also in 1980, Robert S. McCarl issued a report of research on the occupational folklife of the District of Columbia firefighters. Although largely a description of the work techniques, customs, stories, and recreational activities of firefighters, McCarl's monograph does mention some tensions and personnel issues. One is the ambivalence felt by some individuals in the role of officer. Another is the insensitivity of officers, on occasion, toward those whose activities they supervise. Tensions and conflicts undermine morale, erode "the basic fibre and cohesiveness of the occupation," and diminish the quality of fire fighting performance and the effectiveness of the fire fighting force, writes McCarl.[3]

McCarl recommends to higher administrative levels how they might train supervisors in order to improve life in the workplace as well as the effectiveness of the organization in meeting some of the purposes, goals, and objectives for which it was formed and perpetuated. These include officers' training programs that teach more on motivation and human psychology through attention to the kinds of lore he has recorded.

Ironically, folklorists and organizational behavioralists were largely unaware of one another's existence throughout the 1970s and early 1980s. In 1983 an interdisciplinary and international conference brought them together for the first time. The UCLA Center for the Study of Comparative Folklore and Mythology and the Behavioral and Organizational Science Group in the Graduate School of Management jointly sponsored the event. Called "Myth, Symbols & Folklore: Expanding the Analysis of Organizations," the conference's objectives included communicating recent findings in folklore studies and organizational science, encouraging joint research, and developing transdisciplinary methods based in the humanities.[4]

It was at this conference in 1983 that the term "organizational folklore" began to be used in reference to folklore generated in organizational settings, folklore about organizations, and folklore as an example of spontaneous or informal organizing. "Organizational folklore studies" has been described as a field of inquiry utilizing the concept of organization in research on traditional, expressive forms and processes of communication manifested in people's interactions.[5]

The study of organizational folklore logically extends occupational folklore and folklife scholarship as well as the research on organizational culture and symbolism. Some studies of workers' folklore contained implications for better understanding organizational behavior and improving organizations (particularly works by Collins, Nickerson, and Santino[6]), but these were not systematically developed. Students of organizational behavior, who had begun to oppose mechanistic models in favor of the metaphor of organizations as "cultures," did not know about the research on occupational traditions that could yield insights into the expressive, social, and aesthetic side of organization. Knowledge of one another's field can better inform the disciplines and enrich understanding of human behavior in organizational settings. It might also benefit organizations and their members.

Organization Development

The field of organization development (OD) draws on the behavioral sciences for theory and techniques, particularly such disciplines as psychology, sociology, and social psychology. About twenty-five years old, the field has several intellectual roots. One is "laboratory training," essentially unstructured situations involving small groups in which participants learn from their own interactions and the evolving dynamics of the group. Also known as the T-group (T for training), it is an educational vehicle for individual or small-group change—essentially an experience-based method of learning.

Another source of techniques in organization development is the survey feedback method. Researchers obtain data through questionnaires, interviews, or other data-gathering techniques, which they feed back in summary form to everyone taking part in the inquiry. This provides a basis for understanding problems and planning action as well as helping assure participation by all members in improving the organization.

A third source for organization development is the field of organizational behavior. OB concerns individual and group behavior in organizations along with matters of organizational structure, functions, and processes (e.g., leadership, communication, decision-making).

Organization development (OD) is the applied side of research on organizations (although it has a theoretical dimension too). Writing in the *Academy of Management Proceedings* (1971) on the definition and history of organization development, W.H. French and C.H. Bell propose that OD be considered "a long-range effort to improve an organization's problem solving and renewal processes, particularly through a more effective and collaborative management of organization culture—with special emphasis on the culture of formal work teams—with the assistance of a change agent or catalyst and the use of the theory and technology of applied behavioral science, including action research" (p.146).

Settings run the gamut from labor unions to volunteer organizatons, industrial plants, government agencies, research and development labs, schools, and businesses; they include small departments, large divisions, or whole organizations. The objective might be to improve morale, health and safety, group interactions, interdepartmental communication, the effectiveness of an organization, or a combination of these or other goals. OD emphasizes collaboration among parties, an approach recognizing that problems and solutions in most organizations are complex, that no particular group is necessarily *the* problem, and that rarely is there a single, simple resolution to any issue.

If a program is essentially diagnostic, then the "change agent" or "catalyst" (i.e., a third party to the issue and the organization, usually an outside consultant) may play a more active decision-making role in gathering and interpreting data and in feeding it back to those individuals who provided it. At other times, e.g., when organization members are attempting to develop processes to learn to solve their own problems (the long-term goal of OD), the change agent tends to adopt a more passive role, serving as counselor or sounding board for ideas.

Most studies of occupational folklore are descriptive, not clinical;[7] academic, not applied. Some provide insights into human behavior and implications for organization development, but they describe situations rather than solve practical problems. Were their authors to engage in organization development efforts, they would likely proceed as follows (see figure 8.1):

    1. Feed back a summary of their findings (from observation, interviews, and questionnaires) about problems and/or positive matters to organization members participating in the research, which includes a cross-section of personnel (i.e., as broad a range of "stakeholders" as possible);

    2. Facilitate discussion of the feedback and emerging data with participants;

    3. Assist with action planning and implementation;

    4. Take part in the evaluation of development efforts;

    5. Repeat the process, feeding back a summary of findings, facilitating discussion, and so on.

The researchers' participation would have been solicited by representatives of the organization who had sought assistance. Data would not be

Figure 8.1. Action-Research Model for Organization Development

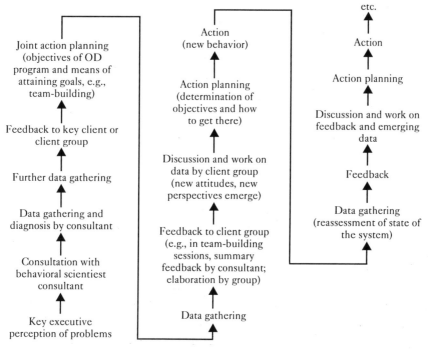

Joint action planning (objectives of OD program and means of attaining goals, e.g., team-building)

↑

Feedback to key client or client group

↑

Further data gathering

↑

Data gathering and diagnosis by consultant

↑

Consultation with behavioral scientiest consultant

↑

Key executive perception of problems

Action (new behavior)

↑

Action planning (determination of objectives and how to get there)

↑

Discussion and work on data by client group (new attitudes, new perspectives emerge)

↑

Feedback to client group (e.g., in team-building sessions, summary feedback by consultant; elaboration by group)

↑

Data gathering

etc.

↑

Action

↑

Action planning

↑

Discussion and work on feedback and emerging data

↑

Feedback

↑

Data gathering (reassessment of state of the system)

Source: W.L. French, "Organization Development: Objectives, Assumptions, and Strategies." Copyright 1969 by The Regents of the University of California. Reprinted from the California Management Review, Vol. 12, No. 2. By permission of The Regents.

presented ex post facto or without members' involvement but would be generated, summarized, and discussed collaboratively as an ongoing process in the spirit of learning, changing, and solving problems. As Raymond Miles warned many years ago, the consultant "must protect those he works with from damage (e.g., the work group being studied must have the right to decide how information collected about it will be used)."[8]

Advocates of organization development point to several unique features of their approach, as indicated in the following list of underlying values and assumptions (which I quote from Gortner et al., *Organization Theory*[9]):

1. Assumptions about people as individuals:

Individuals desire personal growth and development if the environment is supportive and challenging.

Most people are willing to make a higher level of contribution to attaining organizational goals than is permitted by the environment.

2. Assumptions about people and leadership in groups:

One of the most psychologically relevant reference groups for most people is the work group (both peers and superiors).

Most people want to be accepted and to interact cooperatively with more than one small reference group (including the work group, the family, personal friends, and so on).

The formal leader cannot perform all the leadership and maintenance functions in all circumstances; hence, the informal part of the organization is important in groups because different individuals must perform a variety of leadership roles.

Suppressed feelings and attitudes adversely affect problem solving, personal growth, and job satisfaction.

The level of interpersonal trust, support, and cooperation is much lower in most groups than is either necessary or desirable.

The solutions to most attitudinal and motivational problems in organizations involve alteration of mutual relationships by all parties in the system. (Attitudinal and motivational problems are "transactional.")

3. Assumptions about people in organizational systems:

Since organizations are characterized by overlapping work groups, the leadership style and climate of the higher team tend to be transmitted to lower teams.

"Win/lose" conflict strategies between people and groups are not optimal in the long run in solving most organizational problems.

Time and patience are important in changing organizational values and behavior because such changes take a long time.

For any changes to be sustained, the total human resources system (appraisal, compensation, training, staffing, job, and communications subsystems) must change appropriately.

4. Assumptions about values held by members of the client organization:

Members believe in both collaborative efforts and the end products of the organization.

The welfare of all organization members is important, especially to those people having the most power over others.

5. Assumptions (values held) made by behavioral science change agents:

Organized effort exists to meet the needs and aspirations of human beings.

Work and life can become richer and more meaningful, and organized effort more effective and enjoyable if feelings and sentiments are permitted to be a more legitimate part of the culture of organizations.

Equal attention must be given to research and action applying the research.

The goal of organization development is to utilize human resources more effectively. Power equalization and the democratization of work environments may be important but are not exclusive issues in this regard. Better utilization of human resources should increase everyone's power.

First, OD practitioners consider themselves more facilitators than experts at solving the specific problems of a particular organization. Second, practitioners of OD utilize "process consultation." The consultant works with organization members over time to ascertain and discuss issues, to plan and implement action, to evaluate the program that was implemented, etc. Contrast this with the "purchase model"—a client simply buys information or a set of ready-made services—or the "doctor-patient model" in which a client describes symptoms and requests an immediate remedy.

Third, those in OD assume that for an organization to develop, change must occur—most fundamentally in bringing about conscious awareness in organization members of behavioral patterns that help or hinder development. Once informed, people can better reinforce or alter these patterns as appropriate.

Fourth, OD practitioners assume that members of the organization value collaborative effort. As long as one or another party sustains an ideological commitment to the disregard of basic human rights, to chronic dissension and turmoil, to hatred, violence, or destruction, then OD cannot help resolve the conflicts in the organization. With people unwilling to work together to solve problems, organization development efforts can do little more than help clarify issues and suggest ways in which collaboration might bring about change.

Fifth, practitioners of organization development place high value on the welfare of organization members, particularly those who historically have had little empowerment. "People identified with the field of organization development have consistently been advocates of involving people in decisions that directly affect them," writes Burke in *Organization Development: A Normative View*; "we are concerned with *providing people with choices*," he contends.[10] This stands in stark contrast to the unilateral decision-making and policy-setting that occurred in the financial institution I described at the beginning of this chapter—a situation in which people were denied the most fundamental forms and processes of communication and interaction, their folklore.

Folklore in OB and OD

What is the role of folklore in organization development? How can folklorists' concepts, methods, techniques, and questions be applied to help organizations and their members? Folklore can be used as a tool of discovery to uncover assumptions and values, as a diagnostic technique to probe for

sore spots and problems, and as a means of implementing change in organizations by helping to improve communication, morale, cooperation, and
so on.

Folklore as a Tool of Discovery

Given the way most researchers define culture—as a set of assumptions
held by a group of people that are manifested (and communicated to new
members) through the group's values, norms, and artifacts—folkloristics
has a central role to play in research. This is because, first, members learn
most tacit assumptions and ways of doing things in organizations not by
reading printed policy manuals and memos (aspects of the "formal organization") but in firsthand interaction and communication through the stories
that people tell, the figurative language they use, the rituals they engage
in, and the customs that predominate (the "informal organization").[11] Second, much of our behavior in any face-to-face interaction and communication, whether in organizational settings or not, consists of folklore.

Therefore, if researchers want a data base from which to infer the culture, they should consider documenting, describing, and interpreting examples of folklore. This is exactly what happened at Evergreen State College
in Olympia, Washington.

In May 1990, the college advertised the position of ethnographer to undertake a one-year project to document the culture. From the scores of ap-
plicants the selection committee chose Peter Tommerup, a Ph.D. candidate
in folklore and organization studies at UCLA. The project had grown out of
an informal study two years earlier by the Assessment Study Group. Members felt that Evergreen has a culture that affects the way people conceptualize and articulate their educational experiences. The question was, what is
it? Hence, the desire for an ethnography.

According to one of the documents regarding the project, the ethnography had a dual purpose: to describe the nature, and then assess the impact
of, the teaching and learning cultures at the college. The settings to be
researched included various subcultures and countercultures, institutional
forums for academic teaching such as core programs and seminars, and situations in which "nonacademic" learning takes place (e.g., career development, academic advising). "Within these settings, the ethnography will
focus on those cultural symbols, traditions, and practices (e.g., logos, mot-
tos, vernacular speech, metaphors, personal experience stories, legends, rituals, rites of passage, celebratory events, etc.) that are rich in meaning,"
reads the document. "These artifacts will be examined in order to discover
whether they support or thwart the kind of teaching and learning idealized
and described in a variety of mission statements."

The institution would benefit from "a clearer understanding of the nature and value of the formal and informal cultures that have evolved," states the document. Individual participants would benefit from having "the opportunity to reflect on and articulate what they have found meaningful, satisfying, and/or dissatisfying at Evergreen," as well as helping determine what aspects of the culture should be perpetuated and what should be altered. As in the typical OD approach described above, there would be feedback of essential findings in progress, discussion, and action planning (with safeguards regarding data in order to protect participants). As of this writing, Tommerup is completing a final report of his research.

While folklore often mirrors culture, and therefore can be used as a source of information about basic assumptions and values, there are two caveats unknown to many nonfolklorists who study organizational behavior using the culture construct. First, many examples of folklore, especially narratives, are widely spread rather than situation-specific. Some have been documented, such as stories of shop floor accidents that are traditional "numbskull" tales, accounts by flight attendents of supranormal experiences (e.g., sightings of ghosts and other strange phenomena), and narratives concerning encounters of flight attendents and Pullman porters with difficult passengers.[12] The story "Is the Big Boss Human?" revolves around what happens when a low-level employee insists on everyone following the rules, including an unidentified visitor (who, it turns out, is the company president). Variants have been reported from IBM, Revlon, and other organizations.[13] Although they contain particulars to localize them, and therefore sound "true" or plausible, such narratives have their origins at another place and time.

The second caveat is that folklore may not tally with culture but instead serve as a means of projection, fantasy, wish fulfillment, scapegoating, or other psychological mechanism for trying to adapt, adjust, or cope with stress and the vicissitudes of organizational life. Look at how people personalize their workspace. If they work in windowless offices and under considerable stress, they may have posters or postcards of meadows, forests, and faraway places that they stare at when feeling especially tense or troubled. Note placement. Often the images that people look at for inspiration are located higher on the wall, best viewed when one leans back in one's chair and looks up, the typical posture of reverie. Or cartoons and photocopier lore critical of organizational life may be in a private space, surreptitiously viewed in moments of anguish in an effort at catharsis.[14]

Many stories also are projective.[15] William A. Wilson offers numerous, often colorful examples from Mormon missionaries. Although he is dealing with a religious group, there are lessons for other organizations.

One of the most widely told stories Wilson has collected concerns a pair of enterprising elders on a mission who decide to take an unauthorized trip. They prepare their weekly reports to mission headquarters several weeks in advance and give them to their landlady, instructing her to send them each week at the appointed time. She mixes up the reports, sending them out of sequence (or mails all at once); the missionaries are caught. In similar stories the missionaries enter a sporting event against mission rules. Photographs of them appear in the press; the mission president sees them. In yet other narratives, missionaries take part in an event outside mission boundaries, such as a World Series game, and appear in front of a television camera at the moment their mission president back home sits down to watch the evening news.[16]

"Good missionaries, of course, do not do these things—they do not kill investigators' cats, no matter how bothersome, nor violate mission travel rules, no matter how chafing," writes Wilson. But they delight in telling stories about those who do transgress the norms. The narrators "relieve tensions by vicariously living the adventures of the miscreants in the stories without actually performing the acts." Such stories "provide missionaries means of safely expressing frustrations and tensions imposed by the system, thus making easier the missionaries' remaining in the system."[17]

One might question whether members *should* remain in an organization that chafes. Most of us suffer irritations at work, however. Wilson's point is that organizational life is rarely free of tensions and frustrations; folklore may provide a way to let off steam through fictional portrayals of breaking the rules, which exasperated members sometimes wish they, too, could do. In sum, researchers must be aware of the "paradox" of folklore as both tallying with, and not tallying with, the culture. In not mirroring culture, folklore might help uncover problems.

Folklore as a Diagnostic Technique

Stories, language, rituals, customs, festive events, and other forms of folklore develop directly out of individuals' experiences on the job and with one another. Therefore, they are likely to point to sore spots and reveal problems, on the one hand, and, on the other, indicate positive attitudes and supportive conditions or suggest solutions to issues. By observing if ritualistic interaction is positive or negative, whether or not people take part in foodsharing or participate in celebrating events spontaneously, and so forth, one can infer much about morale and climate. Listening to people tell stories, noting rumors, and paying attention to the metaphors and traditional sayings that crop up in conversation will provide a great deal of information about not only assumptions and values but also attitudes, perceptions, fears, and concerns. Thus, folkloristics can help uncover sore spots and various problems and, sometimes, possible causes or cures.

Several aspects of folklore methods and techniques, then, might enrich the research done by organizational behavior specialists as well as assist OD practitioners better understand and help others. Some are the following:

1. Observing the presence *or* absence of particular symbolic content, communicative processes, and interactions. Much talk about beating the system, engaging in prohibited behavior, and so on may be symptomatic of a certain climate. On the other hand, the presence of celebratory events, foodsharing, and play may signal quite a different ambience. The next step is helping members discover and do something about the problems giving rise to tension, stress, poor self-image, low morale, and so on; or, in the opposite case, assisting members in identifying and developing ways to maintain the sense of personal satisfaction and social support.

2. Analyzing the themes of narratives. Stories about dramatic events or "critical incidents" in the organization's history may reflect members' beliefs regarding the environment, the organization's preparedness for and responsiveness to change, and how the organization ought to act. Also, depending on who tells them and in what situation, narratives can reveal what troubles people and what might be done to improve job design, organization functions, and systems of recognition and reward.

3. Noting rumor, photocopier lore, and stories and ritualistic behavior that seem to originate out of uncertainty, anxiety, or stress. By documenting and analyzing these forms and processes, we may better understand some of the sources of organizational tensions and interpersonal conflict, appreciate how people naturally cope and adjust, and perhaps discover causes of stress that can and should be removed.

4. Assessing the consistency between what is professed and what is signaled through actual behavior. Because they look to supervisors and managers for guidance, rewards and leadership, organization members are likely to assign meaning(s) to virtually anything and everything that supervisory personnel do, i.e., to see them as symbols of the organization and their behavior as expressive of assumptions and values. How do organization members interpret the customs, social routines, ritualistic actions, metaphors, and stories of their leadership? What act triggers acceptance, scepticism, rejection?

Particular examples of folklore express aspirations and concerns, characterize perceptions, transmit conceptions and interpretations of events, occupy leisure, or teach and reinforce norms and values. Others project anxieties, express joy and satisfaction, and provide meaning and sense-making. Awareness of multiple meanings of folklore examples in different situations makes it possible not only to infer assumptions or values but also to understand psychological processes helping people cope with the vicissitudes of organizational life. Understanding behavior and discovering conditions affecting it may lead to programs to change the bad and perpetuate the good.

Folklore as a Means of Implementing Change and Continuity

Change seems axiomatic in OD. Folkloristics can contribute to OD theory and practice, first and foremost, through its bias toward continuity. From the beginnings of the field two hundred years ago to the present, folklorists have focused on historical artifacts. In identifying, documenting, analyzing, and presenting certain behaviors as "traditions" or "traditional," folklorists mean that these phenomena have been transmitted intergenerationally and exhibit continuities and consistencies in thought, feeling, and behaving. Sometimes folklorists have considered particular traditions to be not functional, feasible, or appropriate to the present situation (especially customs and beliefs, such as "superstitions," viewed as personally harmful or socially injurious). In other instances they have attributed meaning and value to traditions and traditional symbolic behaviors, even advocating the perpetuation of some.

While many specialists in OD have an intuitive awareness of the existence of traditions, few appreciate the role of folklore in conveying information, transmitting values, reinforcing attitudes, or providing ways to deal with difficult situations. Without folkloristic training, only an occasional organization specialist can recognize when to leave well enough alone, balance change with continuity, or encourage the development and perpetuation of certain traditions. Herein lie ways of utilizing folkloristics to benefit individuals and organizations.

For example, based on his research of the lore of Mormon missionaries, William A. Wilson makes two recommendations. Because folklore makes us aware of ways in which people already are coping with stress, this, "hopefully, will teach leaders not to interfere with processes that are already working quite well," he writes. Also, "to a sensitive observer folklore may suggest ways to remove the causes of the sore spots and, in the process, eliminate the need for coping mechanisms in the first place."[18]

Thus, management support of folklore as natural and normal adaptive mechanisms may be important in regard to morale. Using folklore to identify the sources of problems can lead to remedies. Folklore itself may be curative: Having a sense of tradition in an organization, and possessing traditions, are especially appealing to many members (when these traditions are positive, rather than deleterious). Leaders' encouragement of certain forms and examples of folklore emerging from people's interactions, especially those that seem supportive, can contribute toward developing a climate and culture necessary to organization members' feelings of creativity and community.

Those seeking to affect organizations sometimes use folklore to aid the process. Folklorist Barbara Kirshenblatt-Gimblett admits that as an administrator she helped create folklore to improve organizational climate. "When I began to chair the department, I instituted the 'Seventh Annual' Winter Solstice Party. That was the first time it had been held," she joked. "It has now become the tradition that it is every year the *Seventh* Annual Winter Solstice Party."[19] In his book on organization development Burke describes a brief ceremony in which senior managers, needing to phase out a rocket program, lauded it and the people who had contributed over the years. All drank a toast. They then covered a replica of the rocket with black cloth, symbolically burying it. The ritual attended to a need for closure, transition, and new beginnings as well as honored feelings of self-worth and self-esteem among those who had participated in the program for so long.[20]

In addition, any important precept in an organization is best communicated not through memos or manuals but in stories, metaphorical language, rituals, and other folklore forms in face-to-face interaction.[21] This is especially true for mission, values, and philosophy. A few years ago an organization in Southern California developed a program in which longtime members were brought together with groups of engineering newcomers. The oldtimers told stories about how they had learned the intricacies of organizational life, including the "matrix" system of project organization, and about how they managed to succeed in the company. The program's purpose in educating newcomers by "handing down the old hands' wisdom" was to attempt to eliminate much of the anxiety, confusion, disappointment, and (stress arising in large, complex organizations—especially when values, goals, and ways of doing things change over time, are not explicitly known and understood, or are contradictory.

This program exemplifies the basic purpose of organization development: to enhance the problem-solving and renewal processes in organizations, which includes improving the well-being of members. Implemented by the office of the director of human resources, it proceeded according to standards of conduct established long ago: "OD programs are designed to improve the welfare and quality of work life for *all* the members of the organization," write French and Bell. "They are not a method for giving tools of manipulation or exploitation to any group (say, the managerial group), nor are they a method for improving the welfare of one group at the expense of other groups."[22] Finally, the program achieved these goals through understanding and appreciation of the forms and processes of traditional, symbolic communication and interaction, that is, folklore.

Conclusion

In 1984 James G. Hunt and others edited a volume called *Leaders and Managers* (New York: Pergamon Press, 1984), which contains several articles on symbolism and metaphors. Only a few years earlier such matters "would have been considered too 'soft' for a book purporting to report leadership findings" writes Hunt (p. 275).

While organization research has moved increasingly toward culture and symbolic behavior, folklore studies has expanded in interest and application to organizations. "The broader implication of *organization* was its vision of society," writes Simon J. Bronner (p. 125) in *American Folklore Studies: An Intellectual History* (Lawrence: Univ. Press of Kansas, 1986). "In a modern society that was noted for its increasing individualism, institutional settings define more identities: the office, the military, the city, the media, the school, the profession, the government. More cultural associations are voluntary and overlapping" (p. 126).

Bronner concludes his book on currents and trends in American folklore study by writing that the organizational current "moves to the fore because it proposes to reveal what is of most concern in a future-oriented society—the present state of the modern world and its guiding structures for the future." Moreover, "as folklore studies increasingly moves outside the academy, as it becomes more subject to organizational differentiation, and as it lodges in governmental agencies, foundations, corporations, museums, and libraries, then the keyword *organization* may balloon into a prominent theory of folklore studies" (p. 128).

The concept of organization and skills of administration have become increasingly important to folklorists in their jobs.

Writes Bess Hawes, director of the folk arts division of the National Endowment for the Arts: "I used to think that issues involving structure and organization were not worth spending a lot of time on and that only substance and content were really important. . . . [After several years in federal administration] I certainly have more respect than I had when I came in for the limiting and shaping powers of definition, structure, and form."[23]

In an essay about her experiences as a dean, folklorist Polly Stewart identifies specific skills from folkloristics that can be applied in an academic administrative setting (and by extension to other kinds of organizations) to improve organizational functioning and life at work. "One important skill is analytical," helping faculty and admnistrators "get past the esoteric-exoteric barriers . . . obviously impeding communication," she writes. In addition, "a folklorist in the administration can help administrative colleagues understand the power of an institution's symbology and its effects upon faculty." Third are interactional skills associated with fieldwork through which one can under organizaiton members' feelings, attitudes, and perceptions of one another. One of Stewart's most important discoveries is that "administrators and faculty members would get along a lot better if the former used more skill in helping the latter feel good about themselves."[24]

To conclude, occupational folklorists such as Archie Green have long complained that neither industrial relations specialists nor trade unionists saw substance in folklore, held leaders responsible for cultural matters, or felt the need to add specialists in vernacular expression to their staffs.[25]

Disinterestedness no longer prevails. Folklorists' knowledge, skills, and abilities are needed to help diagnose organizational problems as well as to enhance communication, promote creativity, and maintain a climate of social support. Folklorists can benefit from the fields of organizational behavior and organization development, both as a vehicle for applying insights from research and as a source of understanding about organizations and administration crucial to their survival and the effectiveness of their programs.

Notes

1. Jerry L. Gray and Frederick A. Starke, *Organizational Behavior: Concepts and Applications* (Columbus: Charles E. Merrill, 1977), 2.

2. Richard L. Daft, "Symbols in Organizations: a Dual-Content Framework of Analysis," in Louis R. Pondy, Peter J. Frost, Gareth Morgan, and Thomas C. Dandridge, eds., *Organizational Symbolism* (Greenwich, Conn.: JAI, 1984) 199.

3. See Robert McCarl, *The District of Columbia Fire Fighters' Project: A Case Study of Occupational Folklife* (Washington, D.C.: Smithsonian Institution Press, 1985), 112, and also Robert McCarl, *Good Fire/Bad Night: A Cultural Sketch of the District of Columbia Fire Fighters As Seen Through Their Occupational Folklife* (N.P.: 1980), 128.

4. Arthur Regan, "Myths, Symbols and Folklore: Expanding the Analysis of Organizations," *Folklore and Mythology* 2 (Dec. 1983): 3-4; Michael Owen Jones, "Organizational Folklore Conference," *American Folklore Society Newsletter* 12 (Oct. 1983): 3-4, 6.

5. See, for example, my book *Exploring Folk Art: Twenty Years of Thought on Craft, Work, and Aesthetics* (Ann Arbor: UMI Research Press, 1987), particularly Chapter 8: "Aesthetics at Work: Art and Ambience in an Organization" (p. 155),

180   Michael Owen Jones

and also my article "Informal Organization and the Functions of Folklore in the Writings of Chester I. Barnard, CEO of New Jersey Bell Telephone Company," *New Jersey Folklife* 13 (1988): 10-16.

6. Camilla Collins, "Twenty-Four to the Dozen: Folklore in a Hoisery Mill" (Ph.D. dissertation, Indiana University, 1978); Bruce Nickerson, "Industrial Lore: A Study of an Urban Factory" (Ph.D. dissertation, Indiana University, 1976); Jack Santino, "Characteristics of Occupational Narratives," *Western Folklore* 37 (1978): 57-70; Jack Santino, "The Outlaw Emotions: Workers' Narratives from Three Comtemporary Occupations" (Ph.D. dissertation, University of Pennsylvania, 1978).

7. W. Warner Burke, *Organization Development: A Normative View* (Reading, Mass.: Addison-Wesley, 1987), 145, describes various consulting models.

8. Raymond E. Miles, "Organization Development," in George Strauss, Raymond E. Miles, Charles C. Snow, and Arnold S. Tannenbaum, eds., *Organizational Behavior: Research and Issues* (Madison, Wisc.: Industrial Relations Research Association, 1974), 178.

9. Harold F. Gortner, Julianne Makler, and Jeanne Bill Nicholson, *Organization Theory: A Public Perspective* (Chicago: Dorsey, 1987), 398.

10. Burke, *Organization Development*, 22-23, 79.

11. Jones, "Informal Organization" 10-16.

12. Nickerson, "Industrial Lore"; Jack Santino, "Occupational Ghostlore: Social Context and the Expression of Belief," *Journal of American Folklore* 101 (1988): 207-18; Jack Santino, "'Flew the Ocean in a Plane': an Investigation of Airline Occupational Narrative," *Journal of the Folklore Institute* 15 (1979): 189-208; Jack Santino, "Miles of Smiles, Years of Struggle: The Negotiation of Black Occupational Identity Through Personal Experience Narrative," *Journal of American Folklore* 96 (1983): 393-412; and Jack Santino, "A Servant and a Man, A Hostess or a Woman: A Study of Expressive Culture in Two Transportation Occupations," *Journal of American Folklore* 99 (1986): 304-19.

13. Joanne Martin, Martha S. Feldman, Mary Jo Hatch, and Sim B. Sitkin, "The Uniqueness Paradox in Organizational Stories," *Administrative Science Quarterly* 28 (1983): 438-53.

14. Susan L. Scheiberg, "Emotions on Display: The Personal Decoration of Work Space," *American Behavioral Scientist* 33 (1990): 330-38; Michael Owen Jones, "How Does Folklore Fit in?" Unpublished paper given at the Academy of Management meeting, Anaheim, Calif., August, 1988.

15. Michael Owen Jones, "What If Stories Don't Tally with the Culture?" *Journal of Organizational Change Management* 4, no. 3 (1991): 27-34.

16. William A. Wilson, "On Being Human: The Folklore of Mormon Missionaries," *New York Folklore* 8 (1982): 17-18; and "Dealing with Organizational Stress: Lessons from the Folklore of Mormon Missionaries," in Michael Owen Jones, Michael Dane Moore, and Richard Christopher Snyder, eds., *Inside Organizations: Understanding the Human Dimension* (Newbury Park: Sage, 1988), 277.

17. Wilson, "Dealing with Organizational Stress," 277; Jack Santino, "The Outlaw Emotions: Narrative Expressions on the Rules and Roles of Occupational Identity," *American Behavioral Scientist* 33 (1990: 318-29.

18. Wilson, "Dealing with Organizational Stress," 278.

19. Michael Owen Jones, "Is Ethics the Issue?" in Peter J. Frost, Larry F. Moore, Meryl R. Louis, Craig C. Lundberg, and Joanne Martin, eds., *Organizational Culture* (Beverly HIlls: Sage, 1985), 244.

20. Burke, *Organizational Development*, 119.

21. Shirley A. Arora, "'No Tickee, No Shirtee': Proverbial Speech in Leadership and Academe," in Jones, Moore, and Snyder, *Inside Organizations: Understanding the Human Dimension* 179-89; Caren Siehl and Joanne Martin, "The Role of Symbolic Management: How Can Managers Effectively Transmit Organizational Culture?" in James G. Hunt, Dian-Marie Hosking, Chester A. Schriesheim, and Rosemary Stewart, eds., *Leaders and Managers: International Perspectives on Managerial Behavior and Leadership* (New York: Pergamon, 1984), 227-39; Sonjia Sackmann, "The Role of Metaphors in Organization Transformation," *Human Relations* 42 (1989): 463-85; William Foote Whyte, "Vocational Education in Industry: A Case Study," *Applied Anthropology* 3:4 (1944): 1-6.

22. Wendell L. French and Cecil H. Bell, Jr., *Organization Development: Behavioral Science Interventions for Organization Improvement*, 2nd ed. (Englewood Cliffs, N.J.: Prentice-Hall, 1978), 35.

23. Bess Lomax Hawes, "Aspects of Federal Folklife," *Practicing Anthropology* 1-2 (1985): 4-5 (the quote is on page 5).

24. Polly Stewart, "The Folklorist as Academic Administrator," in Charles Camp, ed., *Time and Temperature: A Centennial Publication of the American Folklore Society* (Washington, D.C.: American Folklore Society, 1989), 18.

25. Archie Green, "American Labor Lore: Its Meanings and Uses," *Industrial Relations: A Journal of Economy and Society* 4 (1965): 51; "Industrial Lore: A Bibliographic-Semantic Query," *Western Folklore* 37 (1978): 213; "At the Hall, In the Stope: Who Treasures Tales of Work?" *Western Folklore* 46 (1987): 167.

For Further Information

"Action research" is an important concept in organization development. In actual practice, research occurs first and then results are fed back in summary form to all participants who discuss and work on the feedback and emerging data. Next, participants plan and implement specific action. This stage is followed by data gathering (a reassessment), which begins the process of research, reflection, and action over again. According to Burke in *Organization Development: A Normative View* (Reading, Mass.: Addison-Wesley, 1987), the concept of action research has two sources. One is John Collier, commissioner of Indian Affairs from 1933 to 1945, who worked to effect change in ethnic relations and who advocated conducting research to determine the "central areas of needed action." The other was Kurt Lewin, a sociologist who conducted many action research projects on such varied topics as leadership, community and race relations, intergroup conflict, and eating habits. See John Collier, "United States Indian Administration as a Laboratory of Ethnic Relations," *Social Research* 12 (May 1945): 275-76; and Kurt Lewin, "Action Research and Minority Problems," *Journal of Social Issues* 2 (1946): 34-46.

There are now hundreds of papers, dissertations, and publications on the study of the cultural and symbolic aspects of organizations (more the former than the latter). For some works concerning "organizational symbolism" or folklore, see Janice M. Beyer and Harrison M. Trice, "How an Organization's Rites Reveal Its Culture," *Organizational Dynamics* 15 (1987): 4-25; David M. Boje, "Learning Storytelling: Storytelling to Learn Management Skills," *Journal of Management Education* 15 (1991): 279-94; David M. Boje, "The Storytelling Organization: A Study of Story Performance in an Office-Supply Firm," *Administrative Science Quarterly* 36 (1991): 106-26; Simon J. Bronner, "Folklore in the Bureaucracy," in Frederick Richmond and Kathy Nazar, eds., *Tools for Management: A Symposium from the Pennsylvania Evaluation Network* (Harrisburg: PEN Publications, 1984), 45-57; M.S. Feldman and J.G. March, "Information in Organizations as Signal and Symbol," *Administrative Science Quarterly* 26 (1981): 171-84; Joanne Martin, "Stories and Scripts in Organizational Settings," in Albert H. Hastorf and Alice H. Isen, eds., *Cognitive Social Psychology* (New York: Elsevier/North-Holland, 1982), 255-303; S.G. Harris and R.I. Sutton, "Functions of Parting Ceremonies in Dying Organizations," *Academy of Management Journal* 29 (1986): 5-30; Michael Owen Jones, "Why Folklore and Organization(s)?" *Western Folklore* 50 (1991): 29-41; L.R. Marcus and M.T. Marcus, "Occupational Folklore," in George H. Schoemaker, ed., *The Emergence of Folklore in Everyday Life* (Bloomington, Ind.: Trickster, 1990), 121-32; Joanne Martin, Martha S. Feldman, Mary Jo Hatch, and Sim B. Sitkin, "The Uniqueness Paradox in Organizational Stories," *Administrative Science Quarterly* 28 (1983): 438-53; Michael Moch and Anne S. Huff, "'Chewing Ass Out': The Enactment of Power Relationships Through Language and Ritual," *Journal of Business Research* 11 (1983): 293-316; Larry F. Moore and Brenda E.F. Beck, "Leadership Among Bank Managers: A Structural Comparison of Behavioral Responses and Metaphorical Imagery," in James G. Hunt, Dian-Marie Hosking, Chester A. Schriesheim, and Rosemary Stewart, eds., *Leaders and Managers: International Perspectives on Managerial Behavior and Leadership* (New York: Pergamon, 1984), 240-52; Louis R. Pondy, Peter J. Frost, Gareth Morgan, and Thomas C. Dandridge, eds., *Organizational Symbolism* (Greenwich, Conn.: JAI, 1983); and Sondra Thiederman, *Bridging Cultural Barriers for Corporate Success: How to Manage the Multicultural Work Force* (Lexington, Mass.: Lexington Books, Heath, 1991).

A few of the many works on "organizational culture" (which may also refer to "symbols," however) include Stephen R. Barley, "Semiotics and the Study of Occupational and Organizational Cultures," *Administrative Science Quarterly* 28 (1983): 393-413; Gibb W. Dyer, *Cultural Change in Family Firms* (San Francisco: Jossey-Bass, 1986); W.J. Duncan, "Organizational Culture: 'Getting a Fix' on an Elusive Concept," *The Academy of Management Executive* 3 (1989): 229-36; Gary Alan Fine, "Negotiated Orders and Organizational Cultures: Qualitative Approaches to Organizations," *Annual Review of Sociology* 10 (1984): 239-62; Lois Friedland, "Anthropology in the Boardroom," *Sky: Delta Airlines In-flight Magazine* (June 1987): 97 ff.; Peter J. Frost, Larry F. Moore, Meryl Reis Louis, Craig C. Lundberg, and Joanne Martin, eds., *Organizational Culture* (Beverly Hills: Sage, 1985); Frederick C. Gamst, "The Concept of Organizational and Corporate Culture: An Ethnological View," *Anthropology of Work Review* 10 (1989): 12-19; James M. Hayes, "Creating a Subculture at the Plant Level," in M.A. Berman, ed., *Corporate Culture and Change* (New York: Conference Board) 50-54; Mariann Jelinek, Linda Smircich, and Paul Hirsch, eds., "Organizational Culture," *Administrative Science Quarterly* 28 (1983); William G. Ouchi and Alan L. Wilkins, "Organizational Culture," *The Annual Review of Sociology* 11 (1985): 457-83; Vijay Sathe, *Culture and Related Corporate Realities* (Homewood, Ill.: Richard D. Irwin, 1985); Edgar H. Schein, *Organizational Culture and Leadership: A Dynamic View* (San Francisco: Jossey-Bass, 1985); S.E. Seashore and D.G. Bowers, *Changing the Structure and Functioning of an Organization: Report of a Field Experiment* (Ann Arbor: Survey Research Center, 1963); Thomas Sergiovanni and John E. Corbally, eds., *Leadership and Organizational Culture: New Perspectives on Administrative Theory and Practice* (Urbana and Chicago: Univ. of Illinois Press, 1984); and Linda Smircich, "Concepts of Culture and Organizational Analysis," *Administrative Science Quarterly* 28 (1983): 339-58.

Some works on organizational behavior and organization development that might interest folklorists are W. Warner Burke, *Organization Development: A Normative View* (Reading, Mass.: Addison-Wesley, 1987); Wendell L. French and Cecil H. Bell, Jr., *Organization Development: Behavioral Science Interventions for Organization Improvement*, 2nd ed. (Englewood Cliffs, N.J.: Prentice-Hall, 1978), 3-46; Harold F. Gortner, Julianne Mahler, and Jeanne Bell Nicholson, *Organization Theory: A Public Perspective* (Chicago: Dorsey, 1987); Jerry L. Gray and Frederick A. Starke, *Organizational Behavior: Concepts and Applications* (Columbus: Charles E. Merrill, 1977); John B. Miner, *Theories of Organizational Behavior* (Hinsdale, Ill.: Dryden, 1980); Henry Mintzberg, *The Nature of Managerial Work* (Englewood Cliffs: Prentice-Hall, 1973); Gareth Morgan, *Images of Organizations* (Beverly Hills: Sage, 1986); William G. Scott and Terence R. Mitchell, *Organization Theory: A Structural and Behavioral Analysis* (Homewood, Ill.: Richard D. Irwin, 1976); James C. Naylor, Robert D. Pritchard, and Daniel R. Ilgen, *A Theory of Behavior in Organizations* (New York: Academic, 1980); and George Strauss, Raymond E. Miles, Charles C. Snow, and Arnold S. Tannenbaum, eds., *Organizational Behavior: Research and Issues* (Madison, Wisc.: Industrial Relations Research Association, 1974).

More recent folklore research on workplace traditions with implications and ramifications beyond the job itself (whether the writer explores them or not) include Mia Boynton, "A Woman in a Man's Sphere: Testimonies from a Woman Steelworker at Buffalo's Republic Steel," *New York Folklore* 14 (1988): 87-101; Robert S. McCarl, " 'You've Come a Long Way—And Now This Is Your Retirement': An Analysis of Performance in Fire Fighting Culture," *Journal of American Folklore* 97 (1984): 393-422; Jack Santino, " 'Flew the Ocean in a Plane': An Investigation of Airline Occupational Narrative," *Journal of the Folklore Institute* 15 (1979): 189-208; Jack Santino "Miles of Smiles, Years of Struggle: The Negotiation of Black Occupational Identity Through Personal Experience Narrative," *Journal of American Folklore* 96 (1983): 393-412; Jack Santino, "A Servant and a Man, A Hostess or a Woman: A Study of Expressive Culture in Two Transportation Occupations," *Journal of American Folklore* 99 (1986): 304-19; Amy Skillman, "The Humor of a Tradition Bearer in the Lumber Yard," *New York Folklore* 14 (1988): 59-71; and the January 1990 issue of *American Behavioral Scientist* edited by Michael Owen Jones and devoted to the subject "Emotions in Work: A Folklore Perspective."

Perhaps of interest to some readers is a special issue of *The Public Historian* devoted to writing business history, applying the historian's skills, training business historians, and anticipating the future of business history. See volume 3, number 3 (Summer 1981). Also see Charles Dellheim, "Business in Time: The Historian and Corporate Culture," *The Public Historian* 8 (Spring 1986): 9-22.

For some anthropological works on organizations, see C. Stewart Sheppard, "The Role of Anthropology in Business Administration," in Bela C. Maday, ed., *Anthropology and Society* (The Anthropological Society of Washington, 1975), 64-75; Frederick C. Gamst, "Industrial Ethnological Perspectives on the Development and Characteristics of the Study of Organizational Cultures," in Tomoko Hamada and Ann Jordan, ed., *Cross-Cultural Management and Organizational Studies* (William and Mary Studies in Third World Societies no. 42, 1990), 13-47; William Foote Whyte, "Organizational Behavior Research—Where Do We Go from Here?" in Elizabeth M. Eddy and William Partridge, eds., *Applied Anthropology in America* (New York: Columbia Univ. Press, 1978), 129-43; Michael K. Orbach, "Anthropologists in the Administrative Process," in William Millsap, ed., *Applied Social Science for Environmental Planning* (Boulder: Westview, 1984), 61-72; and Julia N. Pennbridge, *Industrial Anthropology: A Selected Annotated Bibliography* (Washington, D.C.: Society for Applied Anthropology Mongraph Series, No. 14, 1984).

For more information about "intervention" and so-called "change agents," see Richard N. Ottaway, ed., *Change Agents at Work* (Westport, Conn.: Greenwood, 1979); and *Group Facilitators Intervention Guidebook*, developed by Rollin Glaser and Christine Glaser and available from Organization Design and Development, 2002 Renaissance Blvd., Suite 100, King of Prussia, PA 19406.

Some readers might not be clear on the difference between occupational folklife and organizational folklore studies. The latter is far larger in scope, taking into account concerns, issues, and forces affecting the workplace and the organization as a whole rather than limiting its intellectual horizons to "the shop floor." For example, in his article "Occupational Folklife: A Theoretical Hypothesis," *Western Folklore* 37 (1978): 145-60, Robert S. McCarl conceptualizes workplace traditions in terms of *technique*. He contends that this "*shaping principle* of an occupation" (his emphasis) is at "the critical center" of both work and an understanding of occupational lore. Allegedly a "theory," the principle is claimed capable of "explaining the culture of the workplace." However, technique appears to be only the skills, knowledge, and abilities associated with a particular set of tasks (e.g., "the primary technique of glass work in a molding factory is the smooth coordination and movement of raw glass into the kiln, out again, into the mold and then into the lehr" (149). McCarl's approach, therefore, is simply a job-title orientation. While documenting traditions related directly to job classifications, this approach ignores much folklore and misses many of the forces bearing on traditional, symbolic behavior in organizations.

Moreover, although McCarl often uses the term "community" in his studies, he never defines it. He seems to mean, variously, the larger society, the whole organization of the District of Columbia's Fire Department, only lower-level employees but not administration, only those technicians and officers in the particular firehouse he studied, and only technicians but not officers. In some writings after 1985, McCarl began to use such expressions as "face-to-face work group," "primary work groups in the trade," and "the primary group on the shop floor" to identify the research population of occupational folklife. Although he does not define these terms, he apparently is trying to exclude the "foreman or shop floor manager" and all other management from the category of those "we have chosen to represent" and "of who we are attempting to serve." Obviously he is trying to differentiate occupational from organizational folklore studies on the basis of whether or not management is included, and to try to make a moral or ethical issue out of it. Significantly, however, McCarl's own research included managers and supervisory personnel (i.e., four ranks of officers among firefighters). He showed his study of firefighters' lore first to a captain who, despite McCarl's attempts at anonymity for informants, was able to recognize the sources of many remarks and who became irate over McCarl's complete misunderstanding of the larger organizational framework in which the firefighters' techniques and traditions had developed (see David A. Ryan, "Critique," in Robert S. McCarl, *The District of Columbia Fire Fighters' Project: A Case Study of Occupational Folklife* [Washington, D.C.: Smithsonian Institution Press, 1985], 29-37). In sum, McCarl neither acted within his own parameters of study and reportage nor did he have the necessary conceptual framework to understand the workplace; he needed the kind of approach presented here, namely, organizational folklore study related to the fields of organizational behavior and organization development.

For information about organization development practitioners—their employment, skills, fees, and activities—see Lynda C. McDermott, "The Many Faces of the OD Professional," *Training and Development Journal* (Feb. 1984): 15-19. Some readers might also be interested in Gordon Lippitt, Ronald Lippitt, and Clayton Lafferty, "Cutting Edge Trends in Organization Development," in the same journal for July 1984 (pp. 59-62).

Consulting with organizations (businesses as well as not-for-profit corporations) on the multicultural work force promises to be one of the most relevant and timely applications of folkloristics. Dr. Sondra Thiederman, who earned her Ph.D. in folklore studies from UCLA, has developed a successful consulting firm specializing in this subject (based in San Diego, it is called Cross-Cultural Communications). In her first year she gave nearly fifty workshops and seminars to a wide variety of organizations. She published two books in 1991, both with Lexington Books (The Free Press, Macmillan, Inc., 866 Third Ave., New York, NY 10022). One is titled *Bridging Cultural Barriers for Corporate Success: How to Manage the Multicultural Work Force.* The other is called *Profiting in America's Multicultural Marketplace.*

There are many professional societies and groups for practitioners in organizational behavior, organization development, and related fields. One is the Organization Development Network whose current executive director is Thorne A. Sharon, P.O. Box 69329, Portland, OR 97201 (tel. 503-246-0148). The ODN has more than a dozen regional branches; there is considerable local programming for its two thousand members. With 20,000 members, the American Society for Training and Development has many regional and local offshoots with frequent meetings and programs (as well as a national meeting). For more information, write to ASTD, 1630 Duke St., Box 1443, Alexandria, VA 22313-2043 (tel. 703-683-8100).

The major scholarly society in organizational behavior and administration is the Academy of Management. Membership includes receipt of numerous journals and newsletters and invitations to participate in the annual meetings of half a dozen regional subgroups. Members usually affiliate with several divisions or interest groups, such as Careers, International Management, Management Education and Development, Managerial Consultation, Organization Development, Organizational Behavior, Organizational Communication, and Public Sector. For information, write to the Secretary-Treasurer, Academy of Management, P.O. Drawer KZ, Mississippi State University, Mississippi State, MS 39762 (tel. 601-325-7016). Be sure to request the recently revised *Handbook*, which gives the history and objectives of the Academy, lists its present officers and committees, describes the various professional divisions and interest groups, and identifies the Academy's several publications including its newsletter as well as the *Academy of Management Journal, Academy of Management Review*, and *Academy of Management Executive*.

The Society for Applied Anthropology was incorporated in 1941. Its primary objectives are the scientific investigation of "the principles controlling relations of human beings to one another . . . and the wide application of these principles to theoretical problems." It publishes *Human Organization* and *Practicing Anthropology*. Inquiries regarding membership should be addressed to SfAA Membership Services, P.O. Box 24083, Oklahoma City, OK 73124. Those interested in joining the American Anthropological Association and receiving the *American Anthropologist* and *Anthropology Newsletter* should write to American Anthropological Association, 4350 North Fairfax Dr., Suite 640, Arlington, VA 22203 (tel. 703-528-1902). Write to the same address for information about the American Folklore Society, which publishes the *Journal of American Folklore* and the *American Folklore Society Newsletter*. The AFS also has an Organizational Folklore Section, established in 1983 and directed since then by Richard Raspa at Wayne State University; more recently, an Occupational Folklore Section was founded, initially directed by Robert S. McCarl.

9

Moving Toward Responsible Tourism: A Role for Folklore

Elke Dettmer

Each year millions of people turn into tourists. By the year 2000 tourism is expected to be the largest economic factor worldwide. Tourism serves deep-seated needs of industrial, urban people; it results in culture contacts that have changed folk cultures more profoundly than any revolution or ideology. Unrestrained tourism can cause irreversible damage to fragile natural and cultural environments, the very sources it depends on. Pollution, overcrowded resorts, and resentful native populations are byproducts of developments motivated by profit. Nevertheless many underdeveloped Third World countries and peripheral rural regions of industrialized nations, such as the Canadian province of Newfoundland, which is the focus of this essay, continue to seek in tourism an answer to their economic problems.

Tourism in Canada

Tourism in Canada is considered a major growth industry. However, judging by the Canadian stand I visited in 1987 and 1988 at the International Tourism Exchange (ITB), the largest international tourism trade fair worldwide, which takes place each year in Berlin, the Canadian approach seems locked in the past. Clichés and stereotypes prevail not only in the quaint imitation fort guarded by a couple of mounties which houses the Canadian exhibit but also in the brochure offered to the German public, which appears shabby compared to the glossy materials distributed elsewhere at the fair.

To make matters worse, the brochure is full of errors, at least as far as Newfoundland is concerned. For example, driving along the Trans Canada Highway, the main thoroughfare, is said to reveal all the scenic attractions of the island. In fact, these are largely bypassed. Fogo Island, a place of pictur-

esque outports (fishing villages) and an unusually active folk music tradition, is advertised as a major bird colony, mistaking it for the Funk Islands,
which are way out in the Atlantic and off limits to tourists. The Bakeapple
Festival in Labrador (part of the province "Newfoundland and Labrador"),
celebrating the harvest of a rare and treasured berry, is interpreted to the
German public as a festival of "baked apples"; however, apples do not even
grow in Labrador. These misguided, amateurish publicity efforts were produced in faraway Ottawa, obviously by people who had never been in Newfoundland, who relied exclusively on secondary sources, and who became
hopelessly muddled in the process.

In 1988 a new German travel guide to Canada, part of the popular Poly-
glott series (Kanada mit Alaska), was launched inside the Canadian fort at
the ITB. This is a much more valuable product with practical travel information and additional literary tidbits, such as accounts by early settlers, tales of
Indians and gold miners, and even the description of a drive along the rough
Churchill Road by a member of the German air force stationed in Goose
Bay, Labrador, which lend life to dry facts. However, Atlantic Canada is still
described in the old stereotypes, and the attractions of Newfoundland are
distinctly underrated when compared to its neighbor Nova Scotia, "Canada's
Ocean Playground," a region where tourism has been aggressively promoted
for years. Again it seems obvious that the writer has largely relied on secondary sources for his information on Newfoundland.

Tourism trends in Canada were discussed at the ITB in Berlin in 1987,
when I interviewed Jost Krippendorf, director of the Institute for Leisure
and Tourism Research at the University of Berne, Switzerland, one of the
most outspoken critics and activists in recent rethinking of tourism. Although in spacious Canada tourism overload hardly presents a problem,
Krippendorf feels that the treatment of the Canadian environment is insensitive and that tourism developments are often decided by amateurs who
keep repeating the same mistakes already made elsewhere.

At the 1988 ITB, criticism leveled against Canadian tourism practices
focused on two posters promoting Wardair's new flight route from Hamburg
to Toronto. These featured caricatures of happy Indians, e.g. an Indian who is
holding his ear to the ground, exclaiming: "Ugh! Must be 6:43 p.m. Wardair
flight gets ready to land." Many Europeans are aware of the discrimination
Canadian Indians are subjected to, and the posters were cited as examples of
insensitive advertising at a public discussion of "Tourism: A Blessing or a
Curse for the Hosts?"

Tourism in Newfoundland

Even though Newfoundland has long been presented to American tourists
as a haven of unspoiled natural resources and a unique folk culture, so far

mass tourism has not had a major impact there. However, tourism on the basis of hunting and fishing was promoted to the American elite as soon as the railroad improved transportation in the latter part of the nineteenth century. Such attractions as sightseeing and scientific interests were advertised beginning in the 1920s. Because many Newfoundlanders move to mainland Canada and the United States to find work, special efforts are made to bring them back to the island on their vacations. Homesick expatriates visiting their families and friends, in fact, constitute a large part of the visitors coming to Newfoundland. But the major focus of current marketing efforts are organized American mass tourists, e.g., bus tour customers, who, however, for reasons such as remote location, uncertain climate, and lack of luxury accommodations, have yet refused to make Newfoundland a major travel destination.

Within North America, Newfoundland offers a particularly rich folklore, which has been noticed not only by the folklorists of Memorial University. In tourism advertisements the folklore of the native population is often used as one of the defining characteristics of a vacation destination, as is the case in the promotional catalog *Newfoundland and Labrador*: "Nowhere in North America will you find such rich folklore, such unusual and colorful traditions, or so many people willing to tell you about them" (p. 5). Throughout the catalog the attractive quaintness of the Newfoundland population is advertised by mentioning folk remedies, traditional dishes, ancient dialects, yarns, legends, holiday celebrations, and bonfires as well as community fairs, folk festivals, and craft displays and sales. Special emphasis is given to the music: "Newfoundlanders sing, dance and play more than anyone else; and they do it better. Music is everywhere, and Newfoundland has a wealth of thousands of its own folk songs that is unequalled in North America. Listen to them, sing them, and take them home with you" (p. 2). The congenial attitude toward strangers is particularly emphasized, and Newfoundlanders are described as "the happiest, gentlest, friendliest, and most hospitable people to be found anywhere" (p. 21).

Implications are that professional "folk types" playing out the stereotype will develop once tourists are attracted to Newfoundland in large numbers and want to be entertained according to the expectations raised by such an unrealistic catalog. The initial friendly attitude toward visitors, which, in fact, has been my own experience, invariably changes when tourists become a routine sight. A first sign of organized, standardized tourist encounters is the popular "Screech In" ceremony performed by increasing numbers of more or less commercially inspired entertainers. These performers often wear the stereotypical Newfoundland fishermen's outfit, i.e., oilskins, a southwester, and rubber boots in the promotional event designed to welcome visitors to the island. The tourists are pronounced honorary Newfoundlanders after they have passed the test of kissing a cod fish, speaking a

few words of Newfoundland dialect, and downing a glass of locally popular
"Screech" rum.

In fact, during my research on folklorism in Newfoundland I found the
most blatant examples in the context of tourism. In 1985 I had a chance to
observe folklorism in the making when I visited a new bed and breakfast
place in Upper Island Cove, a picturesque outport within reasonable driving
and sailing distance from St. John's. The owner, a woman who had lived in
Toronto for a long time before returning to her native Newfoundland, had
bought a plain house and with the help of substantial government grants
transformed it into the "Galecliff Lodge." The house now fits a certain
international, i.e., American, standard, filled with appliances, knickknacks,
and fake antique furniture; it no longer resembles the original house nor any
other house in Upper Island Cove. When I arrived with my friends, the yard
was just being bulldozed to make room for a hundred maple trees, a species
not common to the area. Only one rock had resisted all attempts at landscaping. As we discovered when we sat down for dinner, the landlady had managed to make use of this rock.

Next to our plates we found rolled and tied sheets of fake parchment
that contained the "Legend of the Kissing Rock," according to which fishermen of former times kissed their loved ones goodbye on this rock before
venturing out to sea. An entirely concocted "legend," this story bears no
relationship to the reality of a Newfoundland outport, where the sexes lead
quite separate lives that do not include traditions of public displays of affec-
tion. Evidently our hostess cared nothing about authenticity; a clever busi-
nesswoman, she simply made the best of what she considered an eyesore. In
fact, several photos on the wall of guests standing on that rock indicated that
she had created a real attraction, a "sight."

While this may be considered a minor, rather amusing matter, the influence of our hostess was spreading in the community beyond her property.
The evening was beautiful, one of the first warm days after a long winter,
and walking through the village we met people sitting in front of their
homes, who chatted with us as is the custom in Newfoundland outports.
Back at the Galecliff Lodge we commented on the pleasant experience and
our hostess immediately took credit for it by saying that she had told everyone to be nice to her guests. However, visitors bring news and are therefore
generally appreciated in outports; assigning a conscious role to the local
population, to smile for the tourists, is a move toward typecasting the happy, quaint Newfoundlander in the service of commercial interests rather
than encouraging real encounters.

The Galecliff Lodge was opened in 1985 with much fanfare and was
widely touted by the provincial tourism industry as the model of a good bed
and breakfast operation. Fancier than the "hospitality homes" that had once

existed in just about every outport to accommodate visiting businessmen, teachers, clergy, and the occasional tourist, bed and breakfast homes on the scale of the Galecliff Lodge are beyond the means of most Newfoundland families, while government funds are made available only to the select few. In fact, entrepreneurs from outside the province are often given preference over local initiatives. Judging by tourism brochures dating from the 1950s to the present, locally owned and run hospitality homes have steadily declined while new hotels and motels were added to the list of accommodations.

Tourism planners in St. John's seem to base their ideas of how tourism is to be developed on the model of Florida, the most popular travel destination of affluent Newfoundlanders who congregate there by the thousands during the long winter months. A striking example of this attitude is bright blue water slides, largely supported by government funds, which opened across the island in the summer of 1987. In at least one instance such a newly constructed attraction competed directly with an older, local tourism project.

In 1980 an industrious, sociable, middle-aged woman had started to build cabins for rent on her husband's farm in the Humber River Valley. After several years of hard work, without help from the government, she proved successful. Her property includes a brook with a lovely natural swimming hole, used by both her guests and the local youths, whom she employs occasionally for such jobs as cleaning up the environment and constructing simple picnic tables and bridges across the brook. During the annual Strawberry Festival she regularly offers her grounds for picnics and folk concerts. Her cabins are mainly advertised by word of mouth.

Since 1987 the new water slide park less than a mile down the road catches the eyes of tourists before they reach her place. Featuring prefabricated cabins, a bulldozed playground and, in the summer of 1988, the added roadside attraction of a "baby moose" (a pathetic animal crouched in the far corner of a stall), this park is a poignant example of the government's preference for large-scale projects and artificial amusements rather than utilizing, preserving, and enhancing assets unique to Newfoundland, i.e., the spectacular scenery, the rich flora and fauna that can easily be observed in their natural state, and the somewhat slower, traditional lifestyle that offers a contrast to life in the city.

Unfortunately the tourism industry in Newfoundland is dominated by businessmen interested in nothing but profits and by career bureaucrats who are transferred from one department to another without acquiring much expertise and who often do not plan beyond the next election. However, tourism is more than a business, and success cannot simply be measured by statistics. Even if a bus tour brings many visitors to the island, much of the profit reverts to the mainland bus company and to the international hotel chains they tend to use. Paradoxically tourism destroys tourism; destinations lose their attraction when they are overused. Canada has considered tourism a potential gold mine and in recent years has spent much money on its promotion. Instead of development and exploitation at all costs, the tourism industry should be concerned with preservation and careful use of the natural and cultural environment to ensure its future.

A Personal Approach to Tourism

My active involvement in tourism in Newfoundland began quite accidentally. When I traveled across Newfoundland in the summer of 1983 in search of a topic for my Ph.D. thesis I simply fell in love with the place, the Nordic scenery, the relatively unspoiled landscape, and the ready hospitality of the outport. I also realized that the fishery was in decline and that new sources of income were urgently needed to insure the viability of the outports. As an outsider who has traveled extensively and lived in areas much frequented by tourists I soon realized the tourism potential of the island. This was confirmed in 1984, when I returned to Germany and noticed that increasing numbers of Germans travel to Scandinavia, Ireland, and Iceland, areas that resemble Newfoundland in climate and scenery.

Germans now comprise the largest number of tourists worldwide. Most take six weeks' vacation each year; many have become sophisticated travelers who are easily bored with the destinations of mass tourism. After some research I felt confident that at least part of the German tourism market could be interested in Newfoundland, given adequate information and publicity. They would enjoy Newfoundland as it is because of the contrast it offers to industrialized, crowded, polluted Germany. In fact, I decided that affluent, adventurous Germans would be particularly appropriate tourists for Newfoundland.

Unfortunately my vision was not shared by the Newfoundland government employee in charge of tourism marketing to whom I conveyed my ideas after returning from Germany in the fall of 1984. She flatly told me, "We are not interested in the German market!" Instead, the American tourist was the main target, notoriously the most demanding customer in terms of infrastructure and conspicuous consumption. Even two years later, after I had long lost my initial naïveté and enthusiasm and a new director had taken over the marketing position, I was again turned away with the very same words.

In my efforts to promote responsible tourism in Newfoundland I soon learned that folklorists do not carry much clout in the "real world." Even though I referred to my earlier career in business and eventually submitted a marketing plan, strikes against me were my idealistic commitment to a tourism that would benefit the people of Newfoundland who most needed new sources of income and the small-scale developments I advocated, whereas large and expensive schemes appear more impressive and are funded more readily. While I hoped—and still hope—to work for the government (ultimately the only way to be effective), I knew that I first had to establish some credibility beyond mere talk and the letters and proposals I wrote. My goal became to develop a tour of Newfoundland that would prove my points and that could be used as a model for others to follow.

In the next years tourism became my "sideline." Whenever I traveled across Newfoundland for research or other purposes I made efforts to meet local tour operators, to identify potential tourism resources, and to introduce the idea of small-scale developments such as simple bed and breakfast and cabin accommodations, boat rides, and hikes to anyone willing to listen. I appeared on the television news and was written up in the provincial television magazine to spread my ideas to the public. On several occasions I tried experimental tours with friends and designed touring itineraries for visitors.

During my regular visits to Germany I gave public slide talks on Newfoundland. The enthusiastic response further confirmed my belief that Newfoundland would be an attractive vacation destination for many Germans. However, the slide talks did not result in actual travel, and the German travel agents I contacted were either not willing to take any risks or did not see enough profit in the tour I offered to include it in their Canadian programs. Finally in 1987, after a period of trial and error, I found an almost ideal partner in the German nonprofit organization *Naturfreunde* (Friends of Nature). Actively concerned with environmental issues, this association was just starting a program of "soft" tourism, i.e., tourism careful of the natural and cultural environment. The first small tour I designed and guided for them in 1988 proved successful and in 1989 they included my Newfoundland tour in their program. Most importantly, the German travel journalist I had invited to come along on the first tour, whose expenses were paid by the government (a first cooperative gesture), was so impressed with Newfoundland that he wrote several lead articles for major German newspapers.

New Ideas on Tourism

In itself this small tour is not very significant. However, it introduces a different model of tourism to Newfoundland at a time when it is still possible to influence the direction tourism is taking. At this point it is very important to educate all concerned so that they can make informed choices how and if they want to participate in tourism developments. Consequently tour-

Table 9.1. Sample Insights on Tourism

The Host Population:

We need tourism for our economy: it creates jobs and brings income. We know, however, that it also represents a danger to our culture and our environment. We therefore want to supervise and control its development so that our country may be preserved as a viable economic, social, and natural environment.

We want to keep control over our land. We pursue an active planning and land use policy. We limit our new construction by carefully considered zoning policy. We decline to sell land to non-locals. We promote and encourage the utilization of the exisiting buildings and infrastructure.

The Tourist:

Away from home and free: it is very tempting to do things I would never do at home. I shall avoid this danger by observing myself critically while on holiday, and behave with restraint. I want to enjoy myself without offending or harming others.

The areas that I visit are inhabited by people who have a different culture. I want to learn more about the country and its population. I shall adjust to the host population instead of demanding the opposite and acting like royalty. Asking instead of answering, exploring instead of finding.

The Travel Business:

We see our clients as people who enjoy life and who want their holidays to be the "most pleasurable weeks of the year." We also know that there is an increasing number of interested, considerate, and environment-conscious tourists. We shall try to respond to and encourage this trend without "preaching" to our guests.

We shall bear in mind the interests, independence, and rights of the local population. We shall respect local laws, customs, traditions, and cultural characteristics. We shall always remember that we as travel agents and as tourists are guests of the local population.

Source: *Tourism with Insights: Our Proposals* by Working Group "Tourism with Insight and Understanding."

ism has become part of my teaching. I have lectured not only to folklore classes at Memorial University but also to adult education classes and tourism associations, and I have offered workshops on tourism to Rural Development Associations and similar groups. At the same time, tourism is a major focus of my Ph.D. thesis, and over the years I have given a number of scholarly papers on the topic.

Much of my thinking has been influenced by the critical trends I observed at the ITB in Berlin, where worldwide trends in tourism are first noted. I have joined *Gruppe Neues Reisen* (Association for New Travel), a group formed in 1978 by people from various walks of life who are concerned with the problems caused by tourism. At the ITB in 1987 I participated in the critical exhibitions and discussions they produced together with thirteen other international associations as the working group *Tourismus mit Einsicht* (Tourism with Insight and Understanding). In 1988 four more associations had joined the working group at the ITB. This time critical materials included a booklet with thirty proposals, ten each addressed to "the responsible host population," "the tourist," and "the travel business" (see Table 9.1). Jost Krippendorf, one of the most prominent members of the working group, introduced these proposals to the press and leading members of the travel industry in a public discussion. The fact that all accepted these proposals, at least verbally, is an encouraging sign that the tourism industry has entered a new phase where growth is no longer the only objective and that the self-destructive tendencies and the limits of tourism are now widely recognized.

For the host population, proposals include being aware of the dangers of tourism developments and participating in the control over tourism in order to maintain a viable economic, social, and natural environment. Tourism developments should be made by, with, and for the local population. Tourists in turn are asked to behave with restraint, to learn more about the country and its population, and to adjust to their hosts rather than exploit an inherently unequal situation where what constitutes leisure and fun for one is hard work and a burden for the other. Proposals for the travel industry include respecting local laws, customs, traditions, and cultural characteristics; providing clients with comprehensive information about all aspects of the country they want to visit; and advertising honestly and responsibly, avoiding the usual superlatives and stereotypes. Many of these proposals simply make good, common sense. However, if taken seriously, they could change the nature of tourism. It is up to all of us, as tourists, teachers, interpreters, or critical scholars to implement these ideas.

Folklorists' Potential Contributions Toward Responsible Tourism

Rural, peripheral areas far from the industrialized cities—the regions most coveted by tourists—are still the areas most folklorists prefer to study. In fact, more or less accidentally folklorists may become precursors of tourism, preparing its way with the publications, exhibitions, and festivals they help to produce. Fieldwork, too, is a form of tourism: The collecting of folk arts and crafts for museums and archives can be considered an early form of souvenir hunting. In a sense, therefore, folklorists are deeply involved in the rise of tourism.

The few regions that so far have remained relatively untouched by tourism, such as Newfoundland, may now experience accelerated touristic developments. By providing the population with information on the dangers as well as the benefits of tourism and on alternative models, we can help them to avoid mistakes made elsewhere. Above all this is a political issue; only an informed public can make rational decisions and participate actively in the making of its own future. It is not enough for folklorists to introduce regions to tourists; we must be held accountable for what happens to the people afterwards.

With the knowledge acquired by training in folklore combined with additional social and political skills, folklorists can help to change stereotypical perceptions, encouraging tolerance and cultural appreciation instead. Because of their training, values, and orientation, folklorists should be able to bring a different perespective to tourism and, hopefully, a more sensitive approach. As consultants, interpreters, writers, or tour guides, we can provide specialized advice and expertise in regard to traditional cultures and symbolic behavior. This is an important task, given the tremendous impact tourism has everywhere.

For Further Information

A tremendous amount of literature exists on tourism. For example, about five hundred titles are listed in the annotated bibilography, *The Perceptual and Socio-Cultural Dimensions of the Tourism Environment*, published in 1983 by the Travel and Tourism Program of the George Washington University and the International Trade and Tourism Division, Department of Economic Affairs, Organization of American States, Washington, D.C. To mention some of the classics of tourism scholarship, Hans Magnus Enzenberger's essay "Eine Theorie des Tourismus" (in *Einzelheiten* [Frankfurt: Suhrkamp, 1962]) became a precursor of later theories by analyzing tourism (particularly mass tourism) as a reaction to repression. Since the 1970s many more studies of tourism have attempted to analyze the tourist according to his attitude toward vacations, expectations, and motifs for travel. In 1975 L. Turner and J. Ash published *The Golden Hordes: International Tourism and the Pleasure Periphery* (London: Constable), which explores the history and development of tourism as harmful to authenticity and cultural identity. *The Tourist: A New Theory of the Leisure Class* by Dean MacCannell (New York: Schocken, 1976) provides a semiotic analysis of touristic objects, of "sights." An anthology of essays, *Hosts and Guests—The Anthropology of Tourism*, edited by Valene L. Smith (Univ. of Pennsylvania Press, 1977), details the cultural impact of tourists upon the peoples they visit. Many social science journals include articles on tourism. A multidisciplinary publication devoted to tourism, *Annals of Tourism Research* (New York: Pergamon), appears twice each year.

While interest in tourism is rising among North American folklorists, it is not yet considered a special field of study. Particularly Barbara Kirshenblatt-Gimblett has dealt with the thorny issue of authenticity in relationship to tourism. Among German folklorists, tourism has been mentioned in connection with folklorism. Recently a paper by Utz Jeggle and Gottfried Korff, "On the Development of the Zillertal Regional Character: A Contribution to Cultural Economics," which analyzes the process of folklorism culminating in tourism developments, has been published in *German Volkskunde—A Decade of Theoretical Confrontation, Debate, and*

Reorientation (1967-1977) (edited and translated by James R. Dow and Hannjost Lixfeld [Bloomington: Indiana Univ. Press, 1986], 124-39). Another study on "Tourism and Folklorism," a chapter from Hermann Bausinger's textbook *Volkskunde* (Tübingen: Tübinger Vereinigung für Volkskunde, 1979), 159-79, will soon be available in translation as part of the book *Folk Culture in the World of Technology*, to be published by Indiana Univeristy Press. In Germany, folklorist Dieter Kramer introduced a new approach in his book *Der sanfte Tourismus* (Wien: Oesterreichischer Bundesverlag, 1983). Building on the idea of "soft" technology that had become a commonplace in the 1980s, Kramer explores the reasons for tourism developments in the Alpine regions and points to nonprofit organizations, such as the Alpine Club, to counteract purely commercial tourism efforts with socially and environmentally sound "soft" tourism. Since then Kramer has initiated a section on "Tourism and Cultural Relations" at the 1987 meeting of German folklorists and has subsequently called for the formation of a working group *Kulturwissenschaftliche Tourismusforschung* (Scholarly Cultural Research on Tourism).

On yet another level, the work of economist Jost Krippendorf as director of the Institute for Leisure and Tourism Research at the University of Berne, Switzerland, includes suggestions, strategies and scholarly programs for action, although Krippendorf admits that a large discrepancy still exists between scholarly programs and what can be done in concrete situations. One of his books is now available in translation, *The Holiday Makers: Understanding the Impact of Leisure and Travel* (London: Heinemann, 1987). In the United States similar goals are pursued by the *North American Network on Third World Tourism*, which was formed in 1987 by members of the travel industry, ecumenical and academic circles, and other concerned individuals. The contact address is The Center for Responsible Tourism, Virginia T. Hadsell, Director, 2 Kensington Road, San Anselmo, CA 94960.

PART III

Enhancing Identity and Community

10

Serving the Public: An Assessment of Work in Public Sector Folklore

Betty J. Belanus

Folklore applied to the public sector is nothing new in the United States. Whether one traces the birth of this work back to Henry Schoolcraft in the 1840s or Benjamin Botkin in the 1930s, most folklorists will agree that the public sector folklore "boom" of the 1970s and 1980s has firm roots in the history of the discipline. What is relatively new is the large number of academically trained folklorists being hired on a temporary or permanent basis by national, state, regional, and local agencies. The projects and programs these folklorists carry out range from focused internships to general surveys of regional folklore; from the creation of school or museum educational units to being a member of an interdisciplinary "cultural resource management" team.

As an academically trained folklorist who has worked in many capacities in a variety of cultural agencies, I believe that an examination of my own career in public sector folklore serves in some sense as a microcosm of work in the field. Such an examination allows an assessment of the present state of public sector folklore in general, including methods of training future professionals, the types of projects and programs currently practiced, and a forecast of the future of the field. My views represent not only the experience of twelve years in the field, but observation of my fellow public sector folklorists, and a critical stance developed during the writing of my doctoral dissertation evaluating public sector folklore. I will first chronicle and comment on my own career in public sector folklore, and then conclude with the lessons that I feel my own career can offer the field in general.

Academic and Practical Training

Many people working in public sector folklore do not have advanced folklore degrees. However, the "credential" of an M.A. or Ph.D. in the field gives the public sector folklorist a definite advantage—not because it looks impressive on a resume but because of the experience that these degrees represent. Although students interested in work in the public sector may sometimes wonder how the "historic-geographic method" and the "oral-formulaic theory" are going to help them, a solid graduate education in folklore theory and technique offers students a deeper understanding of the material common to both academic and public sector folklore. Work in the public sector requires not only practical experience but a thorough knowledge of the field including all of those seemingly arcane models and paradigms. Besides, academic folklore training has its practical side as well: training in research techniques, the analysis of problems, and the relation of single items to larger contexts.

Even before entering graduate school, students can draw from their undergraduate training in preparing for a career in public sector folklore. My own undergraduate degree in American studies gave me a background in American history, sociology, and literature that proved useful in researching the regions of the United States in which I have worked. Of course, many students do not discover folklore studies, and the possibility of a career in the field, until they are almost through their undergraduate studies. But, fortunately, the interdisciplinary nature of folklore in general, and public sector folklore work specifically, allows a wide range of undergraduate studies to become relevant in a student's later career.

Early exposure to practical work situations, in my opinion, is as important as academic study. As an undergraduate, my first career-related job came in the form of a work-study position at the Northampton Historical Society, Northampton, Massachusetts. In this position, I accessed and cataloged items in the collection, gave tours of three historic houses, and assembled two small exhibitions. I was later able to build on this introduction to museum work in graduate school, working at the Indiana University Museum of Anthropology, History and Folklore (now the Mathers Museum), first as a volunteer, and later as a work-study student and a graduate assistant. The understanding of museum work gained during these years has proven invaluable in developing exhibitions and museum education programs.

During the summer before I began graduate school, I served as a voluntary intern at the Archive of Folk Song (now the Archive of Folk Culture, part of the American Folklife Center) at the Library of Congress for one month. My main project as an intern was preparing a number of boxes of R.W. Gordon's papers for microfilming. (Gordon had been the first head and virtual founder of the Archive of Folk Song in the late 1920s.) This brief experience introduced me to archival work and stressed the importance of making folklore collections accessible to the public.

Once in graduate school, I encountered the attitude among my professors that the ideal for the serious folklorist was teaching on the university level while working on one's own research, publishing widely in academic journals and in book form. I learned at the same time, however, that university teaching jobs were becoming more and more scarce, and that some scholars were being "forced" into public sector positions because of this academic work shortage. By that time I already knew enough about public sector folklore to desire a career in this aspect of the field. Luckily, a number of my fellow graduate students were also interested in public sector work, and we helped each other acquire skills necessary for this work and kept each other informed about summer positions and available grants. Attending graduate school at a large and diverse university offered us opportunities to acquire necessary skills through courses in other departments, according to our interests. Photography and film courses, arts administration courses, and the aforementioned museum studies were some of the academic routes to obtaining these skills. Folklore department assistantships in editing a journal, archiving, and teaching an introductory course were others.

Fortunately for folklore students presently in graduate school, public sector folklore does not hold quite the stigma it had in the recent past. Graduate programs are now actively seeking public sector internships and jobs for their students, enlisting the help of former students such as myself. Nevertheless, students interested in public sector careers are well advised to lay their own groundwork by pursuing the skills needed for such jobs, and keeping well informed of opportunities for part-time and summer employment in the field.

Applications

The first paid position in public sector folklore serves as the "rite of passage" into professionalism. Often, this opportunity comes during the summer while a student is still in graduate school. Such a position usually consists of conducting folklore or oral history fieldwork and either preparing a written report or planning a public program.

My own first paid public sector job was fairly atypical of most. I was hired by a firm called Soil Systems, Inc.—a private company that bid on government contracts to do anthropological surveys and excavations. Under the Moss-Bennett Act of 1974, these companies were eligible to bid on projects that impacted potential archaeology sites by such government actions as the building of a dam. The site was surveyed to determine its importance, and if it was judged to be significant, an excavation was planned. In this case, the Army Corps of Engineers was building the massive Tennessee

Tombigbee Waterway on the Tennessee River through major portions of the South, impacting a large number of important archaeological sites (not to mention farm land, homes, and whole communities) in its wake.

The particular site in question was part of an antebellum northeastern Mississippi plantation site including archaeological remains of slave (and later sharecropper) homes and commercial buildings. My job was to conduct oral history interviews with former residents who remembered living and working in the area when the community still existed. Many people recalled stories transmitted from slave days, and their insight into the later sharecropping community was very valuable to the understandings of the archaeologists' findings. Although bringing interviewees to the field laboratory to identify specific artifacts proved inconclusive, general information about the types of cookware, tools, clothing, and other household goods used within peoples' memories aided in the analysis of artifacts. People also remembered the buildings, their placement and modifications, and their approximate dates of habitation. More important than information about artifacts and buildings, however, was the human dimension the oral histories added to the project. Stories of family and community life, tales of local ghosts and humorous characters, and accounts of the seasonal cycle of cotton cultivation gave flesh and blood to the story told by artifacts, post-holes, and flora and fauna samples.

The atypical parts of this job, as I later found out from more experience in public sector work, were (1) the opportunity to work as part of an interdisciplinary team including historical archaeologists and traditional historians, and (2) the chance to work on a "cultural resource management" project fueled by government funds not often available to folklorists. I was at that time oblivious to the fact that the American Folklife Center had turned down portions of the same Tennessee Tombigee project after lengthy negotiations and moral problems with the nature of the project and its funding. Instead, as a young folklorist with no political savvy, I saw the job as a great opportunity to hone my interviewing skills, test my knowledge of narrative and material culture, and put other information gained in my graduate classes to practical use. The resulting report for the Army Corps of Engineers successfully blended historic archaeology, oral history, and traditional history to form a picture of the Waverly area from the days of slavery through the 1960s. Only later, at a discussion among graduate students and Professor Richard Dorson, did I discover the scandalous nature of the "tainted money" that I had been paid as a participant in this project. Controversy aside, I believe that folklorists have a great deal to offer this type of project that combines the viewpoints of several disciplines. The American Folklife Center itself has participated in many such projects, albeit through other funding sources and with other motives than "salvage archaeology."

My next paid position, as a fieldworker and presenter for the Tennessee State Parks Folklife Project (TSPFP) during the summer of 1980, was a much more typical public sector venture. The TSPFP was conceived of by Robert Fulcher, a state park district naturalist and amateur folklorist. The project was partially funded by the National Endowment for the Arts' Folk Arts Program.

Three academically trained folklorists were hired to collect folklore around two state parks apiece and to plan programs at the parks. Like many other public sector folklorists, Fulcher's goals were to increase awareness of and appreciation for Tennessee traditions, to attract the local community to park programs, and to collect a body of material for future use. He felt that much of the knowledge held by older tradition bearers would die with them, since most younger community members were not interested in or aware of the songs, stories, and occupational and craft skills still practiced or living in memories of older people. He also recognized the fact that local people often viewed park programs as serving only tourists and felt unwelcome. Collecting information that would be placed in the State Library and Archive and presenting programs based on this information in the parks seemed like excellent ways to achieve Fulcher's goals, which were totally within the goals of the NEA Folk Arts Program as well.

As is common in public sector work, we were really doing four jobs in one: collecting folklore by means of audio recordings and photography, preliminary archiving of the material (logging tapes and photos, collecting background information about informants), planning programs, and doing all of the publicity for the programs to insure an audience. Fulcher was an inspiring supervisor who made us feel that the work was urgent and important. This job added to my field collecting experience and taught me presentation and publicity skills (mostly by trial and error). Ultimately, I decided to use the TSPFP as a case study for my dissertation. The writing of the dissertation gave me the chance to step back from a public sector project with which I was intimately involved, and make some critical observations. I will draw from some of these observations in the conclusion of this article.

The next summer I carried out two shorter fieldwork projects, one in Indiana and one in Mississippi, both for arts organizations. Through these projects I was introduced to two frustrating elements all too typical of many short-term public sector positions: lack of time to do one's best and lack of the fulfillment that comes from personal follow-up. During the Mississippi job, I had two weeks in each of two locations to collect information and suggest participants for a week's worth of library programs, to be carried out later that year. This involved going into a countywide area with very little background information, learning as much as possible about the type of traditions found there, and then locating and interviewing individuals who could present these traditions in a library setting. Unlike in my former work in Mississippi and Tennessee, I turned my material over to another folklorist without a chance to process it through publication or presentation myself. Although I met and interviewed many interesting tradition bearers and felt that I made good recommendations for the programs, more time and background in the communities would have made the work more satisfying and relevant to myself and to the communities involved.

In 1982, after finishing my Ph.D. qualifying exams, I took a full-time position as state folk arts coordinator for the Indiana Arts Commission. In this job, I was able to use skills I had obtained in graduate school and during my summer employment. But perhaps even more important was a new skill I learned—the complex negotiations of office politics in the mercurial world of arts administration. I worked in this capacity for a little over two years, during which time I carried out the day to day work of administering grants to communities and created two projects of my own through "special projects" funds from the National Endowment for the Arts' Folk Arts Program.

The first of these projects was a library project based on the Mississippi model. I hired two folklorists to do the fieldwork, thus graduating from fieldworker to administrator and thus perpetuating the aforementioned sins of not allowing my fieldworkers enough time to really dig into the folklore of the counties I assigned them to. As a grant writer and administrator, I found that this was often a necessary evil based on keeping costs down while attempting to serve as wide an area as possible in a limited time frame. I did, however, manage to lay more groundwork for the fieldworkers by visiting the counties and meeting with community leaders beforehand, collecting a list of possible traditions and gathering the names of many potential tradition bearers beforehand. Following the fieldwork period, I used the recommendations of the fieldworkers to plan week-long library programs in six libraries in underserved areas of the state, which pleased the agency. Several of the librarians planned follow-up projects (including one who applied for a grant from the arts commission to fund a booklet on local traditions), which pleased me.

The second project was the creation of four slide-tape programs, which allowed me to do some follow-up on the fieldwork carried out for the library project. (My integration into the arts world through the medium of arts administration was proven when I commissioned an original synthesizer score from a young composer who had applied for a fellowship at the arts commission for one of the programs.) The programs were offered to libraries, schools, clubs, and other organizations around the state at a nominal rental or purchase cost. Although they were never heavily used, I recently checked on the programs and found them still available and intact, despite the fact that the Indiana Arts Commission no longer has a folk arts coordinator. During the course of my work in Indiana, I found that the materials generated by some earlier community projects funded by the Arts Commission had met less fortunate fates, with slides, tapes, and reports relegated to shoe boxes on dusty shelves, or permanently misplaced after a folklorist leaves the project.

After two years, I ventured into another phase of public sector folklore work as an independent contractor. Resigning our full-time jobs, a friend and I began work on a project documenting the folk craftspeople of the state of Indiana, toward a publication and an exhibition. We drew upon much of the fieldwork done during the library and slide-tape projects and other folklore projects carried out in the state over the years. Simultaneously, I became the part-time coordinator of a project administered by the Indiana Historical Bureau called "Folklore in the Classroom." My job was to edit a workbook and set up teachers' workshops. Carrying out our own research and planning an innovative traveling exhibition was very rewarding. Working with teachers and other educators on Folklore in the Classroom thrust me into a new world of folklore and education. However, the pay was low and juggling two projects at once was exhausting.

When funds ran out for the Folklore in the Classroom project, we were still engaged in research, writing, and administering our exhibition as it traveled to six sites in Indiana. I was hired for another part-time contract, this time at the Indianapolis Children's Museum to work on a project called the "Mysteries in History Toolbox"—a resource kit for teachers based on the museum's revamped American history gallery, funded in part by the Indiana Humanities Committee. The kit had sections on artifacts, archaeology, architecture, oral history and folklore, and visual and written documents. I wrote background booklets for each of these subjects and created a number of activities for students. I also helped plan workshops to show teachers how to use the kit.

The pay for this project was even worse than the Folklore in the Classroom job, but the work was interesting and built upon many of my academic and practical skills. For instance, as an undergraduate and graduate student I had always had a special interest in historic photography and its impact on family folklore. One of the activities I prepared for the Toolbox was a series of cards that helped students research their family photographs, taking the history of photography from daguerreotypes to instant photos. More important, I learned more about museum education. Through contact with teachers during the course of preparing both the Folklore in the Classroom material and the Mysteries in History toolbox, I learned that they were anxious to have access to hands-on activities for their classes, and I also learned more about their criteria for using those materials in the classroom.

After the Mysteries in History project ended, I decided it was time to "get serious" about finishing my dissertation. Such a delay in finishing one's degree is a chronic dilemma among public sector folklorists who are seduced by interesting money-making projects or full-time employment in the field. This tends to perpetuate the feeling among more academically-oriented colleagues that public sector folklorists are less serious and less motivated than those who finish their degrees in shorter time periods. The truth is that, in public sector folklore, work experience and completed community projects count more than the Ph.D. Often, finishing the Ph.D. offers no incentive (such as increased salary or standing) but becomes instead a personal goal and opens academic doors should the folklorist wish to teach part-time on the university level.

During the time I worked on finishing my dissertation, I began substitute teaching, which gave me plenty of time for dissertation writing and offered experience in classrooms with students ranging from first graders to seniors in high school. The exposure to a wide variety of teaching techniques, lesson plans, and curriculum materials helped in future folklore and education work. However, I do not recommend substitute teaching for any lengthy time period, since the pay is very poor and many classes seem determined to drive their substitutes mad.

By the time my dissertation was in sight of being finished, finding a full-time job again became necessary to get out of debt and resume my career path. I was hired by the Smithsonian's Office of Folklife Programs as Curator for the Massachusetts Program of the 1988 Festival of American Folklife. I had had some previous experience with the Festival, having worked for two weeks in 1986 as a presenter for the Tennessee Program. The chance to work in Washington, D.C. on a project that I would be responsible for shaping, and the relatively large salary, lured me away from Indianapolis and a possible chance to work at the Children's Museum full-time as Director of the Resource Center.

Planning and executing the program drew on many of my skills, since the work involved supervising an extensive field collection, and synthesizing that collection into a combined exhibition and live presentation. The scale of the program was rather frightening, with over 100 participants, an estimated 1.5 million visitors, and a budget of $600,000. Despite the size of the program, the most problematic aspect was how properly to represent the folklife of an entire state. Since Massachusetts on the whole is a very politically aware state, no matter how many ethnic groups and regions were to be represented, there were always people demanding to know why their particular group or region was being excluded or shortchanged. Also, there was great resentment toward the Smithsonian, a national agency, making the final decisions on how the state was to be portrayed. As curator, I was often torn between the creation of a coherent program, the attempt to include as many groups and individuals as possible, keeping within the budget, and pleasing administrators in our office and at sponsoring agencies in Massachusetts. Fortunately, in the end, the program was well-received by most visitors and administrators, and especially by the participants from Massachusetts.

During the course of the year and half I spent working on the program, I also continued to develop my interest in folklore and education, getting to know some of the education specialists around the Smithsonian, and working with educators in Massachusetts. The acting director of our office encouraged me to apply for a Smithsonian Educational Outreach grant to act as education specialist for the office. Since I wrote the grant, I also wrote the job description and planned to work on projects of my own devising. The job would have seemed like a dream come true, if it had not launched me into another realm of funding snafus—given the fluctuating budget of the Office of Folklife Programs, the job never became permanent, relying on a patchwork of grants, Festival funds, and private money I raised for various projects.

One such project, the Folklore Summer Institute, was definitely worth my tenuous status as a Smithsonian employee. Essentially a training program, the institute allowed a group of "community scholars"—individuals who have been collecting and presenting folklore in their home communities for a number of years—to come to Washington, D.C. to meet with folklore scholars and each other, exchange information and expertise, and learn about resources available for folklore projects. This project involved me in the important work of "empowering" (or, "enabling") community researchers to carry out their own research with the full knowledge, aid, and support of professional folklorists. An extremely varied group of individuals were accepted into the program during the two years I directed it, representing remote rural locations as well as the inner city, working at small museums, local arts agencies, elementary and secondary public schools, social service organizations, photography studios, and volunteer organizations. The groups chosen represented a wide variety of other ethnic backgrounds, and work in the public sector including planning annual festivals, exhibitions, and performances featuring local folk artists, the marketing of folk crafts, the writing and editing of publications, and the creation of curriculum materials. The things they had in common were an interest in preserving and presenting folklore in their communities and the desire to learn how to go about doing so more effectively. The Folklore Summer Institute brought me full circle from my own academic training and experience following the "proper channels" of work in the public sector. These folks were out in their own communities, doing work in many cases *more* effective than most public sector folklorists, and certainly with more lasting impact than much of the work I had done in the course of my career.

After the last Summer Folklore Institute, I became a victim of government funding cutbacks during the fall of 1990 and carried out some contract work for both National Public Radio and the Allegheny Highland Heritage Project in Western Pennsylvania while I was temporarily out of a job at the Smithsonian. Then, I curated another Festival program for the Office of Folklife Programs in 1991, this one on Family Farms in the Midwest. I am currently working on a contract basis with the OFP, continuing the work I began as education specialist. There is a chance that this position will become permanent soon.

A Career in Public Sector Folklore

Though no one career can be said to be "typical" of public sector folklore work in general, I believe that mine offers insight into the evolution, present state, and future problems of the field. Toward this end, I will list several implications for the field as a whole that I feel can be derived from my own experience:

1. The true public sector folklorist is "born, not made." By this I mean that, despite the advanced academic degrees, political know-how, and honed skills of fund-raising and administration, most public sector folklorists who have stuck with the often frustrating trade began their careers *wanting* to work with the general public instead of in the world of academia. They consciously set out, sometimes from their undergraduate years, to gain the skills and experience that would lead them into public sector work. I cannot speak for everyone's motivations in this pursuit, but my own reflect a perhaps idealistic desire to reach as many people as possible with information about tradition bearers and the communities they live in, in order to encourage perpetuation of folklore throughout the United States and the world. One could argue that many folklorists working in a purely academic setting share this desire, and carry it out through teaching and publishing. However, public sector folklorists seek to reach an infinitely wider audience through media concerts and festivals, films, exhibitions, curriculum materials accessible to teachers in public schools, and articles in popular or regional publications. This work, in my opinion, takes different skills and a different type of commitment from those required of a career devoted mainly to teaching and writing on the university level.

2. In order to perpetuate their own careers, and the field in gen-

eral, public sector folklorists need to become masters of many job-
related "worlds." While some public sector folklorists may find a niche
early in their careers and stick with one job (say, working within an arts
agency) their entire work lives, most of us move from one position to
another because of the circumstances of available funding, changes in
personal life, or the desire to try something new and more challenging.
This requires gaining appropriate skills that neither academic training
nor previous experience has prepared us for. Thus, within one career,
we may learn skills as diverse as mastering the nuances of a Stereo
Nagra to obtain a broadcast-quality recording in the field, writing good
exhibition labels, administering a large federal grant, helping a teacher
manage a visit by a folk artist to a fourth grade class, and ushering a
senator through a folk festival featuring his or her constituents. In
short, the public sector folklorist must remain extremely flexible and
willing to learn throughout his or her career.

3. Education, experience, and skill do not necessarily ensure a stable, well-paying job in the location of one's choice in the field of
public sector folklore. Sometimes this is the fault of the folklorist, as
in my case when I took low-paying jobs that interested me, or "went
freelance" in order to choose my own projects and schedule. Unfortunately, more and more often, the relatively small number of available public sector jobs and a current funding squeeze on all levels of
public and private cultural agencies have caused the "choice factor" to
dwindle. Many public sector folklorists find themselves stringing together a series of temporary jobs, or looking outside the field for work
that (ironically) builds on some of the experience they have gained as
public sector folklorists (becoming museum administrators, pursuing
careers in media production or publishing, working as professional
fund-raisers, and so forth). It does not bode well for a field when many
of its most able workers are receiving pink slips and pursuing other
career paths.

4. Public sector folklorists need to broaden their support base,
stretching the field much further than its current boundaries. Many
public sector folklorists have assumed a proprietary stance toward their
work, legitimizing some types of folklore over others and shutting out
local enthusiasts who are not familiar with the materials of "authentic
folklore." I am not advocating that we embrace "fakelore," but I am
appealing for more programs that offer training and a forum for information exchange to "kindred spirits" such as community scholars.
Many projects that I worked on, including the Tennessee State Parks
Folklife Project, imposed a structure created by public sector folklorists and agency administrators on a community, with little recognition

of what that community may have been more interested in receiving from such a project. Working with communities and with people already involved in the collection and perpetuation of folklore on the *inside* of those communities is one way to broaden support and serve the public more effectively.

Since I began graduate school in the mid-1970s, the field of public sector folklore has certainly seen rapid growth and maturation. State folklorists or state folk arts coordinators are now well established in nearly every state and a number of territories of the United States. Some state programs have grown to include staffs of a dozen or more folklorists, and many local agencies have hired folklorists on a more or less permanent basis. More important, perhaps, is the critical assessment that the field has undergone in the past half-dozen years, in publications, at American Folklore Society meetings, and during special conferences. I hope that this assessment of the nature of public sector folklore careers, using my own career as a case study, has added to this critique. The future of public sector folklore work depends on such direct gazes into the mirror, checking flaws as well as admirable traits.

For Further Information

A definitive, critical history of the applied folklore and public sector folklore movements is yet to be written. The first volume devoted entirely to aspects of public sector folklore history and case studies is Burt Feintuch, ed., *The Conservation of Culture: Folklorists and the Public Sector* (Lexington: Univ. Press of Kentucky, 1988). Unpublished treatments of this history can be found in Peter Thomas Bartis's Ph.D. dissertation, "A History of the Archive of Folk Song at the Library of Congress: The First Fifty Years" (University of Pennsylvania, 1982), and my own dissertation, "Evaluating Public Sector Folklore: The Tennessee State Parks Folklife Project" (Indiana University), both available through University Microfilm. Archie Green, who served as lobbyist for the American Folklife Center, has written often on the early history of applied folklore; see his "Introduction," in Linda Coe, ed., *Folklife and the Federal Government* (Washington, D.C.: American Folklife Center, 1977), 1-9, and "Public Sector Attention to Folklife in the United States," in Nicholas Spitzer, ed., *Louisiana Folklife: A Guide to the State* (Baton Rouge: Louisiana Folklife Program/Division of the Arts, 1985), 245-51. Although dated, the debate between socially conscious folklorists and Richard M. Dorson concerning the ideals of applied folklore will still fascinate folklore students; see Dick Sweterlitsch, ed., *Papers on Applied Folklore* (Bloomington, Ind.: Folklore Forum, Bibliographic and Special Series 8, 1971).

Two issues of the *Kentucky Folklore Record* report on work in public sector folklore: Volume 26 (1980) and Volume 32 (1986). The former includes a working definition for professional folklorists, a report on folk arts in the schools programs, and a provocative essay on reasons not to produce a folk festival by folklorists Timothy Lloyd and Charles Camp. The latter volume includes evaluations of programs in the public sector, with an excellent article suggesting goals for public programs by folklorist Doris Dyen. Many publications, films, records, and other products of state folklore programs are listed in Henry Willett, "A Survey of State Folk Cultural Programs," a publication of the Public Programs Section of the American Folklore Society (Jan. 1986), available from the National Endowment for the Arts Folk Arts Program, 1100 Pennsylvania Ave., NW, Washington, D.C. 20506. Ormond Loomis's *Cultural Conservation: The Protection of Cultural Heritage in the United States* (Washington, D.C.: American Folklife Center, 1983) gives a good overview of work in the public sector. The best "finger on the pulse" of public sector folklore since 1984 is the biannual *Public Programs Newsletter*, available by joining the Public Sector Section of the American Folklore Society. The newsletter includes reports on state and national folklore programs, discussions of important issues, job announcements, and listings of new publications and products.

A good introduction to folklore and education projects initiated by folklorists is Marsha McDowell, ed., *Folk Arts in Education: A Resource Handbook* (Michigan State University Museum, 1987). This work includes descriptions of projects (including more information about my own project, "Folklore in the Classroom"), as well as sample materials and an excellent bibliography. Copies of "Folklore in the Classroom" are available from the Indiana Historical Bureau, 140 North Senate, Indianapolis, IN 46204. The "Mysteries in History Toolbox" is administered by the Indianapolis Children's Museum Resource Center, but it does not travel out of state.

The Smithsonian's Office of Folklife Programs offers a number of free publications, including its annual *Festival of American Folklife Program Book* and monographs in the Folklife Studies Series, available from the Office of Folklife Programs, 955 L'Enfant Plaza SW, Suite 2600, Washington, D.C. 20560. The American Folklife Center issues a newsletter, *Folklife Center News*, quarterly, a handsome Annual, and a number of project reports, including Mary Hufford, editor, *One Space, Many Places: Folklife and Land Use in New Jersey's Pinelands National Reserve* (1986), which illustrates the interdisciplinary nature of much of the AFC's work, all available from American Folklife Center, Library of Congress, Washington, D.C. 20540.

11

Promoting Self-Worth among the Aging

DAVID SHULDINER

Within the communities they study, folklorists have long sought out aged members as rich sources of cultural information. In doing so, these fieldworkers have tended to reinforce (or reassert) a traditional veneration of the aging. Yet, equally important, the process of encouraging elders to talk about themselves and their communities has served as an important source of personal validation for older community members. In developing public cultural programs for older adults—first as the Connecticut Humanities Council scholar-in-residence at the Connecticut State Department on Aging [CSDA], and presently as the humanities program coordinator with the CSDA—I have made ample use of the tools of the folklorist's trade in developing curricula and models for educational programs.

Techniques employed by fieldworkers to encourage their research "subjects" to share cultural knowledge are quite applicable to the implementation of educational programs that invite participants to share their own views and memories. I have made use of them in devising strategies for eliciting reminiscence and review of personal and social experience utilizing readings, films, and other materials and formats. In this way, I have stimulated meaningful dialogue on a wide range of subjects, including local history, immigration and ethnicity, and traditional arts and music. In the course of such programming, elders are able to assert their sense of self and community belonging, as reflections of their continued vitality and engagement.

I offer the story of my own involvement in public humanities programs for the aging as an illustration of the ways in which the outlook and methodology of the field of folklore are ideally suited to this collaborative effort of scholarship and public programming. By describing my entry into, and involvement with, the community of elders and the network of those who provide services to older adults, I wish to demonstrate the ways in which my training as a folklorist has been generously applied to a task whose most tangible benefit has been the promotion of self-esteem among the aging through programs that emphasize mental vitality and "wellness."

Roots of the Program

This is also the story of a successful collaboration between two public institutions not usually involved in each other's affairs: a state humanities council and a state agency on aging. It is the tale of the Connecticut Humanities Council's major entry into the aging field, and the Connecticut State Department on Aging's initiation into the humanities, reflecting a growing recognition of the contributions that humanities scholars can make to the aging, and the role that public agencies may play in translating that potential into programs of quality and substance for older adults.

The Connecticut Humanities Council has, in recent years, reassessed its pattern of grant-giving for public humanities projects. Two factors contributed to that reassessment: (1) the rapid increase in population of the state's elderly, and thus the emergence of a growing constituency for its programs; and (2) the large attendance of older persons at council-funded programs, in particular local library-sponsored book discussions. The council made a special effort at program outreach, contacting various aging agencies and community sites, encouraging them to take advantage of program materials offered by the council's Resource Center and to apply for grants to bring programs to sites where elders meet. To accelerate this process, the council took an unprecedented giant step further down the road, through the vehicle of its longstanding "scholar-in-residence" program.

Over the past several years, the Connecticut Humanities Council has collaborated with state agencies and other public organizations in sponsoring scholars-in-residence whose work is intended to bring a "humanistic" perspective to the programs and policies of the institutions to which they are attached. The council did, in fact, indirectly set a precedent in presenting aging concerns through this program with the placing of a scholar-in-residence at Connecticut Public Radio. This scholar (who happened also to be a folklorist), in the course of his activities at the stations, contributed to a twenty-six-part radio series entitled "New Rules for the Old," consisting of interviews with older people in Connecticut from various walks of life. It was a compelling next logical step for the council to reach a statewide audience with its most ambitious venture into aging: a proposal to fund a "humanist-in-residence" with the State Department on Aging.

The Connecticut State Department on Aging (CSDA), for its part, has had a record of developing and supporting innovative programs and approaches to addressing the needs of the state's elderly population, such as job training for older adults, a nursing home ombudsman program, and a minority advisory council. Yet, the CSDA is largely assigned the onerous task of being the "watchdog" agency for the state's aging network, making sure that all funds dispersed and services provided for the state's elderly conform to standards. When approached by the Humanities Council about the possibility of applying for a grant to place a scholar-in-residence with the agency, the CSDA welcomed the possibility of providing a direct community service in the form of humanities programs for elders. However, neither the CSDA nor the Humanities Council had a clear vision of what programs, approaches and subjects in the humanities might best be received by an elder audience, or of the nature and extent of available resources for program development.

A Folklorist in the Community of Elders

As this process was unfolding, my scholarly activity was laying the groundwork for the new career upon which I was about to embark, but as yet knew nothing about. As a doctoral candidate in folklore and mythology at UCLA, I specialized in American immigrant and ethnic history and culture, occupational folklore, and folksong, and I had a growing interest in the field of oral history. For my dissertation I chose to examine forms of expression of ethnic and class identity among a group of elderly Jewish immigrants who were active in labor and political movements in Eastern Europe and the United States. During the process of conducting interviews, mostly with women and men in their seventies and eighties, I grew to appreciate not only the great privilege of sitting at the feet of these repositories of living history but also the importance of providing an opportunity for those with whom I met to share the stories of their lives with me.

In the fall of 1984—a few months after completing my degree in folklore—I responded to an announcement in the *Chronicle of Higher Education* of a ten-month position for a "Humanist in Residence" with a state agency on aging. Typical of the "gypsy scholar" fresh out of the academic mill with yet another arcane degree, I was, at the time, holding down two tenuous part-time jobs—teaching election year politics at a private high school and history at a Jewish Sunday school. The advertisement—surprising for its appearance in an academic trade journal—stirred memories of an earnest but vague yearning to combine scholarly pursuits with community service, a desire difficult to articulate in ways that would lead to gainful employment. The Connecticut Humanities Council, whose mission it has been to bridge the gap between "the academy" and the "the public" had presented, in this brief ad, the seeds of a fruitful synthesis.

At this point I began to reflect not only upon my work among the aging as a scholar (which partly inspired me to apply for the job) but also upon the ways in which my training and outlook as a folklorist might have prepared me for the position offered. To begin with, folklorists and others who conduct fieldwork have long developed skills not only in academic discourse, but also in communication with the "folk"—those members of the general public who have been their primary research subjects. Among that public are members of ethnic and occupational groups whose cultural wisdom and life experience are their "degrees," and whose outlook and forms of expression are the "data" upon which the scholarly species thrive. It is this very mediation between academic community and general audience—between scholarly and conventional discourse—that is the essence of public humanities programming.

From another perspective, it has long been the aged within traditional communities who have been sought after by folklorists as the richest of cultural resources whose memories may yield portraits of worldview, lifestyle, local history, and the like. By seeking out aged community members as sources of "primary data," folklorists have tended to reaffirm a traditional respect for elders as bearers and guardians of communal knowledge. By treating elders as valuable repositories of cultural wisdom, fieldworkers instill in them a sense of worth of comparable importance to the information gleaned from them.

Perhaps one of the most vital roles played by the folklorist is that of stimulating the very process of reflection among interview subjects that has yielded those precious "gleanings from the field." It has long been said that life review and reminiscence are important ongoing activities engaged in by people as they age—a poignant process, not simply of summing things up, but of maintaining a sense of self and community belonging, signalling a continued vitality and involvement in the present. By encouraging elders to talk about "the old ways," folklorists have been made aware of the crucial role that such reminiscing plays in establishing (or reestablishing) vital links between present and past experience. Folklorists with skills in the methodology of oral history would find themselves ideally prepared to develop and lead public humanities programs for the aging, since the techniques used in eliciting life stories may be brought to bear in encouraging elder participants in educational programs to contribute their experiences as vital program components.

The Department on Aging Hires a Folklorist

In October 1984 I went for an interview held at the State Department on Aging's office in Hartford, Connecticut, and conducted by the director of the Connecticut Humanities Council and two administrators from the department. The questions they asked were open-ended—clearly this was a "fishing expedition" for fresh ideas on how to set up a model for humanities programs for older adults. I spoke to them of oral history, of programs that would encourage elders to share memories and traditions. They must have been won over by the folklorist's approach to their problem, for in November, I found myself employed by the Connecticut State Department on Aging as their "humanist in residence."

My marching orders (as the director of the Humanities Council liked to call them) were broad: to develop and implement cultural programs for older adults throughout the state. I worked under the supervision of the director of the Community Services Division of the Department on Aging, but I was (and continue to be) left pretty much to my own devices. As a neophyte, not only in the Nutmeg State but also in the aging field, my first task was to visit local senior centers and other sites where successful programs in the humanities had already been conducted, and to learn from them how they went about finding and utilizing resources for program development. I discovered that much innovative work had been accomplished by a number of inspired senior center directors, therapeutic recreation directors in nursing homes, and the like, and that a variety of resources were known and utilized at various sites in scattered parts of the state.

I began the task of gathering information from these local sources as well as from individuals and institutions across the country. Eventually I compiled an inventory of resources and potential program presenters (*Humanities Programs For Older Adults: A Resource Guide*) that could be distributed to anyone interested in developing humanities programs for Connecticut's elders. (In addition to providing information on films, traveling exhibits, historical societies and museums, as well as speakers directories of local colleges, I also exercised the folklorist's prerogative by listing storytellers, folk singers, and other sources of "vernacular education.") Once again, in the process of developing and presenting programs among older adults in communities throughout the state, the tools of the folklorist's trade were drawn out of their kit bag, sharpened and utilized. I established as a common denominator—and driving force—in my work an emphasis upon interaction between participants and program presenter, much like the conversational style of the field interview that provides a comfortable setting for communication, aimed at stimulating people to share personal experience and integrate it with particular themes addressed (be they subjects about which information is sought from an interviewer or topics of group discussion). In effect, by making life review and reminiscence vital components—standard operating procedure—of humanities programs for older adults, I made an effort to select materials and design program formats that encouraged reflection upon life experiences as a means of stimulating the fullest audience participation. This process was naturally enhanced when the specific subject matter under discussion reflected folkloristic concerns (e.g., local history, traditions, values, and arts).

The first model program I worked on was a film discussion series presented in cooperation with the Stamford Commission on Aging as part of a celebration of Black History Month in February 1985 that also included guest lecturers and a "soul food" luncheon planned by the Commission. Two films on black traditional culture and religion ("Yonder Come Day," a portrait of Bessie Jones, a black American traditional singer from St. Simon Island, Georgia, and "Two Black Churches," a comparison of worship services in rural Mississippi and New Haven, Connecticut) were borrowed from the Connecticut State Library (an invaluable source of program materials) and shown at several sites. Audiences ranged from all black to all Anglo-American and offered a variety of responses. Encouraged to relate what they had viewed on screen to their own experiences, several black audience members offered touching stories of baptisms in a Stamford river, and even one off the shore of Long Island Sound, as well as memorable rites of conversion and recollections of the sense of wholeness that characterized the traditional church-centered community. Though some white audience members found it difficult to accept the demonstrative nature of these black worship services, they came to see, during discussion periods, the ways in which other parts of their lives provided needed outlets for expressive behavior. After viewing the film, "Yonder Come Day," in which children's game songs were depicted, one viewer, an Anglo-American woman, tearfully recalled seeing a game she had taught to her daughter being taught in turn to her granddaughter.

In March 1985 I presented a slide program, "Hartford Changes," borrowed from the Connecticut Historical Society. After consulting with an active member of a social club that meets regularly at a senior center in an outlying community, it was decided that the slides, which depict changes that have taken place in eight Hartford sites during the last 150 years, be shown in such a way that program participants could break in at any point during the presentation to make comments about what they saw on screen. Since most members of the audience were longtime residents of the greater Hartford area and/or held lifelong jobs in the city, murmurs of recognition swept across the room as the photographs depicted scenes that came within the scope of living memory of audience members. The script provided with the slides was utilized only after initial responses were elicited concerning each historic site being viewed. The presentation was rapidly transformed into a moderated collective "oral history" of Hartford's old neighborhoods. The success of this event prompted a request from this group for another program on a different historical theme but using the same format.

Among my special interests as a folklorist have been the nature and role of the traditional arts and music. Materials on this subject in a form readily available for public programs are relatively scarce, so I approached the State Library with the suggestion that they acquire several films about older traditional artists and musicians. They agreed to rent the films so that I could arrange "preview" showings of them before a cross-section of older adults throughout the state. I took this opportunity to organize a film discussion series on "Aging and Creativity," which I brought to audiences at over two dozen sites across Connecticut. Among the films shown were a five-part series entitled "Visions of Paradise"—portraits of older American naive artists (including painters Harry Lieberman and Minnie Evans, and environmental artist Tressa Prisbrey) from Light-Saraf Films; two titles by ethnographic filmmaker Les Blank: "Well Spent Life" (featuring Texas sharecropper/singer Mance Lipscomb) and "Sprout Wings and Fly" (a portrait of Appalachian fiddler Tommy Jarrell); and the Appalshop film "Sourwood Mountain Dulcimers" (with J.D. Stamper and John McClutcheon). Some of the issues raised in discussions were (1) the character of creativity; (2) formal versus nonformal training; (3) the influence of personal and social background in creative expression; and (4) the place of artists in their community and in society at large. Audience members were encouraged to recall lives spent in their communities of origin, and the role that music and traditional arts played as integral parts of social life in an earlier era.

One of the most popular programs that I shared with Connecticut elders was a series of showings of "The Road Between Heaven and Hell: The Last Circuits of the Leatherman," a videotape funded in part by the Connecticut Humanities Council and broadcast over public television. The film looks at the character of folklore and historical memory in stories about a famous tramp who walked a 365-mile route through Westchester County, New York, and southern Connecticut every thirty-four days for some thirty years in the mid- to late nineteenth century. Among those offering commentary in the film about the "Leatherman" (so-named for his raiment, fashioned exclusively from leather remnants) is folklorist Gerald Warshaver, who talks about the ways in which legend attempts to explain the mystery surrounding a real-life figure, as well as the role of legend in conveying a sense of importance to the teller and his or her locale. Following each showing, audience members were invited to share their recollections of incidents relating to the Leatherman (some were old enough to have heard stories of direct sightings of the tramp by elders when they were very young). One person recalled a retired schoolteacher telling her about dismissing class when the Leatherman appeared in town (such an incident was mentioned in the film). Another man mentioned his grandfather—a very matter-of-fact Yankee farmer—who dutifully noted the regular appearance of the Leatherman in his journal over a twenty-year period. After one showing, a man related a story told by his great-uncle whose farm was visited by the Leatherman. The vagabond was asked by the farmer to skin a dead horse that had become bloated; he slit the belly with some difficulty and, being one who rarely spoke, simply declared: "Ripe."

It is worth mentioning an incident reported to me by the director of a senior center where I presented the "Leatherman" film. It was a back-handed compliment of sorts on the program; moreover, it was a tribute to the compelling character of local legend. A group of card players at one senior center where the film was shown refused to break up their game to view the program. They did overhear it, however, and gradually got involved in a discussion about the Leatherman; the center director noted that the card players, as well as those who actually participated in the program, were still talking about it several days later.

Among the most successful printed materials used have been a series of anthologies entitled "Self-Discovery Through the Humanities," issued by the National Council on the Aging. Each unit consists of selected readings from literary works, philosophical essays, poetry, and oral histories addressing a variety of central themes, from American social history, the work experience, and the environment to issues of ethics, the family, and constitutional law. They are designed to be digested in several weekly discussion sessions. Copies of the anthologies are loaned to group participants for the duration of a "course." Discussion leaders' guides (with suggested questions, additional readings and activities, and so forth) are also provided, as well as other materials. One unit, "In the Old Ways," focuses on American ethnic traditions, with individual sessions devoted to the life cycle, food-ways, holidays, and the like.

One highly popular unit of the self-discovery series is "Exploring Local History." As a discussion leader at a senior center in Bristol, Connecticut, which was celebrating its bicentennial in 1985, I led an enthusiastic group of local residents (most of whom were Bristol natives; one of them still lives in the house in which she was born) through this eight-part anthology, which included reminiscences of youthful days spent in towns throughout the United States, photographs of families, and house interiors and local architectural styles, as well as poetry and short stories. We visited the Bristol Historical Society, whose docents took us on a guided tour, in period dress, of their museum. We also took a walking tour of Federal Hill (two blocks up from the senior center), original site of the town green, where troops trained during the Revolutionary War and around which the town's central figures built homes and churches. In one session, participants were asked to draw floor plans of their childhood homes; in another they were invited to bring in old family photographs and memorabilia.

Among the most exciting projects with which I have been involved were ones in which I acted as consultant to a theater scholar, Christine Howard Bailey, who specializes in "oral history theater" among older adults. A group of participants in the Parkville Senior Center in Hartford, Connecticut, were invited to explore the social and historical roots of their community through the vehicle of a dramatic presentation based upon their own memories. The project, sponsored by OPUS/Arts and Aging (a nonprofit organization that places artists-in-residence at selected sites in the greater Hartford area) received private funding for theater training sessions, and a grant from the Connecticut Humanities Council to conduct oral history workshops and individual interviews in which the life stories of workshop participants, as well as other community members, were recorded. These narratives were transformed into a script that served as the basis for "Parkville Days," a play that was performed at several local sites, as well as taped by Hartford Community Television (along with a group interview of the cast and "crew"). In post-performance discussions, audience members were invited to contribute their memories about the Parkville neighborhood.

On the heels of this enthusiastically received venture, another oral history theater production about Jewish farmers in Colchester, Connecticut (also funded in part by the Connecticut Humanities Council) was completed and performed in Colchester and in Hartford. Dr. Bailey has most recently completed a production recalling the events of "The Flood of 1955" as witnessed by the residents of Winsted, Connecticut, and enacted both by residents of Winsted (including a sizable "Greek chorus") and members of the original troupe from "Parkville Days" (some of whom, having acquired the acting bug, have appeared in as many as four oral history theatre productions).

With the "humanist-in-residence" program with the State Department on Aging in Connecticut, a great precedent has been set for the active involvement of folklorists and other humanities scholars in the educational enrichment of the lives of that community of elders whose cultural riches have been so often tapped by them. Turning the tables in more than one way, the valorization of my role as folklorist/educator brought me as much self-esteem as I hope to have instilled in elder humanities program participants.

On another level, the project has provided a model with far-reaching implications for the development of meaningful and challenging—yet accessible—public agency-sponsored humanities programs reaching a broad cross-section of the aging community. The National Endowment for the Humanities rewarded the Connecticut Humanities Council for its initiative in funding public humanities programs for elders by granting it an "exemplary project award" in recognition of the success of the "humanist-in-residence" project. The State Department on Aging in its turn embraced the goals of this project by giving it permanent status with the creation of the staff position of humanities program coordinator within their Community Services Division. Under this new title, I have acted as overall project director of the Humanities Council's NEH-funded project, which has brought over one hundred scholar-led book and film discussion series, as well as traveling exhibits, to sites throughout the state.

In addition, I have begun to collaborate more actively with scholars in the region to develop and fund a wider range of innovative, and culturally enriching, educational programs. Among these is a project—funded by the Connecticut Humanities Council—to develop an anthology of readings on Connecticut Life and culture consisting largely of primary materials: extracts from oral histories, diaries, journals and archival documents. (Among the proposed chapters are those on Native Americans, immigrants and ethnics, legend, folk songs, and traditional arts.) A precedent has been set in Connecticut for humanities scholars—folklorists, philosophers, historians and the like—working with state aging agencies to reach a special audience whose wellspring of experience may provide rewards both for those offering programs and those who follow the path of lifelong learning.

For Further Information

The booklet *Humanities Programs for Older Adults*, mentioned in this chapter, is designed primarily for use by program planners in Connecticut. However, a separate short work has been prepared, based on the Connecticut model, that offers a general approach to establishing public humanities programs for elders in any region. It presents a selected list of potentially helpful national institutions, a "generic" guide to finding local program resources, and profiles of successful projects from several states. Entitled *Humanities for Older Adults: A Brief Guide to Resources and Program Development*, it is available at no cost by contacting the Humanities Program Coordinator, Connecticut State Department on Aging, 175 Main Street, Hartford, CT 06106 (tel. 203-566-4810).

There are at present no books or articles that deal specifically with the application of the skills and insights of the folklorist to the development of humanities programs for older adults. But the materials described in this chapter all reflect in one way or another issues and subjects of concern to folklorists. As mentioned, NCOA's "Self-Discovery Through the Humanities" contains at least two units with much folklore material: "Exploring Local History" and "In the Old Ways." Copies of these and all of the NCOA anthologies are available on loan to any community group for use in programs for older adults (or for intergenerational programs). Many states have local repositories of NCOA materials.

For further information, contact the National Council on the Aging, 600 Maryland Avenue, S.W., Suite 100, Washington, D.C. 20024 (tel. 202-479-1200.

A few of the publications about older people and their lore are Roger D. Abrahams, *Almeda: A Singer and Her Songs* (Baton Rouge: Louisiana State Univ. Press, 1970); Joanne Bock, *Pop Wiener: Naive Painter* (Amherst: Univ. of Massachusetts Press, 1974); Sara Selene Faulds and Amy Skillman, "Biographies," in Simon J. Bronner, ed., *American Folk Art: A Guide to Sources* (New York and London: Garland, 1984), 96-116; Simon J. Bronner, *Chain Carvers: Old Men Crafting Meaning* (Lexington: Univ. Press of Kentucky, 1985); George Carey, "The Storyteller's Art and the Collector's Intrusion," in Linda Dégh, Henry Glassie, and Felix J. Oinas, eds., *Folklore Today: A Festschrift for Richard M. Dorson* (Bloomington: Indiana Univ. Press, 1976), 81-91; Richard M. Dorson, *Negro Folktales in Michigan* (Cambridge: Harvard Univ. Press, 1956); Verni Greenfield, *Making Do or Making Art: A Study of American Recycling* (Ann Arbor: UMI Research Press, 1986); Alan Jabbour, "Some Thoughts from a Folk Cultural Perspective," in Priscilla W. Johnston, ed., *Perspectives on Aging* (Cambridge, Mass.: Ballinger, 1981), 139-49; Michael Owen Jones, *Craftsman of the Cumberlands: Tradition and Creativity* (Lexington: Univ. Press of Kentucky, 1989); Jennie Keith, "'The Best Is Yet To Be': Towards an Anthropology of Age," *Annual Review of Anthropology* 9 (1980): 339-64; Roberta C. Krell, "Folklore and the Elderly: Aging, Creativity, and Community" (Ph.D. dissertation, University of California, Los Angeles, 1986); and Barbara Myerhoff, *Number Our Days* (New York: Dutton, 1979).

The reader might want to examine several other works as well. Charles L. Briggs's "Treasure Tales and Pedagogical Discourse in *Mexicano* New Mexico," *Journal of American Folklore* 98 (1985): 287-314, indicates how the "elders of bygone days" teach younger generations. See also Bess Lomax Hawes, "Folk Arts and the Elderly," in Thomas Vennum, ed., *Festival of American Folklife Program Book* (Washington, D.C.: Smithsonian Institution, 1984); Mary Hufford, Marjorie Hunt, and Steven Zeitlin, eds., *The Grand Generation: Memory, Mastery, Legacy* (Washington, D.C.: Smithsonian Institution, 1987); Sharon R. Kaufman, *The Ageless Self: Sources of Meaning in Late Life* (Madison: Univ. of Wisconsin Press, 1986); Barbara Kirshenblatt-Gimblett, "Objects of Memory: Material Culture as Life Review," in Elliott Oring, ed., *Folk Groups and Folklore Genres: A Reader* (Logan: Utah State Univ. Press, 1989), 329-38; Patrick B. Mullen, *Listening to Old Voices: Folklore, Life Stories, and the Elderly* (Urbana: Univ. of Illinois Press, 1992); and Dana Steward, *A Fine Age: Creativity as a Key to Successful Aging* (Little Rock: August House, 1984).

While aging itself is not usually the central theme of programs I have organized, I have sought out materials for discussion programs that feature positive portraits of older persons. As an example, for a film discussion series on "Traditional Arts and Music" ("traditional" being broadly defined to include naive, environmental, outsider, and so forth), one may choose among a wide variety of film portraits of older artists and musicians. Appalshop (P.O. Box 743A, Whitesburg, KY 41858 [tel. 606-633-0108]) alone has several titles. Among them are "Chairmaker" (22 min., color, 16mm/video), which depicts eighty-year-old Dewey Thompson talking about and demonstrating his craft of furniture building; "Oaksie" (22 min., color, 16mm/video), a portrait of basketmaker, fiddler and harp player Oaksie Caudill; "Quilting Women" (28 min., color, 16mm/

video), which traces the art of quiltmaking from piecing to the finale of a quilting bee; "Sourwood Mountain Dulcimers" (28 min., color, 16mm/video), featuring master dulcimer player J.D. Stamper passing on his skill to a young musician, John McCutcheon.

The Center for Southern Folklore (P.O. Box 40105, 1216 Peabody Ave., Memphis, TN 38104 [tel. 901-726-4205]) is another good source of films. It distributes such titles as "Leon 'Peck' Clark: Basketmaker" (15 min., color, 16mm/video), which presents scenes of basketmaking blended with reminiscences of Leon and Ada Clark's long life together; "Four Women Artists" (25 min., color, 16mm/video), a look at the memories and traditions of novelist Eudora Welty, quilter Pecolia Warner, embroiderer Ethel Mohamed, and painter Theora Hamblett; and "Bottle Up and Go" (18 min., color, 16mm/video), showing the lifestyle and music of a rural Mississippi black couple, Louis and Annie Mae Dotson.

Les Blank's Flower Films (10341 San Pablo Ave., El Cerritto, CA 94530 [tel. 415-525-0942]) is another treasure trove, featuring such portraits of elder musicians as "Hot Pepper" (54 min., color, 16mm) celebrating the Louisiana zydeco music of Clifton Chenier; "Sprout Wings and Fly" (30 min., color, 16mm), a document of old-time Appalachian fiddler Tommy Jarrell; and "A Well Spent Life" (44 min., color, 16mm), a tribute to the legendary Texas songster Mance Lipscomb.

Well worth viewing is a series of five films on older American naive and environmental artists, collectively titled "Visions of Paradise" (29 min. each, color, 16mm). Individual tiles include: "The Angel That Stands By Me," a portrait of an 88-year-old black visionary artist from Wilmington, North Carolina; "Grandma's Bottle Village," featuring 84-year-old Tressa Prisbrey's famous compound of fifteen houses constructed of bottles and full of creatively displayed found objects; and "Hundred and Two Mature" depicting Harry Lieberman, at age 102, sharing his art, philosophy, and love of life.

Another film worth mentioning for its sensitive portrayal of the creativity of people who happen to be old is "Water from Another Time" (29 min., color, 16mm/video), a documentary set in south central Indiana, that introduces three older artists: Lotus Dickey, composer and banjo player; Elmer Boyd, diarist and clock repairer; and Lois Doane, poet, painter, and batik maker. Produced by filmmaker Richard Kane and folklorist Dillon Bustin, it is available from Terra Nova Films Inc. (9848 S. Winchester Ave., Chicago, IL 60643 [tel. 312-881-8491]).

A film recently produced by Wes Graff for the University of Vermont is worth noting. "On My Own: The Traditions of Daisy Turner" (28 min., color, $1/2''$ and $3/4''$ video) is a portrait of a remarkable 102-year-old black woman, living in rural Vermont, who shares a rich body of family traditions and stories with Vermont folklorist Jane Beck. Many other films on older creative individuals are available; a good clearinghouse for information on films dealing with aging (including elder traditional artists) is the Educational Film library at the Brookdale Center on Aging of Hunter College, New York City (tel. 212-481-4330).

12

Reflecting and Creating an Occupation's Image

SUE SAMUELSON

When folklorists move from academe or public sector work to take jobs in the business world, the path is not always a straight one. Before assuming my current public relations position with an association representing county governments, I meandered through several fields of folklore-related activity. Those jobs included government contract work, consulting for arts organizations, and temporary teaching positions. I had seven jobs or consultancies in the three years following completion of my doctorate in folklore. These post-Ph.D. travails were not what I expected, but they represent a common pattern for young scholars, a kind of school of hard knocks I once heard described as the "purgatory of itinerant employment."

Finally I did come to rest somewhere, as the communications specialist for the Pennsylvania State Association of County Commissioners (PSACC) in Harrisburg, Pennsylvania. The PSACC represents the chief elected officials in Pennsylvania's sixty-seven counties plus their chief administrative and legal officers, known respectively as chief clerks and county solicitors. Its membership totals about 350 people. The association provides lobbying, education, and research services on a nonprofit, nonpartisan basis. As communications specialist, my responsibilities include writing and editing a monthly newsletter and producing less frequent publications such as conference programs, yearbooks, a history of the association, and various reports and surveys. A second major task is meeting planning, which includes promoting spring, summer, and fall conferences and coordinating their speakers, special events, trade shows, and hospitality activities. My third responsibility is supervising the office's main computer system as well as a second system that operates a telephone-based electronic bulletin board for our members.

Although relevant in several respects, the word "folklorist" is not in my job description; neither is "association management and public relations" likely to occur to folklorists as an employment opportunity. While I know of folklorists who do possess public relations and computer skills, they exhibit them either in government agencies or in business settings, not associations. Perhaps my nearest role models are the folklorists who have become involved in the study of corporate culture for I bring similar types of skills and tools, analytical and applied, to a new arena. Not only do I serve PSACC members as a technician but I also serve as a guide to help them understand their professional identity and their role in Pennsylvania's political networks. The commissioners ostensibly have the same occupation and address many of the same issues (taxes, prisons, elections, courts, social services, environmental concerns), but they need encouragement and a sense of common purpose in order to succeed in their jobs. The association, and my work in it, facilitates a feeling of belonging, of working together to achieve mutual goals. The PSACC is an organization with its own traditions and sense of history.

What Do Associations Do?

Folklorists and people working in related fields may best understand the role of associations by considering their own membership in professional societies such as the American Folklore Society, the American Anthropological Association, or the Modern Language Association. Collectively known as trade and professional associations, these groups represent a mind-boggling array of occupations, hobbies, and special interest groups. They include doctors, restaurant owners, stamp collectors, peach growers, retired persons, teachers, bankers, journalists, and dog owners. There are 21,000 national associations in the United States alone, representing more than 173,000,000 individuals and firms. Approximately 567,000 people are employed by national associations, for an aggregate payroll of $15.6 billion. On the local, state, and regional levels, there are about 500,000 additional associations, although some have little or no paid staff, according to the American Society of Association Executives.

Association management is an industry in itself and is one of the growth areas for employment in the 1990s. Association staffs have their own support groups, such as the American Society of Association Executives (ASAE) and its state and local chapters. ASAE is particularly known for its CAE program, a course of study, training, and testing, plus practical experience, which leads to a member's designation as a Certified Association Executive.

Trade, professional, or special interest associations perform a variety of functions and employ a wide range of people. Their emphasis is on external and internal promotion of the group's cause, product, or service. Associations seek visibility and understanding of what their members do. This goal

frequently manifests itself in lobbying state or federal agencies or legisla-
tures for money, changes in regulations, or creation of new programs. External activities include outreach efforts to educate a broader public about the
group's concerns. Such activities include outright marketing campaigns,
such as the Beef Industry Council's ads describing beef as "Real Food for
Real People," or more altruistic concerns such as health screenings by the
American Heart Association.

For the folklorist, one of the most intriguing aspects of associations is
their internal work. Associations stimulate a sense of identity, of working
toward common goals. They are excellent vantage points from which to observe group patterns of work or behavior. Associations formalize the idea of a
folk group, a collection of people sharing a common bond and expressing it
in a variety of ways. This may be accomplished via political action or presentation of information or opinions. But association members also share speech
or slang expressions, stories and anecdotes, group history, ceremonies and
festivities, songs and costumes; all are genres easily recognized as traditional
expressions of group identity or behavior.

Folklorists have frequently studied work groups with a well-established
sense of tradition, a long history, and/or obvious symbolic displays of group
identity such as sailors, loggers, miners, cowboys, and railroaders. In recent
years more modern professional groups have become the focus of folklorists'
attention (e.g., trial lawyers, doctors, firefighters, even folklorists themselves), along with special interest groups such as science fiction fans. But
researchers have paid scant attention to associations representing these
groups. I would have ignored them too had I not stumbled into this job. I
recognized the potential power of an association to shape (or reshape) its
members' perceptions and actions, and the behavior of a "folk" group. This
power is bestowed, however, by the group itself. The association must respond to its members' basic beliefs and ways of acting or else the formal
organization will be abandoned. The following review of my work with the
PSACC details some methods in which occupational identity, group awareness, and expressive behaviors are displayed, acknowledged, reinforced, or
modified in an association setting.

The Role of a Folklorist

Many of the activities and events that can influence the county commissioners' sense of identity either originate in or are delegated to my office.
My title, communications specialist, makes this rather obvious. It would be
difficult for commissioners, chief clerks, and solicitors to share common
goals and a sense of cohesiveness if they did not communicate with one

another, especially since the 350 members are scattered among 67 counties. Social, economic, and political issues can vary dramatically from county to county. What binds commissioners together are (1) statutory designations of the responsibilities of the office of county commissioner; (2) commissioners' expressed need to unite against a common enemy, usually proposed legislation or state agencies' regulations; and (3) their desire for continuing education on how to do their jobs more effectively. By law, commissioners share the same duties. But the creation of new laws and regulations often makes their jobs more complex. There is no "school" or established course of study for new commissioners, except the training offered by the PSACC. By law, anyone can be a commissioner as long as she or he has been a resident of the county for one year, is eighteen years of age, and has not been convicted of certain crimes. Commissioners' jobs are considered full-time, but commissioners often continue to practice their other occupations, whether they are farmers, lawyers, teachers, sales representatives, mechanics, dentists, nurses, or truckers. Given these disparate backgrounds the Pennsylvania State Association of County Commissioners is even more important in coordinating group efforts toward mutual goals and in creating a sense of common ground.

If commissioners must work together, they need to feel connected to one another. The association serves as a focal point, disseminating information and coordinating public and private action to accomplish collective objectives. Each staff member supplies special skills in this regard. My contribution to developing this sense of purpose and group identity for commissioners concentrates on three areas: meetings, publications, and informal contacts. In folklorists' terms, I work primarily with ceremonies and festivities and oral history, as well as what I call informal encouragement of group identity.

Association Ceremonies

The commissioners are physically in the same place at the same time only three times a year. These infrequent contacts are of necessity very intense. Much information is conveyed and actions are planned within a limited amount of time. Part of my job is to convince the members to attend these meetings. I then help orchestrate the events so that the attendees have ample opportunity to meet one another, share information (often anecdotal and repeated, and in the form of stories), make contacts, agree on joint action, and recognize the group's success and individuals' contributions.

The highlight of the year is the PSACC's Annual Conference (known in the vernacular as "the convention"), which has been held continuously since 1887. It is attended by about 250 members plus spouses, children, other county and state officials, and vendors, bringing the total attendance to approximately 550. It begins on a Sunday afternoon in early August, followed by three and a half days of speakers, breakout sessions, committee meetings, the annual business meeting, luncheons, receptions, awards ceremony, trade show, sporting events, and tours, and culminating in the annual banquet. The association's budget for this meeting is approximately $70,000 and does not include commissioners' room and travel costs. (Commissioners are reimbursed by their counties for their expenses but must pay for family costs.) Interestingly, one of the reasons the commissioners sought legislation that "officially" created the PSACC in 1913 was to authorize the expenditure of public funds to defray these convention costs.

The annual conference is anticipated by the membership all year. An illustration of the members' involvement in the event is that they in fact select the site. This is done three years in advance and is based on recommendations from the executive committee. The members do not blindly follow the committee, however. While paying heed to the need to rotate locations throughout the state, and selecting from downtown, suburban, and resort properties, the membership has been known to override committee choices.

The annual conference is recognized as the one event that brings most everyone together. The importance of this concept is dramatically expressed by the desire to be "under one roof," meaning all participants housed in one hotel. This qualification often conflicts with the conference's other requirements. The association needs a facility with at least 310 rooms and extensive meeting and banquet space. Outside of downtown Pittsburgh and Philadelphia, there are only a handful of hotels, mainly resorts, that can meet this requirement. If we were to abide strictly by our members' preferences there would be a conflict with rotating the conference to various parts of the state. But when the "one roof rule" was first broken by selecting two hotels in Erie (a somewhat hard-to-reach city in the northwestern corner of the state) for the 1989 annual conference, there was, and continues to be, considerable grumbling and threats of boycotts. However, the selection of an unfamiliar site has encouraged other groups of counties to lobby for conferences in their areas where multiple properties will have to be used. The situation reveals an issue of fundamental importance—the need for unity (being together) and the desire for fairness (going to all parts of the state). A few counties cannot dominate an issue, including the choice of sites for the Association's major meeting.

Once a site is selected the planning of the annual conference reverts to the staff, with guidance from the executive committee (officers, regional representatives, committee chairs). My main responsibilities include (1) coordinating the program of speakers, sessions, meals, and special events as well as producing a printed program; (2) scripting introductory remarks and major presentations such as the awards luncheon and banquet; (3) directing the trade show with approximately thirty-five vendor booths; (4) soliciting sponsors for conference items and events (briefcases, printing costs, coffee breaks, meals, receptions, outings); (5) coordinating evening hospitality suites; and (6) working with other staff on family and recreational events.

This type of work draws on my own talents and interests in planning and attending to detail, but it also is affected by my training as a folklorist, particularly my professional interest in festival, ritual, and ceremony. I have long been interested in American celebrations, from major holidays to smaller expressions such as birthday parties. As a potential avenue of research, conventions intrigue me as a kind of "secular ritual" or a celebration of special identities, from Beatles fans to Shriners, plastic surgeons, or Daughters of the American Revolution. Now, instead of doing "pure" research, I find myself putting my knowledge of celebratory behavior to work.

What I do is more than just the nuts and bolts of meeting planning. I have to consider what the members want to accomplish in terms of group action, training, or information sharing. It is not enough just to bring them to the same place and engage in the same activities. There has to be occasion for personal interaction, for recognition of special achievements, for humor, and for venting frustration at the people and things that get in the way of commissioners doing their job. Despite the possibility of the press perceiving the convention as a perk or junket, we must offer many types of social events as well as formal sessions with speakers and panel discussions. People talk more over a meal or on a boat trip than they do sitting in neat rows in a meeting room. We schedule "cracker barrel" discussions in which a panel of commissioners introduces topics of general concern and the attendees can complain, compare notes, and offer alternative approaches, often expressed in the form of stories, traditional expressions, and other folklore. We encourage audience participation routines in selecting banquet entertainment because commissioners love being in the limelight, especially among a group of their peers. This tendency is also reflected in the annual awards luncheon in which commissioners are recognized for things as varied as their commitment to conservation and transportation safety to their prowess on the tennis court or the golf course. Recognition of incoming and outgoing officers occurs at the annual banquet. Both events, held on the same day at the end of the conference, instill feelings of pride, accomplishment, and success in a group endeavor. They do not occur, however, without a lot of behind-the-scenes work. Yet ultimately the success of the ceremonies is in the hands of those who attend. They never falter in their mission to congratulate themselves and the individual contributions of service to the group.

The success of the annual conference and the staff work involved in producing is evident in the high attendance, the year-round anticipation, and the compliments the staff receives. But to provide continuity in bringing the members together, the Association also produces two other conferences, one in spring and one in late fall. They are smaller (200-250 attendees) and shorter (one and a half days) and are always held in Harrisburg so that commissioners can meet with legislators and in order to reduce pressure on the staff. These meetings have many of the same goals as the annual conference—information sharing, networking, informal discussion over meals or in hospitality suites. They are less intense but serve to keep the feeling of community alive in the intervals between the annual conferences. Folklorists might compare the situation to the effect of meetings of local and regional folklore societies, often held in the spring as a way of bringing people together at a time other than the American Folklore Society meeting in October.

When I plan a conference I do not spend much time consciously thinking about applying the theories of festivity I learned in school. But familiar patterns of celebratory behavior are an integral part of the conferences. These include feasts (the banquet); a sense of being in a special, well-bounded time and place; a spirit of playfulness (outings to baseball games or theme parks or on-site events such as barbecues); an occasion for excess (after-hours drinking); egalitarian participation (all members are welcome), and functions as a seasonal marker (looking forward to August as "convention time").

These components are built into the meetings. They are expectations that must be met, slots that must be filled. I acknowledge the importance of the commissioners' conference traditions but also conduct the backstage mechanics by which the public event is produced. Since I know what the members like and want in their meetings, my work is similar to that involved in any celebratory function—publicizing the event, procuring food and drink, coordinating entertainment, planning the program, and ensuring ritual correctness. It is on a larger scale than a birthday party or family holiday observance but makes use of the same planning skills and reveals many of the goals common to celebrations everywhere.

Association Publications and History

A second major area of my job that involves reinforcing the commissioners' sense of group identity is in publications. It is not the regular publications that accomplish this as much as some of the specialty items I have produced. A monthly newsletter does help to maintain communications and keep ideas flowing. It establishes ties between individual members and the idea of the association, specifically the information coming from the headquarters, the staff, the corporate entity that serves them. The newsletter examines common problems and goals, but issues of group identity and behavior are not paramount (except perhaps in photographs or publicity items relating to the conferences). The publication that has done the most for Association/commissioner identity is the *Centennial History of the Pennsylvania State Association of County Commissioners*, published in 1986 as part of the organization's 100th anniversary celebration. I conducted the oral history interviews that served as the basis for writing the history. A grant from the Pennsylvania Historical and Museum Commission subsidized the cost of tapes and my travel around the state to interview current and former county commissioners and PSACC staff about the association's history and the changes experienced in the position of county commissioner. In addition to the interviews I also collected archival evidence on the association's past—yearbooks, membership directories, minutes of meetings, platform statements—and did background reading on the growth of county government and on state and local relations in general.

Published in an 8 1/2" x 11" paperback format, the book has twenty-six pages and eight photographs. It reviews the growth of the Association from an informal self-help group founded in the late nineteenth century to its "re-creation" by the state legislature in 1913, its use of volunteer staff and administration by committee in the 1940s and 1950s, the acquisition of a paid staff in the 1960s, and tremendous growth in size and clout in the 1970s and 1980s. These changes are paralleled by the assumption of new responsibilities on the part of commissioners, beginning with social pressures created by increasing populations in the post-World War II era, the Great Society programs emanating from Washington, changes in the state constitution in 1968, and the growth of state-mandated human services programs in the 1970s.

Production expenses for the book were subsidized by a corporate contribution. It was published in time for the 1986 Annual Conference, the association's 100th such meeting. A special yearbook with individual county pages featuring group photos and text on county history and tourist attractions was also published for the first time since the mid-1970s. (Publication had ceased because of problems with IRS regulations that have since been resolved.)

The history was very well received and has gone into a second printing. Since there is frequent turnover in the commissioner's office (a rate of about 40 percent in each of the last quadrennial elections) there are few commissioners who have been in office for more than eight or twelve years, although there are some members who were honored in 1986 for twenty, thirty, and even fifty years of service (the latter was a chief clerk). Given the limited time in office and the fact that many commissioners' contact with the association is limited to newsletters and meetings, the centennial publications provided a significant opportunity to instill a sense of history in the members, not only with regard to the office of commissioner but also in terms of the association. This point is an important one that became much clearer through the solicitation of oral history. There is identity as a county commissioner and identity as an association member. The first is broader, more open to variation and idiosyncrasy. It depends on citizens' perceptions of the office and the officeholder and it is influenced by local political networks and social and economic climates. Commissioner identity is shared with fellow commissioners, but the sense of being a *group* is nurtured within the context of the association. It is in association activities that commissioners more clearly display their sense of cooperation and mutual efforts. And it is the Association staff that produces the ceremonies and written texts and orchestrates opportunities for replaying personal experiences.

As the researcher and author of the *Centennial History* I made considerable use of my fieldwork experience in developing contacts in a community and conducting interviews, as well as using technical skills involving photographic and sound recording equipment and doing tape transcriptions. I needed to know about the grants process (sources, budgets, follow-up reports) and about archival procedures. On a limited scale, I produced the kind of company history that has been popular with businesses in recent years. Since "doing a history" is so much more understandable to people than "collecting their folklore," it was an excellent way of getting to know commissioners and understanding the workings of the association, both for me and for them. It was also published at the same time as a special *Report of the Committee on the Future of Counties*, a document produced by PSACC officers and staff that detailed the current state of many county programs and offered recommendations for change. *The Centennial History* and the Committee on the Future's report complemented each other during the association's 100th year. The group's strength was enhanced by an awareness of where it had been and by presenting a blueprint for what it wanted to be.

Informal Exchange

In addition to formal actions on my part as the communications specialist, I also find myself dealing with the issue of association culture or commissioner culture on a more informal basis. I come into contact with commissioners frequently, usually on the phone but sometimes on their home turf, as when I interviewed people for the oral history, or at committee meetings or conferences. When they request information or answer my own questions the issue at hand is not only the particular problem being addressed but also how the response is conveyed. I act as a clearinghouse or point of reference but often suggest they contact other commissioners for advice or examples on how a problem was solved elsewhere. Information sharing is also encouraged in high-tech fashion with Access, the association's electronic bulletin board that commissioners can use with a touch-tone phone. They can record requests for information or listen to updates on legislative activities, conference agendas, and committee meetings. It will never replace the face-to-face interaction and exchange of ideas found at the conferences. But as an association service, it does call attention to the organization as an entity that responds to commissioners' problems or need for information.

Other Skills

In addition to my particular job responsibilities outlined above and the adaptation of folklore-related concepts and methods, I also use some general skills that I acquired or refined in the process of getting my Ph.D. These include the ability to research an issue, gather background information and raw data, and then analyze and interpret it. My writing skills are obviously necessary for the publications I produce, although writing newsletters is a far cry from obtuse academic prose. (I did get my start on newsletters, however, by producing a folklore department newsletter when I was at UCLA and editing *The Digest*, a foodways newsletter, while I attended the University of Pennsylvania.) The application of research abilities, analytical thinking, organizational skills, attention to detail, and written and verbal communications skills to "real world" jobs is nothing new for ex-academics. It is not what many expected to do with their training, but, because of the state of the academic job market, well-trained people have been forced to examine other opportunities. By and large they have thrived in them.

Organizational Communications and Folklore

The opportunities for professionally trained folklorists have been steadily expanding over the last ten or fifteen years. Employment can be sought in federal, state, and some local agencies, in museums, arts organizations, and even in the corporate sector. Folklore, which started as a field of study and then turned into a profession, has now become an industry. Its interdisciplinary nature produces workers who are well prepared to succeed in more than one setting.

I believe I am the only folklorist working in a trade association; I am not the only one employed in a situation where my primary occupational identity is not as a folklorist. I describe myself as a PR person, or as being in association management. I took this job in part because I was disillusioned with trying to get a more recognizable "folklore job" that would pay a decent salary and last for more than twelve months. But despite my serendipitous employment opportunity with the PSACC I have found ways to put my training to good use. I have to be careful about how I present things sometimes, especially to fellow staff members. I often warn them when I am about to start "talking like an anthroplogist." (Many people have little idea what a folklorist is. The identities "anthropologist" and "historian" are fraught with problems, too, but sometimes seem preferable, depending on to whom one is speaking.)

I was lucky to have job skills that are in demand in the association management marketplace (and in the public and private sectors). I know something about computers and word processing. I had an internship in a corporate setting (producing a multi-ethnic festival for employees). I can write a clear and grammatically correct sentence. My having written a dissertation demonstrates an ability to take on a project and complete it.

Association managers will rarely understand the value of hiring an employee with folklore training without an effective presentation by the job-seeker. The same situation exists with regard to executives in other industries who are hiring specialists in organizational communications. They need to be convinced that someone with a folklore background will be a better choice than other candidates with more mainstream experience. Points to keep in mind for such "presentations of self" include:

1. The interdisciplinary nature of folklore can be conveyed as the potential for versatility on the job. Associations are almost always understaffed so someone hired to edit a newsletter may soon find herself writing summaries of research reports or producing a specialized publication. A prospective employee needs to emphasize the many things a folklorist does: researching background data, writing grant proposals, going to new communities and getting to know people, conducting interviews, making public presentations, analyzing data, and preparing material for publication. Since it is obvious that this individual is changing career areas, it is important to stress the ability of the folklorist to evaluate and adapt to new situations, again by offering fieldwork examples. Because of her or his educational background, it is usually obvious that a folklorist has the intellectual capacity to handle a new job. What needs to be demonstrated are the accompanying social skills and commitment to accepting new responsibilities.

2. Folklorists in career transitions are fortunate that the concept of corporate (or organizational) culture has become more than just a buzz-

word. Because of publicity in the popular press, most executives understand basic notions of worker identity, at least as it applies to large organizations. They may not have applied such concepts to members of their own association (or company) but will probably understand the train of thought when a folklorist-potential employee presents it. By doing so, the folklorist demonstrates creativity and an openness to new ideas. An employer will value these with regard to any worker but may also be intrigued by the potential application of the concept of cultural identity to the members of a specific association.

The folklorist, however, still needs to provide concrete examples of how cultural identity can be assessed and utilized for the association's purposes, such as increasing membership, planning more effective educational programs, or initiating outreach efforts to the general public. By administering questionnaires, conducting interviews or small group discussions with an association's members, or researching an association's history, the folklorist can elicit concrete evidence of what members think is important about their work (or hobby or cause) and determine what kinds of support and services are needed to nurture that identity.

3. In addition to the folklorist's general understanding of notions of community is the ability to recognize associated forms of expression, such as stories, songs, customs, and ceremonies. Again, the association employer will want the folklorist to provide examples of practical applications to a particular group of people and the organization that represents them. In such instances, the folklorist-worker should be prepared to discover and describe the ways in which people express themselves within the context of the association and how new forms might be created, introduced, and evaluated for success or failure. What must be emphasized is the folklorist's contribution to the success of an association via increased membership and participation in association activities. These changes affect the bottom line in terms of dues, conference registration fees, and subscriptions to publications. The folklorist can contribute innovative approaches that are also income producing. The executives of non-profit associations understand this outcome as well as any other manager.

Conclusion

Although a folklorist may be intrigued, and ultimately satisfied, by the possibilities presented by nontraditional employment, there are less positive aspects to be considered as well. For me, it is not always easy to accept the fact that I have abandoned the academic career path that once seemed so certain. While I envision a good future for myself in association management

I sometimes wonder if I made the right choice. The demands of my new field also limit my involvement in the old. I go to fewer folklore meetings, do less research and writing, find myself somewhat out of touch with colleagues. But by choosing employment in association management I also anticipate gaining more experience in the very issues that induced me to study folklore. Perhaps that is the festival specialist in me dreaming about the future, but it always has been an integral part of my personality to love parties and celebrations. It is what led me to studying festivals in the first place. Although I cannot discount the effect my training has on my job performance, I must acknowledge preexisting inclinations as well.

This is an issue to be considered whatever folklore students and scholars set out to do. We are attracted to folklore for very personal reasons, and they will continue to affect our choice of what to do with it. I have always been interested in what makes people come together, how they form bonds and live and work and play together, be it families or friends or colleagues. By a very roundabout way I have now found an environment that allows me to satisfy my curiosity about issues of personal significance, and for which I have the training and skills to explore. No matter what the area of expertise, any worker would be grateful for such a reward.

For Further Information

Most of the general works on nontraditional employment for former academics are focussed on corporate jobs. One book that reviews several university programs for "retooling" people with Ph.D.'s is *Teaching and Beyond: Nonacademic Career Programs for Ph.D.'s*, edited by Kevin P. Reilly and Sheila A. Murdick (Albany, N.Y.: Teaching and Beyond Project of the University of the State of New York, 1984). As a basic guide for job hunting, resume writing, and image building I have relied on Marcia R. Fox's manual, *Putting Your Degree to Work* (New York: Norton, 1979). A broad model of my involvement in creating and reinforcing an organization's image is that advanced by Terrence E. Deal and Allan A. Kennedy in *Corporate Cultures: The Rites and Rituals of Corporate Life* (Reading, Mass.: Addison-Wesley, 1982).

The American Society of Association Executives (1575 Eye St., N.W., Washington, D.C. 20005) has produced several publications of interest to readers interested in the profession, including *Principles of Association Management, A Professional's Handbook*, 2nd ed. (1988), *Fundamentals of Association Management: Conventions* (1985), *Policies and Procedures in Association Management* (1987), *Managing Membership Societies* (1979), and *A Coming of Age, A History of the Profession of Association Management* (1987). Also of help is a pamphlet entitled "A Career Guide to Associations" published by the Greater Washington Society of Association Executives.

For job-hunting purposes an excellent source is the *Encyclopedia of Associations*, 22nd ed. (Detroit: Gale Research Company, 1988).

One of my first forays into the use of folklore beyond the ivory tower was as an expert witness in a trial involving the display of nativity scenes on government property. A review of my experience can be found in Sue Samuelson, "Folklore and the Legal System: The Expert Witness," *Western Folklore* 41 (1982): 139-44.

There are several theoretically-inclined sources that examine concepts of festivity that can be applied to conventions and meeting planning. They include Richard Allen Chase, "Fairs and Festivals," *Man-Environment Systems* 7 (1977): 117-44; Harvey Cox, *The Feast of Fools* (Cambridge: Harvard Univ. Press, 1969); and Sally F. Moore and Barbara Myerhoff, eds., *Secular Ritual* (Assen/Amsterdam: Van Gorcum, 1977).

Folklorists have studied many groups of people, social settings, and sets of experiences. Much of the research is reported at scholarly meetings before it is published, if it is published at all. At the American Folklore Society meeting in 1976, for example, Michael Taft read a paper on "Draft Dodgers in Canada: A Large, Uncommunicative Group." Among the presentations at the AFS meeting in 1984 were Charmaine Grey, "Another Man's Treasure" (on garage sales); Karin E. Becker, "Getting the Moment: Newspaper Photojournalists at Work"; Robert Modrow, "Survival Symbols: Managing the Culture of a M.A.S.H. Unit"; Joseph P. Goodwin, "Real Men Don't Use Vaseline: Humor and Conflict in the Gay World"; and Roberta Krell, "The Folklorist and the Elderly." At the 1985 AFS meeting there were papers on the traditions and lore of lawyers, punk rock performers and followers, the elderly, textile mill workers, housewives, and the ill and disabled.

For published sources, see Jan Harold Brunvand, *The Study of American Folklore: An Introduction* 2nd ed. (New York: Norton, 1978), especially Ch. 3, "Folk Groups: Bearers of American Folk Tradition"; Richard M. Dorson, ed., *Handbook of American Folklore* (Bloomington: Indiana Univ. Press, 1983), particularly articles in the section called "American Settings"; and Elliott Oring, ed., *Folk Groups and Folklore Genres* (Logan: Utah State Univ. Press, 1986).

For publications about folklorists themselves as subjects of research, see Richard Reuss, "That Can't Be Alan Dundes. Alan Dundes Is Taller Than That!" *Journal of American Folklore* 87 (1974): 303-17; Richard A. Reuss and Jens Lund, eds., *Roads into Folklore: Festschrift in Honor of Richard M. Dorson* (Bloomington: Folklore Forum Bibliographic and Special Series, No. 14); and Lee Haring, "'. . . And You Put the Load Right on Me': Alternative Informants in Folklore," in Gerald Cashion, ed., *Conceptual Problems in Contemporary Folklore Study* (Bloomington: Folklore Forum Bibliographic and Special Series, no. 12, 1974), 64-68.

A panel at the American Folklore Society meeting in 1986 combined the topic of folklorists as subjects of research with issues of applied folklore. Called "Music, Live and Analyzed: Folklorists as Performers," the panel was chaired by Graham S. Kash with Thomas A. Adler as discussant. Twenty-minute presentations included "Folklorist as Performer: Pros and Cons," by Richard Blaustein; "Performing Blues for Fun and Profit," by David Evans; "The Folklorist as Guest Artist in the Public Schools: Music to Teach and Entertain," by Bettye C. Kash; and "Harping on Harmonica Tradition," by Graham S. Kash.

13

Helping Craftsmen and Communities Survive: Folklore and Economic Development

Patricia Atkinson Wells

In the two decades following the publication of Michael Owen Jones's seminal article "Folk Craft Production and the Folklorist's Obligation" (1970), folklorists have been plagued by the problem of how simultaneously to insure the economic survival of individual folk artisans and to preserve the traditions and culture of which they are a part. Much has been written on the history and impact of crafts assistance programs in the United States and on the role of the folklorist in marketing folk art, most notably in a special issue of *New York Folklore* (1986). However, we are still faced with the fundamental dilemma—are individual economic security and cultural survival mutually exclusive? Do we imperil tradition when we advocate expanding a maker's market? Can we mitigate or minimize the effects of our well-meaning cultural intervention and, if so, how?

Another group of professionals, with very different training, expertise, and purview have encountered a parallel problem in their work. I am speaking of rural development specialists. Like folklore studies, rural development is an interdisciplinary field. Depending on the region and the project, agronomists, economists, environmentalists, sociologists, bureaucrats, capitalists, and a host of other specialists may all be concerned with or involved in the development of a rural area. (Although I am focusing on rural development, folklore studies relates to the broader concept of "community development" inasmuch as folklorists can go into any community, rural or urban, and contribute to the analysis and solution of many of the community's problems and needs.)

A tension exists between the very real problems of contemporary rural economies and the need to develop public policies that sustain rural ways of life. The problem, then, is how to strengthen communities economically while preserving their culture and environment.

Historically, rural economies have been founded on land-based businesses, such as forestry and agriculture, and home-based businesses, including the production of handmade objects. The small family farm is no longer economically viable in many areas of the country, and large-scale farming has also become a financial disaster for many in the wake of changing government policies. Rural development specialists are looking increasingly at the raising of specialty crops and rare livestock breeds, as well as the production of fine foods and indigenous crafts, to provide economic bases in rural areas while sustaining the aesthetic qualities of country living.

This chapter is a brief analysis of the politics of economic development in a rural area of western Massachusetts. The nexus of rural development and folklore—crafts marketing—presented through a case study, serves as the focal point.

The Hilltown Projects

As stated previously, the economic development of rural areas is a thorny problem. Many small towns suffer from economic decay and would welcome growth and new jobs. On the other hand, growth often threatens the quality of rural life. Land is developed or put to uses that may not be in the long-term public interest, and the aesthetic qualities of the countryside rapidly alter amid added roads and housing developments. Community economic development, no matter how benign or well-intentioned, is a type of cultural intervention and, as such, has the potential to enhance or disrupt the life of the community.

The Hilltown Community Development Corporation

The Hilltown Community Development Corporation (HCDC), a private nonprofit organization dedicated to rural economic development, was founded in 1981 after a study conducted by the Center for Rural Communities at the University of Massachusetts (Amherst) showed a hidden economy of small businesses within a ten-town area of Hampshire County known as "the Hilltowns." Business owners in these sparsely populated areas face obstacles inherent in every business (such as arranging credit and financing, promotion, marketing, and advertising), as well as the difficulties created by the very rural nature of the area. In addition, the majority of Hilltowners do most of their business *outside* the hilltowns, in the nearby urban centers of Pittsfield and Northampton.

Funded primarily through grants from state agencies, the HCDC's mission was, and is, to support and build on the Hilltown economy by "helping people to help themselves." They set about this by offering a wide range of loan programs, technical assistance and courses to educate the small business person, pilot studies and programs to begin or expand land-based businesses, the publication and distribution of a Hilltown Business Directory, and, more recently, through job training and housing rehabilitation programs.

The Hilltown Artisans Guild

In 1984, I went to work as a consultant and project director for the HCDC. I was selected for this position because my particular combination of skills and experience *as a folklorist*—among which were a knowledge of traditional arts, crafts and festivals; experience with community, educational, and cultural organizations; and the ability to communicate through writing, editing, teaching, and public presentations—were deemed desirable by the HCDC and appropriate to the particular job. I was charged with organizing a nascent association of artists and craftspeople with a view toward forming a marketing cooperative. The HCDC had previously incubated a successful association of local bed and breakfast operators and was also attempting to organize marketing groups for agricultural producers—focusing on the maple and honey industries.

Spurred by the suggestions of a board member who was both a craftsperson and a small business owner/operator, the HCDC held an open meeting to determine the number of craftspeople living and working in the Hilltowns, the range of crafts represented, and whether there was an interest in, and need for, the formation of an organization of Hilltown craftspeople.

Nearly fifty people attended this meeting, many bringing samples of their work. These products ranged from clothing to pottery, stained glass, jewelry, weaving, painting, and sculpture. They also included "folk arts" and other revivalist Americana like tole paintings and quilts as well as authentic traditional forms such as baskets and wood carvings. Some artists had been academically trained; some had learned their crafts traditionally within their families or as apprentices; others were self-taught. Some had well-established businesses, while others were attempting to make the transition from avocation to vocation with their crafts. Their needs were correspondingly varied. Some people were looking primarily for an informational and/or communicative network through which to share problems, advice, and strategies; some were in need of business counseling or aid in finding a market for their products; and some were looking for potential collaborators to help them develop and market new product lines. *All* seemed to believe in the power of an organization to achieve their desired goals. The Hilltown Artisans Guild was born.

Though I expected to use my administrative experience in helping this group organize, I initially gave little thought to the ways in which my folkloristic training might be of use. In my two-year tenure as "coordinator" of the Hilltown Artisans Guild, I found myself relying increasingly on techniques and perspectives of folklore study, particularly in matters of organization development and policy analysis. I was simultaneously a fieldworker, a cultural architect, and a cultural interpreter. My job was to help clarify and codify the identities, needs and desires of individuals into an ethos for the Hilltown Artisans Guild and to serve as the spokesperson and liaison for the group.

The executive director of the HCDC had great plans for the Hilltown Artisans Guild, including the opening and operation of a cooperative gallery and shop with ongoing crafts demonstrations, and mail-order marketing through a Hilltown catalog. Her ideas were, to a large extent, predicated on what was potentially "fundable"—for the kinds of pilot projects that government agencies would grant operating and administrative funds. Politically, the HCDC needed to establish a track record of highly visible and successful projects and of successful funding proposals. The Hilltown Artisans Guild seemed a natural for grant support for several reasons: (1) crafts marketing deals with the production and aesthetic qualities of material objects and is therefore highly visual; (2) most craftspeople have low incomes, and many of the Hilltown Artisans could be officially designated as "rural poor"; (3) precedent has been set historically for crafts assistance programs in community economic development; and (4) tourism and the marketing of native products had strong support in the state administration of the time. In fact, there was just one stumbling block to the merchandizing of Hilltown crafts—the Hilltown Artisans Guild. Guild members were neither willing nor able to engage in such grandiose schemes at this early stage in the development of their organization.

Unshared Visions

In her cogent article "Unshared Visions: Folklife and Politics in a Rural Community" (1988), Jean Haskell Speer analyzes the politics of public programming in a three-year oral history and folklife project in a rural area in Virginia. She discusses the conflicting public and private agenda for cultural change and points out that within a community there are both congruent and divergent points of view, cultural assumptions and cultural self-images. Speer also makes reference to the "public persona" of the project—the public presentation or collective vision of the project's accomplishments as opposed to daily operations, conflicts and challenges, decisions and dilemmas that reveal the political dimension of the project.

The concepts of public persona and unshared vision are germane to the study of any organization and are particularly important in understanding the relationship of external (or exoteric) agencies and/or projects to the community or communities that they intend to serve.

Members of the board of directors and administrative officers of the Hilltown Community Development Corporation, as it existed in 1984-1985, were primarily non-native Hilltowners. Former urbanites who were part of the latter-day back-to-the-land movement, the prime movers were political activists and therefore well-versed in government bureaucracies and grantsmanship. While they *did* represent the most recent wave of migration to the Hilltowns, and the transition of many of those towns from farming communities to bedroom communities, they were not representative of the traditional native residents in those communities they wished to serve. While these newcomers were sincere in their wish to preserve country living, they were often at odds with native Hilltowners over what aspects of rural life were valuable and worthy of preservation. The HCDC was distrusted as a bunch of "do-gooders" by many of the more conservative Hilltowners, who viewed government grants either as charity or a waste of tax money—to be despised and avoided. Despite the number of Hilltowners who became voting members of the HCDC (over 300), the organization and its projects and programs were regarded by many Hilltown residents as having little to do with them, and not to be taken too seriously.

My position as coordinator of the Artisans Guild was rather unusual. Although I am not a native, I did marry a fifth-generation native Hilltowner. We were living on the family farm and I had worked with and studied Hilltowners and Hilltown culture for nearly a decade. Thus, I was accorded a sort of "honorary native" status. I knew and understood native points of view, although I did not necessarily share them.

Developing the Hilltown Artisans Guild into an organization that had meaning for, and provided the desired services to, its members was a long and challenging process. Though members agreed that they wanted to form a guild, there was a lack of agreement regarding the function of that guild. Predictably, the group went through a period of idealism, intense enthusiasm, and energy, followed by one of disillusionment and frustration, culminating in a new vision of purpose and priorities—a commitment to practical and do-able goals and objectives. This pattern of development was complicated by pressures from the parent or sponsoring organization (HCDC) to meet *its* goals and objectives for the guild.

Crafts Marketing: The Hilltown Solution

Though all marketing has sales as an ultimate goal, the variables of what goods and where, how and by whom they will be sold make the development of marketing strategies highly individual. What works for commercial products is not necessarily appropriate for fine handcrafted objects; nor is the way to sell a quilt necessarily effective for baskets or jewelry. How then does one form a marketing plan for an organization of people who make a diverse variety of items?

The HCDC's solution was to focus on *place*. The work of guild members would be sold under a Hilltown label and logo from a central location— a Hilltown gallery and/or a catalog. However, this plan did not take into account the enormous difficulty of mass-producing handmade objects; nor did it satisfy the makers' desire to have their products reflect their personal identities rather than a somewhat anonymous "Hilltown" designation. For the artists, *individual* identity and recognition in relation to their art held primacy; for the HCDC, *group* identification was primary.

Another approach is that of developing new products—as in so-called "tourist art"—which can be sold as souvenirs of a particular locale.

Folklorists who have advocated the involvement of their profession in the marketing of folk art have tended to approach the problem from two tacks: (1) directly, either as agents for craftspeople and their wares, or as entrepreneurs, actually buying and reselling objects; and (2) more circumspectly, attempting to broaden the market for folk arts by educating the general public regarding the forms and their aesthetic qualities and the complexity and skill required in the technical processes of object production, through exhibits, demonstrations, fairs and festivals, and folk artist residency programs. While the long-term goal of changing the status accorded folk artists and their creative output is both necessary and laudable, such programs do little to help the individual folk artist sell his or her wares.

With the Hilltown Artisans Guild, we tried yet a third approach. Rather than selling their products or attempting to create a market for them, we provided the artists and craftspeople with business and marketing education and aided individuals in making their own *informed* marketing decisions.

The University of Massachusetts (Amherst), through the Department of Continuing Education, has an excellent Arts Extension Service that specializes in arts advocacy and teaches a variety of arts management courses. Working with their director and chief education officer, I was able to develop a series of workshops to fit the specific needs of the Hilltown Artisans. The workshops included such topics as pricing, targeting markets, test marketing and market surveys, product development, promotion and publicity, portfolio development, how to work with an agent, display techniques, how to sell at fairs and festivals, and the jurying process (and how to survive it).

Rather than becoming a *marketing* association as originally envisioned by the HCDC, the Hilltown Artisans Guild was primarily an educational and advocacy organization. The guild became a network for information exchange and mutual support and, as a body, was able to tap into larger art and craft networks. For example, the organization joined the American Craft Council and received its journal (*American Craft*), newsletter, and quarterly information on major shows. Through such professional publications, the guild was able both to advertise its existence and to research other community-based craft organizations and fairs or festivals that might be appropriate markets for guild members' wares. Having an organizational identity also allowed the Hilltown Artisans to be computer-listed by the Arts Extension Service in a New England-wide data base of arts service/advocacy organizations. Through this channel, the guild was placed on a variety of mailing lists and received notices of arts and crafts activities from sources throughout the region.

By means of a monthly newsletter, guild members were kept abreast of the activities of individual members—who was showing where, who was having an open studio on what date, who had received travel/study fellowships, and so forth—and both current and future educational, marketing, and financial opportunities. Information on fairs and festivals, newly opened or recently discovered galleries and shops, professional studio courses, arts administration workshops, apprenticeships, grants and fellowships were featured and updated in the newsletter.

Guild members held a meeting each month, with the site rotating and a different Hilltown hosting each meeting. In addition to conducting business and socializing over shared foods, an individual guild member would present a program at each meeting. Programs included a slide/lecture by a potter on her experiences as a potter's apprentice in Japan, a workshop on production sewing by a quiltmaker, a slide/lecture on mosaic techniques as taught in Ravenna, Italy, a demonstration of the techniques of metal sculpture, and a program on herbs and dried flowers, to cite just a few. This kind of programming allowed Guild members to learn more about one another, to ask questions about each other's work—both technically and in regard to marketing—and to share knowledge and experience with their fellow artisans.

By providing individual artists and craftspeople with business and marketing education, the HCDC was implementing a method that helped to ensure self-determination for the Artisans Guild. Artists and craftspersons to whom purity of tradition is important learned how to target and reach markets that would allow them to continue the production of traditional objects. Some were able to place their work in galleries and shops that feature traditional art, while others—through "networking"— became associated with living history museums such as Hancock Shaker Village and Old Sturbridge Village, teaching and/or demonstrating the tools and techniques of their art as well as selling pieces through museum shops and catalogs.

On the other hand, artisans who wished to be more receptive to the demands of consumers gained knowledge of market surveys, product development, and test marketing. One potter scouted crafts fairs in the region to find out what sold, and where, then created a "bread and butter" line of simple, inexpensive dishes intended for daily use that could be both made and sold in greater volume than her more complex and individual pieces. The sales of this line could then support her more artistic and expensive works, which she previously could create only as commissioned pieces because of the cost and time involved. An herbalist, tapping into the commuter market, developed an all-natural car deodorizing product which she called "Car-Pourri" and which sold in country stores, gift shops, and the like. Another potter and a sculptor who worked in metal collaborated on a line of bird baths, which could be sold in galleries and at craft fairs but also by lawn and garden businesses. With emphases on communicative networks and education, individual members of the Hilltown Artisans Guild were equipped to make their own marketing decisions.

Folklore and Community Development: Shared Concerns

In approaching the marketing of folk art, the folklorist's central concern has been the development of strategies and policies that improve the life of the folk artist economically while simultaneously conserving traditional culture and protecting traditional forms of expression from commercial exploitation.

The development of rural communities has raised similar issues; *cultural* conservation has become as important a concern as the preservation of the environment.

In what ways can the principles and techniques of folklore study contribute in the evolution of policies for community development that help to strengthen rural culture while simultaneously recognizing the needs of and assisting individual members of the community?

Strategies

"Rural development" and "economic development" are not identical. The economy is one facet of a culture, albeit an important and influential one. "Rural development" entails the cultivation and strengthening of rural culture as a whole. Strategies for rural development must flow from the answers to the following questions:

1. What are the important characteristics and traditions of the area/ community that must be preserved and/or developed?

2. What type of economy will weaken local culture? What type will strengthen it?

3. Why is an understanding of tradition, expressive forms, and sym-

bolic interaction and communication vital to serving the community?

Forms of folklore generated in community settings constitute a source of information regarding the values, attitudes, and tastes of those communities. Oral forms such as stories and jokes may also provide insight into both existing and desired conditions and relationships. Celebrations, festivals and rituals, as well as helping fulfill needs for fellowship, reward and recognition, may reenact community myth—the "public persona" of the community. Through observation, analysis, and understanding of traditional expressive behavior, rural development specialists will be better able to enact policies and invent strategies that address the complex needs of the community.

Knowing the cultural characteristics of a community or area can also help organizations and agencies in the development of *their* public persona and in creating programs and policies compatible with community ethos.

A cultural profile of the Hilltowns would include the following:

1. There is a strong tradition of self-help, of taking care of one's emotional and economic needs oneself or in association with family and friends:

2. Cooperation is of great value and importance;

3. The tradition of local democracy, as exemplified in the town meeting, is still strong;

4. Value is placed on technical expertise in hand work;

5. Efficiency is regarded as necessary—"Waste not, want not;"

6. Family is the central core of people's lives;

7. Value is placed on unpretentiousness—competition for material wealth and its symbols is viewed as a threat to community comfort and equality;

8. The elderly are valued for their knowledge and expertise, and as living links with the history and traditions of the community.

Knowing these things about Hilltown culture, I was able to apprise the HCDC of economic development plans for the Artisans Guild which were at odds with Hilltown ethos, and evolve policies that centered on cooperation and self-determinism in the marketing of art and craft. The Hilltown Artisans Guild, four years later, is a viable, independent organization whose foci are still education and communicative networks. Individual artisans have bettered their lot without the negative impact on their communities that increased tourism or mass production might have had.

How are the administrators of rural development projects and agencies to go about getting this kind of cultural information? One way is to sponsor or engage in community-based oral history and folklife projects. This kind of public recognition of the importance of their history and culture not only stimulates the community to present what they feel is of value but demonstrates the agency's awareness of and commitment to indigenous culture. Such projects can be undertaken in partnership with local community groups of all ages. Scouts, 4-H clubs, church groups, arts councils, and local historical societies can provide both volunteers and a wealth of local knowledge. Another way is to integrate the board of directors, project staff, or advisory group with "natives." Representatives of the rural culture are the best sources of information about that culture.

Folklore, or traditional human expression, can be regarded as a resource in solving both interpretive and managerial problems. In developing public policies that sustain rural ways of life, an understanding of folklore serves as the key both to rural culture and to ways of preserving that culture that are both effective and acceptable to members of the community.

For Further Information

Several works are helpful in providing introductions to folklore: Barre Toelken, *The Dynamics of Folklore* (Boston: Houghton Mifflin, 1979); Jan Harold Brunvand, *The Study of American Folklore: An Introduction*, 3rd. ed. (New York: Norton, 1986); and Richard M. Dorson, ed., *Folklore and Folklife: An Introduction* (Chicago: Univ. of Chicago Press, 1972). Although differing in scope and organization, each of these introductions offers an overview of the field of folklore and provides useful bibliographic materials.

Each of the above-mentioned introductions contains information on conducting field research. However, for a more comprehensive guide, see Bruce Jackson, *Fieldwork* (Urbana and Chicago: Univ. of Illinois Press, 1987). *People Studying People: The Human Element in Fieldwork* by Robert A. Georges and Michael O. Jones (Berkeley and Los Angeles: Univ. of California Press, 1980) is particularly helpful in clarifying the concepts and processes of fieldwork as a human endeavor and provides an understanding of the ways in which researchers and the people they study interrelate.

For understanding the problems of marketing folk art and craft, and/or the role of the folklorist in the marketing process, see Michael Owen Jones, "Folk Craft Production and the Folklorist's Obligation," *Popular Culture* 4:194-212, and "'If You Make a Simple Thing, You Gotta Sell It at a Simple Price': Folk Art Production as a Business," *Kentucky Folklore Record* 17:73-77; 18:5-12, 31-40; Rosemary O. Joyce, "'Fame Don't Make the Sun Any Cooler': Folk Artists and the Marketplace," in John Michael Vlach and Simon J. Bronner, eds., *Folk Art and Art Worlds* (Ann Arbor: UMI Research Press, 1986), 225-4l; and Rosemary O. Joyce, ed., "Marketing Folk Art" (special double issue) *New York Folklore* 12 (1986). See also A.H. Walle, "Mitigating Marketing: A Window of Opportunity for Applied Folklorists, *New York Folklore* 12 (1986): 91-112. Further information on tourist art may be found in Nelson H.H. Graburn's *Ethnic and Tourist Arts: Cultural Expressions of the Fourth World* (Berkeley and Los Angeles: Univ. of California Press, 1976).

For more information about folk art and material culture, see works cited in such publications as Simon J. Bronner, ed., *American Folk Art: A Guide to Re-*

sources (New York: Garland, 1984); Michael Owen Jones, *Exploring Folk Art: Twenty Years of Thought on Craft, Work, and Aesthetics* (Ann Arbor: UMI Research Press, 1987); and Thomas J. Schlereth, ed., *Material Culture: A Research Guide* (Lawrence: Univ. Press of Kansas, 1985). For further materials on the study of folklore in America, see Simon J. Bronner, *American Folklore Studies: An Intellectual History* (Lawrence: Univ. Press of Kansas, 1986).

Numerous volumes have been written from a variety of perspectives on the topic of community development and rural development. Some works that provide a helpful introduction to the field, along with bibliographies, are Allen David Edwards and Dorothy G. Jones, *Community and Community Development* (The Hague: Mouton, 1976); Ted K. Bradshaw and Edward J. Blakely, *Rural Communities in Advanced Industrial Society: Development and Developers* (New York: Praeger, 1979); William Wishart Biddle, *The Community Development Process: The Rediscovery of Local Initiative* (New York: Rinehart and Winston, 1965); William R. Lassey, *Planning in Rural Environments* (New York: McGraw-Hill, 1977); and Larry R. Whiting, ed., *Rural Development Research Priorities* (Ames: Iowa State Univ. Press, 1973). For perspectives on the human and cultural aspects of development, see Ward Hunt Goodenough, *Cooperation in Change: An Anthropological Approach to Community Development* (New York: Russell Sage Foundation, 1963); Guy Gran, *Development By People* (New York: Praeger, 1983); Polly Hill, *Development Economics on Trial: The Anthropological Case for a Prosecution* (Cambridge and London: Cambridge Univ. Press, 1986); and Mark Shoul, "Position Paper on Rural Development" (unpublished paper; Miller's River Self-Help Project, 1985).

In the current decade, folklorists have become increasingly active in the advocacy of cultural conservation and in trying to affect public policy relating to development and land use. Some works that reflect the political nature of cultural intervention and cultural conservation are Burt Feintuch, ed., *The Conservation of Culture: Folklorists and the Public Sector* (Lexington: Univ. Press of Kentucky, 1988); Carl Fleischhauer and Charles Wolfe, *The Process of Field Research: Final Report on the Blue Ridge Parkway Folklife Project* (Washington, D.C.: American Folklife Center, 1981); Benita J. Howell, "Folklife Research in Environmental Planning," in William Milsap, ed., *Applied Social Science for Environmental Planning*, ed. William Milsap (Boulder, Colo.: Westview, 1984), 127-39; Mary Hufford, *One Space, Many Places: Folklife and Land Use in New Jersey's Pinelands National Reserve* (Washington, D.C.: American Folklife Center, 1986); Ormond H. Loomis (coordinator), *Cultural Conservation: The Protection of Cultural Heritage in the United States* (Washington, D.C.: American Folklife Center, 1983); and David E. Whisnant, *All That Is Native and Fine: The Politics of Culture in an American Region* (Chapel Hill: Univ. of North Carolina Press, 1983). See also Jean Haskell Speer, "Unshared Visions: Folklife and Politics in a Rural Community," in Burt Feintuch, ed., *The Conservation of Culture: Folklorists and the Public Sector* (Lexington: Univ. Press of Kentucky, 1988), 154-65.

About the Authors

MARJORIE BARD, who has both the M.A. and the Ph.D. degrees in folklore and mythology from UCLA, has long been concerned with the process of dual victimization by individual(s) and state, and has worked within shelters and the criminal branch of the Los Angeles City Attorney's Office as a domestic violence victim advocate. The only academician invited to lead a workshop and to present a paper at the 1987 Governor's Conference on Crime Victims, she discussed the correlation between victimization and homelessness and proposed innovative models for self-sufficiency communities. She has recently published a book-length work on the stories of homeless women entitled *Shadow Women: Homeless Women's Survival Stories* (1990). She is also interested in stress-related and supranormal incidents that create physical and psychic impairment. Currently she is in law school while also participating in transorganizational consulting.

BETTY J. BELANUS is currently an education specialist at the Office of Folklife Programs at the Smithsonian Institution. She served from May 1987 to August 1988 as the curator of the Massachusetts Program for the Smithsonian's 1988 Festival of American Folklife. She holds a B.A. degree in American studies from Smith College and an M.A. and Ph.D. in folklore from Indiana University. She has worked on educational projects at the Children's Museum in Indianapolis and is the editor of the teacher workbook *Folklore in the Classroom* (1985), published by the Indiana Historical Bureau. She served as the Indiana state folk arts coordinator for the Indiana Arts Commission for two years. She has conducted folklore fieldwork in Indiana, Tennessee, Mississippi, and Massachusetts and has acted as a consultant for folk arts and education projects in Indiana, Missouri, and South Carolina. During the winter and spring of 1987 she gained some firsthand education experience "in the trenches" as a substitute teacher for several Indianapolis-area public school systems.

KRISTIN G. CONGDON, whose graduate degrees are from the education department at the University of Oregon, holds the William and Alice Jenkins Endowed Chair in Community Arts at the University of Central Florida. She is coeditor of *Art in a Democracy* (1987), and has published articles in *Journal of Aesthetic Education, Art Education, Studies in Art Education, Journal of Multi-cultural and Cross-cultural Research in Art Education, Visual Arts Research,* and *The Journal of the Caucus on Social Theory and Art Education,* among others. She has produced two videotapes on artists and their work and was a project director in February 1978 of the exhibition, "Boats, Bait, and Fishing Paraphernalia: A Local Folk Aesthetic," in the School of Art Gallery, Bowling Green State University.

ELKE DETTMER, a native of Germany, received her M.A. in folklore at the University of California, Berkeley, in 1982 and has recently completed her Ph.D. dissertation at the folklore department, Memorial University, St. John's, Newfoundland. Her major areas of interest are folklorism and tourism. She has published and lectured both in Germany and North America and has recently translated Hermann Bausinger's classic study, *Volkskultur in der technischen Welt* (Folk Culture in the World of Technology), published (1990) as part of the "Folklore Studies in Translation" series, Indiana University Press. At present she is working on a social science project researching "Women's Economic Lives" in three Newfoundland communities.

SARA SELENE FAULDS has a B.A. in public service/urban and community development from UCLA. After completing required coursework for the M.A. in folklore and mythology, she took her M.A. in architecture and urban planning from UCLA (1980). She has served in many roles for the City of Santa Monica: As vice-chair of the Architectural Review Board, executive board member of the Third Street Development Corporation, and as a liaison to the Santa Monica Arts Commission. She was elected to the board of directors for the Santa Monica Heritage Museum and to two terms as a director of the Ocean Park Community Organization. She has worked in property management for a management company and as a consultant, advising on design and location of development. She is presently employed with Weyerhaeuser Mortgage Company as an administrator working on special projects from the space planning and design of office space to the development of employee incentive/recognition programs. She is also exploring the dynamics of office relationships.

JUDITH E. HAUT earned her doctorate in folklore and mythology from the University of California, Los Angeles. Her dissertation, "Children's Belief: A Folkloristic Study of Conceptualization, Experimentation and Communication," examines some of the learning strategies children employ outside of school. After obtaining an M.A. in folklore from UCLA, she taught at the University of Guam from 1976 to 1980. In addition to teaching folklore courses there, she was the project coordinator for an interdisciplinary pilot program integrating fundamentals of English with a core humanities curriculum, and she wrote one of the textbooks for the course, *People and Their Society* (1978; rev. 1979). In addition to teaching part-time, she continues to write and consult on the subject of folklore and education.

JO FARB HERNANDEZ is the director of the Monterey Peninsula Museum of Art in Monterey, California. Previously she served as director of the Triton Museum of Art in Santa Clara, California (1977-1985); she also has had museum experience at the Dallas Museum of Fine Arts and the Museum of Cultural History in Los Angeles. She holds an M.A. in folklore and mythology (with a concentration in folk art) from the University of California, Los Angeles. Curator of over 150 exhibitions, she is author of such titles as *Day of the Dead: Tradition and Change in Contemporary Mexico* (1979), *Mexican Indian Dance Masks* (1982), *Crime and Punishment: Reflections of Violence in Contemporary Art* (1984) and *The Artist and the Myth* (1987), as well as editor of numerous others. She is president of the California Association of Museums, has served on the board of directors of the Western Museums Conference and numerous California Arts Council grant panels, and has given presentations regularly at professional meetings of the American Association of Museums, the Western Museums Conference, the American Association for State and Local History, the California Folklore Society, the American Folklore Society, and other organizations, as well as lectured at universities and museums nationwide.

BENITA J. HOWELL, associate professor of anthropology at the University of Tennessee, Knoxville, is a native of Asheville, North Carolina. She holds an undergraduate degree in English from Duke University and a Ph.D. in sociocultural anthropology from the University of Kentucky. After completing a dissertation on Native American trickster mythology from the Pacific Northwest, she became involved in Appalachian studies, initially through directing the Big South Fork folklife survey described in this volume. She edited *Practicing Anthropology* between 1986 and 1990. Her research includes community history and cultural tourism projects sponsored by the Tennessee Humanities Council and exploration of federal land management agencies' relations with local communities through comparison of a U.S. Forest Service recreation area, Mount Rogers in southwest Virginia, with Big South Fork in Tennessee and Kentucky. Recent publications on cultural conservation include "Appalachian Tourism and Cultural Conservation," in her edited volume, *Cultural Heritage Conservation in the American South* (1990), and a chapter on cultural conservation and ethnographic research in the U.S. National Park System in *Reconfiguring the Cultural Mission*, forthcoming from the University of Illinois Press.

After serving as state folklorist of Pennsylvania (1969-1970) DAVID HUF-FORD joined the folklore faculty at Memorial University of Newfoundland. In 1974 he earned his Ph.D. at the University of Pennsylvania and joined the behavioral science department of the Pennsylvania State College of Medicine located at the Milton Hershey Medical Center, where he is pro-fessor of behavioral science and medical humanities with a joint appoint-ment in family and community medicine. He is also director of the Doctors Kienle Center for Humanistic Medicine and holds adjunct appointments at the University of Pennsylvania in nursing, social gerontology, and folklore. Hufford's recent work on belief includes "Commentary: Mystical Experi-ence in the Modern World" in Genevieve Foster's memoir, *The World Was Flooded with Light*; "Inclusionism vs. Reductionism in the Study of the Cul-ture Bound Syndromes," *Culture, Medicine and Psychiatry* (1989); and "Rea-son, Rhetoric and Religion: Academic Ideology vs. Folk Belief," *New York Folklore* (1985).

MICHAEL OWEN JONES earned his M.A. and Ph.D. in folklore from Indiana University (1966, 1970). Since 1968 he has been on the faculty at UCLA, offering courses on folk art and technology, folk belief and custom, food customs and symbolism, American folklore, film and folklore, field-work, applied folklore, and organizational culture and symbolism. From 1984 to 1991 he served as director of the UCLA Center for the Study of Comparative Folklore and Mythology. Among his publications are *Why Faith Healing?* (1973), *The Hand Made Object and Its Maker* (1975), (coauthored) *People Studying People* (1980), (edited) *The World of the Kalevala* (1987), *Ex-ploring Folk Art* (1987), (coedited) *Inside Organizations* (1988), and *Craftsman of the Cumberlands* (1989). He has also edited special issues of *Western Folklore* on foodways (1981) and *American Behavioral Scientist* on emotions in work (1990).

Born in 1956, SUE SAMUELSON died of cancer on January 17, 1991. At the time that she wrote the article for this book (1988), she was communica-tions specialist for the Pennsylvania State Association of County Commis-sioners in Harrisburg, Pennsylvania. She also was a part-time lecturer in American studies at Pennsylvania State University, Harrisburg. She had also taught at Rutgers University and worked for the Library of Congress. Her degrees included a B.A. in anthropology from the University of California, Berkeley, an M.A. in folklore and mythology from the University of Califor-nia, Los Angeles, and a Ph.D. in folklore and folklife from the University of Pennsylvania. Her publications and research interests embraced American holidays, regional identity and folklore, the folklore of adolescents, and the role of folklorists as expert witnesses in litigation. In 1988 she moved back to her childhood home in Northern California where she continued her link with trade organizations, working as a communications specialist for a national association of trade associations. She also taught a course on foodways in the anthropology department at the University of California, Berkeley. For more information about her career, see the obituary by Simon Bronner in the *Journal of American Folklore* 104 (1991): 341-44.

DAVID SHULDINER is the humanities program coordinator for the Connecticut State Department on Aging. Born and reared in Los Angeles, California, he earned bachelor's and master's degrees in anthropology from California State University, Los Angeles, and a doctorate in folklore and mythology from the University of California at Los Angeles, where he specialized in occupational lore and American immigrant and ethnic history and folklore. His dissertation was based on oral histories of elderly Jewish immigrants who were active in the Jewish Labor Movement. Among many affiliations with folklore, oral history, aging, and activist organizations, he is a member of the Gray Panthers, an intergenerational activist group founded by older Americans.

A folklorist and arts administrator currently based in Tennessee, PATRICIA ATKINSON WELLS is an adjunct faculty member at Middle Tennessee State University. She serves on the folk arts panel of the Tennessee Arts Commission, and on the board of directors of the Arts and Humanities Council of Murfreesboro and Rutherford County. She has authored papers and articles on topics ranging from the functions of seemingly dysfunctional behavior in a Girl Scout camp to issues in developing arts organizations and action plans for marketing. At the time of this writing, she is a doctoral candidate in folklore and mythology at UCLA. Her dissertation focuses on the culture and traditions of the Hilltowns in Massachusetts, where she spends part of each year.

Index

University of Pennsylvania, folklore
department at, 11
University of Texas, folklore and
ethnomusicology interdepartmental
program at, 11
unshared visions, for development,
243-44
urban design, 4, 150-61
Urban Folklore Conference (1980), 159
Urban Gateways (Chicago), 18
urban legends, 74
Urban Traditions (Chicago), 9, 18, 30
Utah Arts Council, 18
Utah State University: folklore joint
program at, 11; Fife Conference, 30

value, in traditions, 3, 27-28, 41
Vanishing Hitchhiker, The (Brunvand), 60,
71, 74
Venice, California: urban design in,
153-55, 156, 157
Vermont Arts Council, 18
Vermont Folklife Center, 18
Viehmsnn, Katherina, 1
Vietnam War: folksongs of troops in,
31-32 n 2; storytelling about, 78, 88
"Visions of Paradise" (film), 220
Volkskunde, 1

Walle, Alf H., 28, 29
Warshaver, Gerald, 220

Watson, Doc, 8
"Well Spent Life" (film), 220
Western Folklife Center (Salt Lake
City), 18
Western Folklore, 27, 60
Western Kentucky University, folk
studies program at, 9, 11
Whisnant, David E., 19, 28
Whyte, William Foote, 24
Widner, Ronna Lee, 39
Williams, Michael Ann, 96
Williams, Phyllis H., 6
Wilson, Joe, 17
Wilson, William A. (Bert), 4, 30,
173-74, 176
women, as artists, 137-38
Works Progress Administration, Federal
Project Number One, 7
World Music Institute (New York
City), 18
World's Columbian Exposition
(Chicago, 1893), 5

Yoder, Don, 2, 11
"Yonder Come Day" (film), 219
Young, M. Jane, 24

Zeitlin, Steve, 18
Znaniecki, Florian, 6
Zora Neale Hurston Festival of the
Arts and Humanities, 146